Dominik Ohrem (ed.)

American Beasts
Perspectives on Animals,
Animality and U. S. Culture, 1776–1920

Dominik Ohrem (ed.)

American Beasts

Perspectives on Animals, Animality and U. S. Culture, 1776–1920

Neofelis Verlag

German National Library Cataloguing in Publication Data
A catalogue record for this book is available from the German National Library:
http://dnb.d-nb.de

www.neofelis-verlag.de

Cover Design: Marija Skara
Editing & Typesetting: Neofelis Verlag (mn/ae)
Printed by PRESSEL Digitaler Produktionsdruck, Remshalden
Printed on FSC-certified paper.
ISBN (Print): 978-3-95808-037-9
ISBN (PDF): 978-3-95808-100-0

Contents

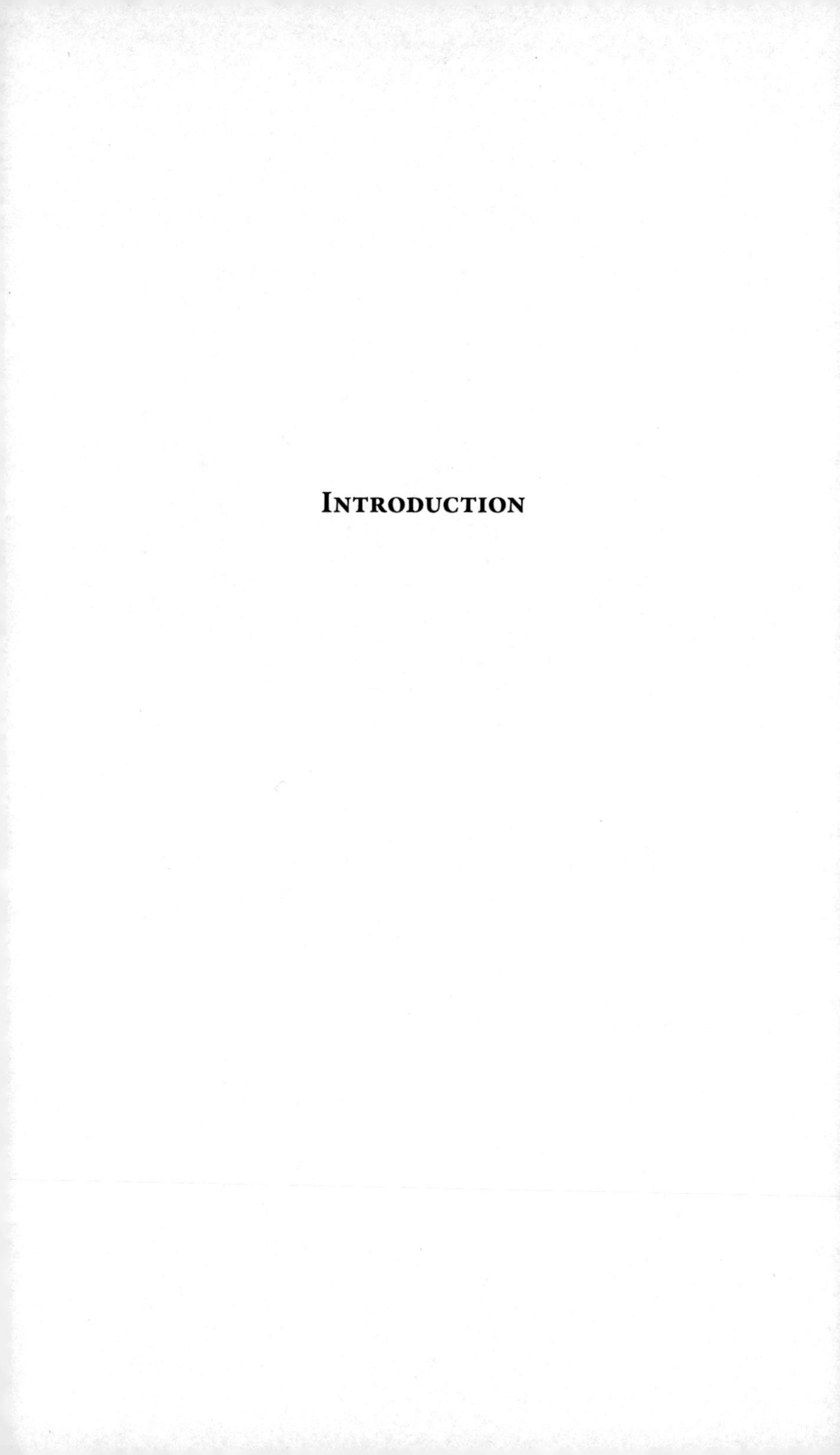

Introduction

A Declaration of Interdependence

American History and the Challenges of Postanthropocentric Historiography

Dominik Ohrem

> [O]ur thinking gets nowhere without the presupposition of the interdependent and sustaining conditions of life.[1]

Declaring In(ter)dependence

"It has been well known for some time in certain circles," the humorous lead article of the January 1857 issue of *Harper's Magazine* informs us, "that a movement was on foot for the emancipation of the brute creatures (so called) from the thralldom of man." Years of correspondence between animals from different parts of the world – "Africa, the Rocky Mountains, the Jungles of India" as well as "the various Menageries" – have shown that there was a unanimous desire for freedom, the logical consequence of which had to be a concerted effort of rebellion on the part of those creatures so unjustifiably made subject to the will and whims of Man.[2] It is decided that "the first blow should be struck in

1 Judith Butler: *Notes Toward a Performative Theory of Assembly*. Cambridge: Harvard UP 2015, p. 119.

2 The Animal Declaration of Independence. In: *Harper's New Monthly Magazine* 14,80 (January 1857), pp. 145–163, here p. 145. Throughout this chapter, the

America"[3] while its human inhabitants are preoccupied with the presidential election, and so the insurgent animals, after freeing some of their fellow nonhumans from P.T. Barnum's American Museum and Isaac van Amburgh's traveling menagerie, hold an assembly in Hoboken, New Jersey consisting of delegations from all over the world and of "members of nearly every respectable family in the Animal Kingdom."[4] The purpose of the assembly, we are informed, is the election of a president of animalkind and a declaration of independence from oppressive humanity. A general awareness about "the importance of the work in hand" suffuses the assembly, with "exclamations of friendship on every side" and the "noblest spirit of conciliation" prevailing over various interspecific difficulties as well as the more meaty complications of predator-prey relations, and thus, while "an enthusiastic Wolf did strangle a Lamb, and a Fox, in a fit of absence of mind, choked a fat Duck, these accidents were rightly ascribed to the force of habit, and did not mar the harmony of the proceedings."[5]

Nonetheless, parliamentary professionalism is frequently put to the test by the diversity of perceptions, motivations and expectations tied to the debating creatures' respective lifeways and their relations both to each other and to the human species, a problem which also complicates the choice of candidates for the presidency. The Buffalo, acting as chair of the assembly, begins by emphasizing the illegitimacy of human sovereignty, for "[h]ad not one of his own race described him as a biped without feathers? And should a biped command quadrupeds?"[6] – a rather thoughtless remark, from which the Eagle naturally takes offense. The Lion and the Monkey are proposed as candidates for the presidency, while the Horse raises his voice in support of the Dog, stressing his leadership qualities – "coolness, watchfulness, bravery, skill, and strength" –, important qualifications given the uncertain times ahead. But the Hyena objects: had the Dog "not notoriously taken the side of their oppressors from time immemorial?" How could this willingly

capitalized 'Man' will be used to refer to the hegemonic concept of the human that both emerges from and underwrites the historically specific intersecting discourses of (not only) race, gender, class and species in the West.

3 Ibid.

4 Ibid., p. 148.

5 Ibid.

6 Ibid. The Buffalo's remark is a reference to Plato's definition of the human being.

Fig. 1
"The Lion entreats the assembly to believe that it is not vanity or ambition which induces him to solicit their suffrages."

Illustration in *Harper's New Monthly Magazine* 14,80 (January 1857).

obedient "slave of man" be competent to lead them? Instead, admitting that tyrannical Man had at least "given them a hint of which they should profit" by referring to one animal as "the King of Beasts," he supports the candidacy of the Lion.[7] After some back and forth, it is the rather inconspicuous Penguin, however, who wins the nomination and, in a monarchical twist somewhat unexpected given the hitherto republican outlook of the proceedings, is crowned king of animals.

While the Penguin's initial proposal for the overthrow of human rule envisions a policy of "'masterly inactivity,'"[8] we soon learn that the assembly has been adjourned to reconvene in Nebraska Territory for the purpose of organizing a much less passive form of resistance: a war of independence. The meeting begins with a number of resolutions read by the Magpie, the most important one emphasizing all nonhuman creatures' right and duty to challenge human dominion and "assert our paramount claims to the exclusive enjoyment of the earth; to resume our freedom in the forests, or the plains, or the swamps, as we please, and to lead the life which is best suited to our instincts."[9] Further resolutions are read which, among other things, pronounce that "all things shall be in common between us," that, in the interest of the community, carnivores "are earnestly solicited to try a vegetable diet," and that,

> as we may not succeed in exterminating the human race for some time to come, a prize of $500 be offered to the human creatures for the best poem descriptive of our declaration of independence [...,] for the best essay on the Rights of Brutes [...] [and] for the best argument to show, from Grotius, Puffendorf [*sic*], and other authorities, that we are entitled to our independence."[10]

After some further squabbles, debates and developments, among which are the founding of the newspaper the *Daily Barker and Biter*, a duel between the Cock and the Hare, the short-lived appointment of the Cock as commander-in-chief, and a passionate speech by the Crocodile lamenting his fellow creatures' seeming indifference towards the degraded condition of the Turtle, the account of the proceedings ends abruptly – not without the author ominously informing us, however, that, according to "an old acquaintance among the beasts, [...] the

7 The Animal Declaration of Independence, p. 151.
8 Ibid., p. 153.
9 Ibid., p. 154.
10 Ibid., pp. 154–155.

Fig. 2
"The Menagerie."
The writing above the human heads reads
"Do not irritate the animals".

Illustration in *Harper's New Monthly Magazine* 14,80 (January 1857).

animals may shortly be expected to act on the offensive, and that they intend to establish zoological gardens for the accommodation and exhibition of various specimens of men."[11]

In its mode of tongue-in-cheek lightheartedness, the *Harper's* article envisions the (im)possibility of a world in which humans not only have to respect the autonomous lifeways of other animals but, much more radically, are forced to submit to the animals' claim to an "exclusive enjoyment of the earth," a world in which humans find themselves crammed into cages for the enjoyment and 'education' of creatures at best superficially concerned with their well-being, helplessly exposed to their gazes. The article, in other words, imagines a fundamental inversion of the power relations between humans and animals – an idea which is, of course, humorously dispelled in the very moment of its articulation. A short note in the *Western Literary Messenger* mentioning recently published magazine issues praises *Harper's* lead article as "ingenious," promising that "[e]verybody will read it and laugh over it."[12] The humorous effect of the article is obviously achieved through its depiction of the animals' peculiar mimicry of human politics and its allusions to contemporary (human) political affairs, such as the struggle between proslavery and abolitionist forces,[13] – transposed onto, and frequently derailed by, the vicissitudes of animal life, interspecies relations and species-specific behaviors – and by the "honorable brutes"[14] scrupulous adherence to the polite formalities of political rhetoric and ritual. The general absurdity of animals engaging in political thought and interaction (using human language) – a capacity that has since Plato and Aristotle figured as one of the decisive markers of the supposed uniqueness

11 The Animal Declaration of Independence, p. 163.

12 *Western Literary Messenger* 27,5 (January 1857), p. 239.

13 More specifically, the article alludes to the conflict brought about by the *Kansas-Nebraska Act* of 1854 and its violent eruption in the events of 'Bleeding Kansas.' We learn, for example, that a monkey, passing through Missouri, is apprehended because he is accused of being a Free Stater on his way to Kansas, while two baboons share a similar fate because the Free State Committee suspects them of having pro-slavery designs. In another scene, the Wooly Horse, supporting the Crocodile's intervention with regard to the deplorable condition of the Turtle, echoes abolitionist rhetoric when he criticizes that some members of the very same assembly which came together to fight for the "natural liberty of brutekind" were so shamefully indifferent to the actual plight of one of their own: "Was [the Turtle] not a beast and a brother?" (Animal Declaration, p. 160).

14 Ibid.

of the human *zoon politikon*[15] – is further accentuated by the article's more specific topic: Given that the actual – human – American *Declaration of Independence* has been widely regarded as the political embodiment of Enlightenment rationality, with its emphasis on human dignity and natural law reaffirming the conviction that humans surpassed all other earthly creatures, and that, qua their being human, they deserved unique moral and legal consideration, an *animal* Declaration of Independence must seem particularly oxymoronic.[16] Of course, as is the case with the dominant strands of Enlightenment thought more generally, the universal figure of Man so prominent in the rhetoric of the Declaration was in fact a violently particularized type of being that only encompassed those humans who found themselves safely within the bounds of the hegemonic normative framework of humanity. For many if not most contemporaries, it was thus among the self-evident truths that the unalienable rights demanded by natural law and supposedly inseparable from the very condition of being human not only stopped short of considering nonhuman life in any capacity but also, and much more glaringly, the lives and rights of 'animalized' humans, in particular the hundreds of thousands of enslaved black people whose degraded condition remained unchanged by solemn proclamations of human equality. While animals, lacking reason, unable to rise above their own instincts and passions, supposedly existed for the use and benefit of humans, similar arguments were brought forward in defense of slavery and of the fundamental inequality of whites and people of color as well as men and women in order to perpetuate existing relations of power in American society. 'Naturally' *dependent* beings such as women, children, enslaved people and, of course, animals were not supposed to declare independence, a status rightfully belonging to that specific class of humans – white, property-holding men – uniquely capable of rational, autonomous self-government. As the racialized, gendered and classed metaphysics of Man at the center of the American *Declaration*

15 See Christopher La Barbera: *States of Nature. Animality and the Polis.* New York: Lang 2012; Richard Sorabji: *Animal Minds and Human Morals. The Origins of the Western Debate.* Ithaca: Cornell UP 1993.

16 It might serve as an interesting side note that Wesley J. Smith, in the preface to his polemic *A Rat Is a Pig Is a Dog Is a Boy. The Human Cost of the Animal Rights Movement.* New York: Encounter 2012, cites the *Declaration of Independence* to defend the 'self-evident truth' of human exceptionalism against the idea that the "human being is merely another animal in the forest" (ibid., p. xvi).

of Independence forcefully suggests, any concept of 'human' independence is thus always already challenged by the differential operations of power that inform the relations of inequality between different groups of humans, an inequality that not only complicates any such universalist rhetoric but arguably points to its strategic function in the perpetuation of these relations.

The example of the discourse of reason and the way it was woven into the fabric of eighteenth- and nineteenth-century racism, sexism and speciesism points to the similarity of their mechanisms of exclusion and to the fact that the power asymmetries they sustained were, although in different degrees of visibility, premised on a dominative and exclusionary concept of the human. It is this concept – Man – which, albeit not always in an unproblematic fashion, also constituted an important implicit or explicit focus of abolitionist, women's rights and early animal rights discourse, explaining the frequent intersections between these social movements in and beyond the antebellum era.[17] With its copious use of the language of rights, the *Harper's* article thus also alludes to the animal rights debates emergent at the time. In 1865, one year before he founded the American Society for the Prevention of Cruelty to Animals (ASPCA), former diplomat Henry Bergh had already acquired a substantial number of signatures for his *Declaration of the Rights of Animals*, establishing a clear connection between his own animal advocacy and the rhetoric of the *Declaration of Independence*. But American animal advocacy discourse, including the language of rights, in fact dates back much further to the early national period. In September 1791, Brown University graduate and prospective minister Herman Daggett delivered a speech on "The Rights of Animals" – a title clearly alluding to Thomas Paine's famous *Rights of Man*, published in two parts in March 1791 and February 1792 in London – "in favor

17 For histories of American animal advocacy and its interrelations with other social movements, see Diane L. Beers: *For the Prevention of Cruelty. The History and Legacy of Animal Rights Activism in the United States*. Athens: Ohio UP 2006; Brigitte Fielder: Animal Humanism. Race, Species, and Affective Kinship in Nineteenth-Century Abolitionism. In: *American Quarterly* 65,3 (2013), pp. 487–514; Susan J. Pearson: *The Rights of the Defenseless. Protecting Animals and Children in Gilded Age America*. Chicago: University of Chicago Press 2011; Janet M. Davis: *The Gospel of Kindness. Animal Welfare and the Making of Modern America*. Oxford: Oxford UP 2016. For a transatlantic perspective on the interrelations between abolitionism and animal advocacy, see Kevin Hutchings: *Romantic Ecologies and Colonial Cultures in the British Atlantic World, 1770–1850*. Montreal: McGill-Queen's UP 2009, chapter 4.

of a certain class of beings, whose rights have seldom been advocated."[18] Because, Daggett explains, the ethical consideration humans extend to others always manifests itself "in proportion to the nearness of the relation," the plight of those "who belong to a different class, or circle in society" is seldom of any relevance to us, and this is particularly true with regard to the "lower order of sensible beings," who "are considered as moving in a very different sphere, and belonging to a community of a far different nature from that of ours."[19] But there is no reason to assume, Daggett continues in obvious reference to the *Declaration of Independence*, that

> the UNALIENATED rights of a beast, are not as sacred, and inviolable, as those of a man: or that the person, who wantonly commits an outrage upon the life, happiness, or security of a BIRD, is not as really amenable, at the tribunal of eternal justice, as he, who wantonly destroys the rights and privileges, or injuriously takes away the life of one of his fellow creatures of the HUMAN race.[20]

Humans, even though, or perhaps precisely because, they are seemingly superior to nonhuman beings, "owing to education, and to certain contracted habits of thinking and acting,"[21] often fail to recognize other earthly beings as fellow creatures towards whom they have an ethical obligation. But, he argues emphatically, that animals "are sensible beings, and capable of happiness, none can doubt: That their sensibility of corporeal pleasure and pain, is less than ours, none can prove: And that there is any kind of reason, why they should not be regarded with proportionable tenderness, we cannot conceive."[22]

While Bergh referred to his *Declaration of the Rights of Animals* as "a species of Declaration of Independence"[23] that would eventually be mentioned alongside Thomas Jefferson's original, such a comparison

18 Herman Daggett: *The Rights of Animals. An Oration, Delivered at the Commencement of Providence-College, September 7, 1791*, p. 3. The published version of the speech is available online here: http://name.umdl.umich.edu/N18673.0001.001 (accessed September 26, 2016). Biographical information about Daggett can be found in Samuel Bradlee Doggett: *A History of the Doggett-Daggett Family*. Boston: Rockwell & Churchill 1894, pp. 151–152.

19 Daggett: *The Rights of Animals*, p. 4.

20 Ibid., p. 9.

21 Ibid.

22 Ibid., pp. 6–7.

23 Quoted in Roderick Frazier Nash: *The Rights of Nature. A History of Environmental Ethics*. Madison: University of Wisconsin Press 1989, p. 46.

indicates (besides an obvious overconfidence) a certain lack of awareness about the irony that any such declaration could only ever be articulated in the mode of an *in behalf of*, pointing to the fundamental dependence of animals' independence on the paternalistic benevolence of human spokespersons like Bergh. After all, Bergh's declaration was signed neither by paw nor hoof but by human hand, relying on the established authority of a human John Hancock.[24] It is in a similar sense, then, that the aspirations towards independence articulated by the *Harper's* creatures are made a mockery of by their obvious dependence on human systems and modes of (linguistic and political) representation, on established human cultural institutions, and on the human politics of naming. This dependence becomes evident with particular irony in the animals' decision to commission the philosophico-juridical services of humans to substantiate their claims to independence from them and to do so by consulting the works of precisely those early modern theorists of natural law who not only often lent ideological support to European colonialist endeavors and their concomitant exploitation of natural resources and destruction of indigenous environments, habitats and species, but who also reiterated, now with the authority of early modern juridical discourse, the concept of human dominion over all other creatures. As Samuel Pufendorf – who, in contrast to other thinkers such as Hugo Grotius or John Locke, actually critiqued European colonial practices – asserts in *Elements of Universal Jurisprudence*, "[natural] law is to be derived from man's own nature alone and not drawn from brutes or inanimate things,"[25] and it does, indeed, not apply to them: "anyone may when he pleases [...] kill any animal or compel it to render services to him, [...] because there is no community of right between man and brutes."[26] However, if the idea of an animal *Declaration of Independence* suggested by the *Harper's* creatures seems absurd, this is not simply because animals are supposedly purely instinctual, non-rational, non-cultural beings of a 'lower order' but because any form of

24 As the motto of the prominent 'animal advocacy' magazine *Our Dumb Animals*, founded in 1868 by Boston lawyer George T. Angell, reads: "We Speak For Those Who Cannot Speak For Themselves."

25 Samuel Pufendorf: Elements of Universal Jurisprudence. In: Id.: *The Political Writings of Samuel Pufendorf*, ed. by Craig Carr, trans. from the Latin by Michael J. Seidler. New York: Oxford UP 1994, pp. 29–92, here p. 62.

26 Ibid., p. 82.

'animal' declaration would be a near impossible political feat given the often conflict-ridden diversity of nonhuman ways of being and inhabiting the world the article itself frequently alludes to. In the way it is premised on and reproduces the general singular of 'the animal,' Jacques Derrida would no doubt identify this idea as a *bêtise*, an asininity, thus indicating its unmistakably human origins.[27]

As a point of departure for the present volume and as an alternative to the problematic aspects of the ideas of both human *and* animal independence, I would like to focus on a notion of creaturely *inter*dependence that offers both a conceptual-analytical perspective for postanthropocentric historiography and articulates a normative claim and challenge. Such a perspective would constitute an attempt at thinking in broad and inclusive terms about the complex webs of relations weaving together living beings on earth, but it would also have to be shaped by an awareness about the inadequacy of both the concepts of 'the human' and 'the animal' to address the ontological and political differentiality of the phenomena these terms refer to. Positioning itself in the midst of these tensions and contradictions, it would have to be shaped by a firm alliance with the perspectives and politics of other academic fields to which the question of the animal is, or should be, of importance – such as the study of race, gender or sexuality. A critical discussion of the question of the animal can thus never be a solipsistic endeavor, because the very concept of animality is characterized by an intersectionality that accounts for both its ambiguity and elusiveness and its historical efficacy. Inseparable from this critical engagement with animality, one of the important tasks of postanthropocentric historiography is to articulate a critique of the concept of Man, which, just like its conceptual counterpart, needs to be considered not only in its species but also in its racial, gender and other dimensions, because it is only through their interpenetration and dynamic co-articulation that Man is able to sustain itself and its hegemonic status.[28] What this also means is that an

27 See Jacques Derrida: *The Animal That Therefore I Am*, trans. from the French by David Wills. New York: Fordham UP 2008, pp. 31–32.

28 Ecofeminists such as Val Plumwood, for example, have long emphasized this intersectional nature of the Western 'master model' of the human. See, for example, Val Plumwood: *Feminism and the Mastery of Nature*. London: Routledge 1993. In her guide to (feminist) intersectionality studies, Nina Lykke argues that animals and the more-than-human "ought to be much more integrated into explicit feminist theorizing of intersectionality." (Nina Lykke: *Feminist Studies. A Guide to Intersectional*

ontology and ethics that foregrounds the idea of interdependence in an attempt to think creaturely life beyond anthropocentric dichotomies needs to be careful not to ignore the very different realities of exposure to violence, oppression, inequality and marginalization that shape *human* life on earth. It needs to be careful, in other words, not to reintroduce the concept of Man through the backdoor in the very attempt at thinking beyond it.

"We are dependent on animals," Kelly Oliver writes in *Animal Lessons*, "and animals are dependent on their environments and one another."[29] Oliver's rather uncontroversial statement points to a problem that troubles the notion of creaturely *inter*dependence as it is used here: While it is obvious that human life has in many ways and from its very beginnings always depended on the lives of animal others, it is not entirely clear how this also applies the other way around. Part of the problem is, of course, the inevitable undercomplexity of thinking in terms of 'animals' in the first place. Different species have (had) different relationships with different groups of humans, with different degrees of proximity and intensity of interaction, and with different potentials for conflict and conviviality. But beyond this, doesn't the idea of creaturely interdependence itself constitute an act of epistemic violence in the way it conveniently glosses over the fundamental power asymmetry that has allowed humans to *force* other creatures into this kind of relationship? Have humans not, either directly (for example, through processes of domestication) or indirectly (through the massive transformations of or intrusions into their habitats), *made* other species dependent on them throughout the historical and deep historical process? While this is no doubt a valid argument, the idea of creaturely interdependence I would like to suggest here is based on an acknowledgment of, and takes as its analytical framework, the historically evolved status quo in which human and animal lives are interwoven in often unprecedented and

Theory, Methodology and Writing. London: Routledge 2010, p. 81.) It should be noted, however, that the concept of intersectionality is not without its problems. See, for example, Jasbir Puar: "I Would Rather Be a Cyborg than a Goddess". Becoming-Intersectional in Assemblage Theory. In: *philoSOPHIA* 2,1 (2012), pp. 49–66.

29 Kelly Oliver: *Animal Lessons. How They Teach Us to Be Human*. New York: Columbia UP 2009, p. 44. Also see id.: Earth Ethics and Creaturely Cohabitation. In: Dominik Ohrem / Roman Bartosch (eds): *Beyond the Human-Animal Divide. Creaturely Lives in Literature and Culture*. Basingstoke: Palgrave Macmillan (forthcoming).

highly intricate ways, the extent and implications of which are not yet fully within our grasp.[30] While the relationship between humans and domesticated species as it has evolved over the centuries is today characterized by a "cooperative dependence from which neither can escape,"[31] the complexity of human-animal interdependence in the Anthropocene cannot be limited to such more obvious examples. This is because in an era in which the intended or collateral effects of human agency extend to the most remote spaces of the earth, even wild creatures, not to mention the many synanthropic species living in human-created and human-dominated environments, are rarely able to escape their influence. In a sense, the lifeways or survival of many species is thus increasingly dependent on what humans do *not* (allow themselves to) do, that is, on the ways in which they regulate (or fail to do so) the expansive and destructive operations of capitalist modernity.

On the other hand, thinking in terms of creaturely interdependence also means that human societies and histories must themselves be understood as *more-than-human* down to the very core of their existence. Human beings are not apart from but a part of what philosopher Roberto Marchesini has termed the "theriosphere," and this is not limited to aspects of biological life and evolutionary kinship with other species but also includes the 'loftier' realms of thought and imagination, which have traditionally been regarded as an "emanation of the anthroposphere."[32] As Marchesini reminds us, nonhuman creatures have always functioned as "great sources of fervid creativity for our species" and their influence reaches into even the deepest recesses of what is supposed to be uniquely human and exclusively associated with the possibilities of the human mind and forms of human intersubjectivity.

30 Even our 'human' bodies – "porous ecosystems swarming with bacteria, fungi, protozoa, and viruses" (Edmund Russell: Coevolutionary History. In: *The American Historical Review* 119,5 (2014), pp. 1514–1528, here p. 1515) – are expressions of continuous processes and relations of creaturely interdependence, even if the kinds of microorganisms involved in these relations are rarely thought of as 'creatures' and in many ways pose unique challenges for creaturely ontologies.

31 Juliet Clutton-Brock: *Animals as Domesticates. A World View through History.* East Lansing: Michigan State UP 2012, p. 133.

32 Roberto Marchesini: The Theriosphere. In: *Angelaki* 21,1 (2016), pp. 113–135, here p. 114. With regard to my above remarks, however, I want to add that we would have to think in more detail about the extent to which the *anthropos* inhabiting the "anthroposphere" is always already defined by more than its species identity.

Animals

> inform our ideas through an infinity of models, thematic variations, existential possibilities, and exemplifying arguments […]. They also give life to new ways of interpreting the world and acting on it. Animality is therefore the archetype that permits, through the non-arbitrariness of its sign, the grammar of the processes of abstraction. […] Our life as humans is surrounded by animal knowledges, is sustained on hybridization with animals, is founded on animal signs.[33]

If in Western philosophical discussions of animality the "heart of the matter" for the most part hasn't been "the animals outside but rather our own immanent animal nature, lived as both an origin and an ongoing inheritance, as our immemorial past as well as what we must transcend in order to be human in the present,"[34] the "animals outside" – their bodies, lifeways and behaviors as well as the (lack of) interiority to which these exterior expressions supposedly testified – have nonetheless served as constant points of reference for delineations of human specificity. In this sense, even the many historical manifestations of anthropocentrism and human exceptionalism remain unwillingly but inevitably expressive of a human dependence on animal life that is also *conceptual* and *epistemological* in character, that involves not only the human's evolutionary deep history but also the cultural history of human self-knowledge and subjectivity.

A postanthropocentric historiography of creaturely interdependence takes as both its central premise and its analytic focus the fact that neither humans nor nonhumans can be understood as fully autonomous history-making subjects, thus underscoring the constitutive importance of the relationality of human and animal historical becomings. In tandem with the various forms of net- or 'meshwork' thinking that have shaped interdisciplinary debate throughout the last decades, relationality might indeed be characterized as something of a postanthropocentric core concept or *episteme* that reaches well beyond the specific concerns of animal studies – and this includes a shift in perspective from the dominant idea of relationality as a result of (intentional) processes of relating to an affirmation of its ontological "primacy."[35] Relationality lies beyond the frustrating impasse of sameness or difference; it allows

33 Marchesini: The Theriosphere, p. 115.

34 Ted Toadvine: The Time of Animal Voices. In: *Konturen* 6 (2014), pp. 22–40, here p. 23.

35 See Andrew Benjamin: *Towards a Relational Ontology. Philosophy's Other Possibility*. Albany: State University of New York Press 2015.

us to cope with the problem that humans and other species both *do* and *do not* inhabit the same world, that they are animate, embodied, earthly beings in lived relations with other creatures whose ways of being-on-earth can nonetheless vary significantly in their adherence "to multiple and discordant spatio-temporal rhythms,"[36] in terms of their sensori-motor makeup and skills, and in many other ways. While, as Marchesini points out, the "unknowable animal" may indeed be a "humanistic invention,"[37] given the fact that human 'access' to nonhuman ways of being must at least to some extent always remain indirect, mediated or partial, most animal historians would probably agree that, however translated into actual animal historical practice, relationality represents something of a conceptual and methodological *sine qua non*. After all, their work is not so much focused on writing an "impossible"[38] history of animals but on writing the history of human-animal *relations* – and this includes the ways in which historical human-animal relations have been shaped by a *disavowal* or marginalization of this relationality in human cultural, philosophical, scientific and other discourses, including the discursive practices of Western historiography itself.

Historiography's Animals

> As history [...] relates to human conduct, it must begin to exist as soon as man begins to act or to extend his ideas beyond his mere animal existence.[39]

It is one of the enduring legacies of the Western historical tradition that its conceptions of human historicity have always been based to a significant extent on the philosophical 'handling' of animals as humans' non-historical others. In keeping with the dominant strands of Western thought, historians and philosophers of history have mostly relied on, and often aggressively reaffirmed, the essential ahistoricity of animal life, with 'the animal' (in the Derridean general singular) functioning as a crucial oppositional figure underwriting the emergence of Man

36 Jamie Lorimer: *Wildlife in the Anthropocene. Conservation After Nature*. Minneapolis: University of Minnesota Press 2015, p. 5.

37 Roberto Marchesini: The Therioanthropic Being as Our Neighbour. In: *Angelaki* 21,1 (2016), pp. 201–214, here p. 204.

38 Erica Fudge: A Left-Handed Blow. Writing the History of Animals. In: Nigel Rothfels (ed.): *Representing Animals*. Bloomington: Indiana UP 2002, pp. 3–18, here p. 6.

39 The Philosophy of History. In: *North American Review* 39,84 (July 1834), pp. 30–56, here p. 32.

as a distinctly historical being – as both the agentic subject of history proper and the proper object of historical inquiry. The work of the influential British historian and philosopher of history, Robin George Collingwood, is one of the more recent examples in which the question of animal (a)historicity implicitly informs, and is sometimes explicitly contrasted with, the notion of human historical life. In the posthumously published *Principles of History* Collingwood defines the "object of historical knowledge" as "*Res Gestae,* understood as the deeds, or past actions, of human beings not in their capacity as animals of a certain species but in their capacity as rational animals."[40] While Collingwood concedes that not all humans are at all times equally successful at being rational animals and, indeed, that humans in general are never more than "feebly, intermittently, and precariously rational,"[41] it is the supposedly uniquely human *capacity* for rational thought that renders *Homo sapiens* a cultural and thus historical being.

> [I]t is in virtue of his [*sic*] rationality that [Man] not only eats but dines, not only copulates but marries, not only dies but is buried. On a foundation of animal life his rationality builds a structure of free activities, free in the sense that although they are based on his animal nature they do not proceed from it but are invented by his reason on its own initiative, and serve not the purposes of animal life but the purposes of reason itself.[42]

His acknowledgment of human animality notwithstanding, Collingwood's emphasis on reason as constitutive of human historicity (and, by extension, of being human more generally) is accompanied, or even enabled, by the presupposition of a fundamental discontinuity with the constraints of animal existence. The "free activities" which characterize human life – "free" because they are more than merely instinctual and predetermined by an organism's biological makeup and environmental embeddedness, as is supposedly the case with all nonhuman animals – may be "based on his animal nature," but they do – crucially – *not* "proceed from it." Rather, "on its own initiative," the capacity for reason gives birth to what seems to be an autonomous sphere of genuinely *human* existence in and of itself, and for Collingwood it is precisely this discontinuity with the merely animal, biological, natural

40 Robin George Collingwood: The Principles of History. In: Id.: *The Principles of History and Other Writings in the Philosophy of History*, ed. by William H. Dray / Jan van der Dussen. New York: Oxford UP 1999, pp. 3–115, here p. 48.

41 Ibid., p. 47.

42 Ibid., p. 46.

that makes possible, legitimizes and guides the work of the historian. In a passage from what is probably his most influential work, *The Idea of History*, Collingwood admits that the notion that humans are the only animals capable of thought "is no doubt a superstition," a concession, however, which is then immediately qualified by the assertion that the human is the only animal who "thinks enough, and clearly enough, to render his actions the expressions of his [*sic*] thoughts" and not merely of "impulse and appetite."[43] Distinguishing between the 'outside' and the 'inside' of historical events, Collingwood explains that while "[t]he processes of nature" are to be understood as "sequences of mere events," the same is not true for historical processes: "They are [...] processes of actions, which have an inner side, consisting of processes of thought; and what the historian is looking for is these processes of thought."[44] While the notion of human-animal difference Collingwood subscribes to is clothed in the Darwinian garb of a difference in degree rather than a radical difference in kind – what Leonard Lawlor calls "metaphysical separationism"[45] –, his defense of the sphere of historicity against the intrusion of natural and animal life processes and forms of being relies on the traditional emphasis on reason as a marker of human uniqueness. In fact, for Collingwood the rational agency of humans that lies at the heart of his conception of history as (only ever) the history of thought is based on a conception of the human as semi-transcendent, independent being defined by a self-enclosed interiority that remains largely unaffected by environmental factors and forms of nonhuman agency. As he puts it in one of his earlier essays,

> Man is not confronted by changing circumstances outside himself; or if he is, that belongs to the mere externals of his life. The essential change is within himself; it is a change in his own habits, his own wants, his own laws, his own beliefs and feelings and valuations; and this change is brought about by the attempt to meet a need itself arising essentially from within. It is because man is not content to react automatically to the stimulus of nature that he is man, and not a plant or a mere animal.[46]

43 Robin George Collingwood: *The Idea of History* [1946], ed. by Jan van der Dussen. Oxford: Oxford UP 1994, p. 216. Collingwood's book was constructed from various manuscript sources after his death by his pupil Thomas M. Knox.

44 Ibid., p. 215.

45 Leonard Lawlor: *This Is Not Sufficient. An Essay on Animality and Human Nature in Derrida*. New York: Columbia UP 2007, p. 24.

46 Robin George Collingwood: The Theory of Historical Cycles [1927]. In: Id.: *Essays in the Philosophy of History*, ed. by William Debbins. Austin: University of Texas Press 1965, pp. 76–89, here p. 86.

As is the case with other thinkers of the Western tradition, in Collingwood's thought the question of the (in)accessibility of nonhuman modes of being encompasses and interrelates epistemic and evaluative aspects. It may be a "superstition" that animals have *no* thoughts whatsoever, but if past actions are "only knowable to [the historian] as the outward expression of thoughts,"[47] the reason they are potentially accessible and thus lend themselves to historical inquiry is because they are not expressive of just *any* kind of thought but of a higher kind of thought that is clearly *recognizable as* thought. We might criticize Collingwood for half-heartedly attempting to fit animals into his rigidly rationalist historiographical framework, and for (unsurprisingly) finding them lacking instead of questioning the framework itself, but this would miss what I think might be the more crucial point: that the always already 'deficient' or 'lacking' animal is, in fact, the enabling precondition of this very framework and its 'exorcism' a crucial self-constitutive performance of Western historiography as such. Collingwood's philosophy of history, that is, relies on an a priori idea about one or several qualities which, in their absence, exclude animals as historical agents before actually considering how the past actions the historian is supposed to work with might also be interpreted in a way that testifies to nonhuman forms of historical agency.

But if Collingwood conceives of the historical process as something propelled forward by the workings of the human mind, the problems it encounters and poses to itself, and the solutions it is able to come up with, the intimate connection between humanity and historicity by means of the pivotal role of thought on which this bond so crucially hinges is haunted by a certain provisionality, a residue of undecidability. For as much and as stubborn as his philosophy of history is centered on the anthropocentric discourse of reason, Collingwood is careful enough to acknowledge that where exactly reason begins – and thus, according to his own philosophical framework, the possibility of history emerges – is not so easy for us to determine. "Perhaps rationality, in some very primitive shape, is as widespread as life itself," Collingwood writes in one of his unpublished manuscripts, which means that, ultimately, "any formula in which we try to define the minimum that we mean by thinking must be altogether arbitrary, and will define only a certain

47 Collingwood: *The Idea of History*, p. 115.

stage in its development."[48] Despite the way it is tied to a hierarchization of thought processes from primitive (animal, 'savage') to higher (human, 'civilized'), the question of the recognizability of thought as it is raised and frequently resurfaces in Collingwood's philosophy of history also figures as an admission of the limitations of human understanding and as a hint towards the fact that to a certain degree animals' ways of being-in-the-world remain enigmatic to us. If human rationality is more akin to an unstable potentiality than a consistent actuality, "flickering and dubious," such a form of rationality "can certainly not be denied to animals other than men. Their minds may be inferior in range and power to those of the lowest savages," Collingwood continues in a rhetoric symptomatic of the discursive intimacies of race and animality,

> but by the same standards the lowest savages are inferior to civilized men, and those whom we call civilized differ among themselves hardly less. There are even among non-human animals the beginnings of historical life: for example, among cats, which do not wash by instinct but are taught by their mothers. Such rudiments of education are something *not essentially different* from an historic culture.[49]

Interestingly, in *Principles*, when he briefly turns to the question of the possibility of animal history, Collingwood refers to the animal stories of Ernest Thompson Seton, published around the turn of the twentieth century and widely read in the United States and elsewhere. Because of their allegedly sentimental or unrealistic portrayals of the natural world and the mental and emotional lives of animals, popular books such as Seton's *Wild Animals I Have Known* (1898) and similar works by other authors such as Jack London and (especially) William J. Long became the object of heated criticism in the context of the infamous 'nature fakers' controversy of the early 1900s.[50] Covered by high-profile magazines such as *Science*, at the heart of this from today's perspective perhaps rather curious debate were crucial post-Darwinian questions about human-animal kinship and difference that in many ways became

48 W. J. van der Dussen: *History as a Science. The Philosophy of R. G. Collingwood.* The Hague: Nijhoff 1981, p. 176.

49 Collingwood: *The Idea of History*, p. 227, emphasis added.

50 For a historical discussion of the controversy and those involved, see Ralph H. Lutts: *The Nature Fakers. Wildlife, Science and Sentiment.* Charlottesville: University of Virginia Press 2001; id. (ed.): *The Wild Animal Story.* Philadelphia: Temple UP 1998.

particularly relevant in the Progressive Era and its debates about the meaning of evolutionary theory.[51] As we might expect, Collingwood is skeptical about the authenticity of Seton's and other animal stories and the way in which "[Seton] professed to reconstruct, from such evidence as that of their tracks, the processes of reason which had determined the actions of various wild animals."[52] "If genuine, these were real history of *Res Gestae*," but, Collingwood continues in a relatively cautious phrasing that nonetheless veers in the direction of a 'nature fakery' accusation, "many readers must have doubted whether they were not sentimentalized portraits falsified by a desire to find in the wild animals he loved a resemblance to human beings closer than actually exists."[53] And yet, indicative of how, despite his anthropocentrism, the question of the animal ultimately remains unresolved for Collingwood precisely because he is a critical thinker, we should note the rather remarkable statement with which he concludes his short-lived foray into the (im)possibilities of animal history: that, in the end, "this is clear, that the question whether history of non-human deeds is possible is to be answered not by arguing, but by trying to write it."[54]

Re-Encountering (American) Animals

> The ancients, one would say, with their gorgons, sphinxes, satyrs, mantichora, etc., could imagine more than existed, while the moderns cannot imagine so much as exists. [...] We are as often injured as benefited by our systems, for, to speak the truth, no human system is a true one, and a name is at most a mere convenience and carries no information with it. As soon as I begin to be aware of the life of any creature, I at once forget its name.[55]

When Progressive-Era Americans like John Burroughs and Theodore Roosevelt condemned the animal stories of Seton and others as misleadingly anthropomorphic 'nature fakery,' in their highly publicized

51 For an excellent discussion of the role of animality in the Progressive Era, see Michael Lundblad: *The Birth of a Jungle. Animality in Progressive-Era U. S. Literature and Culture*. Oxford: Oxford UP 2013; John Bruni: *Scientific Americans. The Making of Popular Science and Evolution in Early Twentieth-Century U. S. Literature and Culture*. Cardiff: University of Wales Press 2014.

52 Collingwood: The Principles of History, p. 47.

53 Ibid.

54 Ibid.

55 Henry David Thoreau: *The Journal, 1837–1861*, ed. by Damion Searls. New York: New York Review of Books 2009, p. 605.

reactions to the works of these writers they exemplified the often unprecedented intensity of debate that surrounded the figure of the animal and the contested meanings of animality in nineteenth-century American culture. The controversy was complex enough and tackled a number of different issues, many of which had already been the subject of debate in the earlier decades of the century. Was it the rigorousness of scientific inquiry or the poetic creativity of imaginative literary writing that offered the most appropriate avenue to the interpretation of animal lives? To what extent were animals to be understood as endowed with the capacities for rational thought, emotion and morality? Were they "reasonable agents"[56] in Collingwoodian terms or more like instinct-driven body-machines, and what were the ethical implications of both views? Did animals have language, and, if yes, how did it 'work' and could it be understood by humans?[57] How could animal life and human-animal relations be conceived in Darwinian terms? The concept of human evolutionary kinship with animals that was anticipated to some degree by post-Enlightenment scientific endeavors in developing fields such as comparative anatomy and in the form of pre- or proto-Darwinian evolutionary thought meant that Western humanity found itself in an increasingly uncertain position on the Great Chain of Being, ushering in what Raymond Corbey has aptly described as a "cosmological sea-change."[58] Because this emergent cosmology "no longer explained humans *meta*physically [...] but traced their origin to the physics of lowly animals," humans were forced "into reluctant retreats from, and renegotiations of, the notion of their own specialty."[59] Indeed, few would have disagreed with him when, in an 1872 review of Louis Figuier's book *The Human Race*, pioneering American anthropologist Lewis Henry Morgan claimed that "the special creation of

56 Collingwood: The Principles of History, p. 46.

57 For the question of animal language in nineteenth-century America, see Susan Pearson: Speaking Bodies, Speaking Minds. Animals, Language, History. In: *History and Theory* 52,4 (2013), pp. 91–108. As Seton argues, while animals such as rabbits "have no speech as we understand it," they do have "a way of conveying ideas by a system of sounds, signs, scents, whisker-touches, movements, and example that answers the purpose of speech." (Ernest Thompson Seton: *Wild Animals I Have Known*. New York: C. Scribner's Sons 1898, pp. 93–94.)

58 Raymond Corbey: *The Metaphysics of Apes. Negotiating the Animal-Human Boundary*. Cambridge: Cambridge UP 2005, p. 34.

59 Ibid., original emphasis.

man" was "the question of questions in modern science."[60] Morgan's assessment, formulated over a decade after the publication of Charles Darwin's *On the Origin of Species* (1859) and a year after that of *The Descent of Man* (1871), testifies to the gradual emergence of a Darwinian or post-Darwinian conception of human life in which the specificity of Man had to be reconfigured in a way that understood the human being as, above all else, a living creature defined by an evolutionary kinship with other animals. American botanist Asa Grey, with whom Darwin had already shared his thoughts on evolution in their personal correspondence in the years leading up to the publication of the *Origin*, became an outspoken proponent of Darwinism and – from his review of Darwin's book in the *Atlantic Monthly* to the defense of Darwinian theory against famous Harvard biologist Louis Agassiz – played an important role in enabling Darwinism to gain a foothold in American science and society.[61]

Robert MacDonald has succinctly interpreted animal stories such as Seton's as a "revolt against instinct."[62] But the critique these stories articulate of the determinist reduction of animal life to this vague category as well as the debate about (animal) instinct versus (human) reason more generally in fact reaches back well into the antebellum

60 Lewis Henry Morgan: The Human Race. In: *The Nation* 15,387 (1872), p. 354.

61 For the influence, reception and adaptation of Darwinian evolutionary theory in the U.S., see the contributions in Jeannette Eileen Jones / Patrick B. Sharp (eds): *Darwin in Atlantic Cultures. Evolutionary Visions of Race, Gender, and Sexuality*. New York: Routledge 2010; and in Tina Gianquitto / Lydia Fisher (eds): *America's Darwin. Darwinian Theory and U.S. Literary Culture*. Athens: University of Georgia Press 2014. Darwin's arguments about the biological continuity between animal and human life and in particular his arguments in *The Descent of Man* were widely (mis)interpreted in a way that, instead of challenging the hegemonic concept of Man, served to underpin and legitimize the widespread anthropocentric and racialized ideas of human civilizational progress. As historian Richard Hofstadter has argued in a seminal 1944 book on the topic, by the turn of the century social Darwinism had become the dominant form in which evolutionary theory exerted its influence on American social and political life. However, not only did many progressives (such as feminist reformer Jane Addams) reject this interpretation of Darwinian theory, as John Bruni points out in his study of Progressive-Era intersections of evolutionary thought and literary writing, the notion of a commanding influence of one particular variety of evolutionary thought is misleading and overlooks the polymorphism of the period's ideas about evolution and its implications regarding the specificity of human life. See Bruni: *Scientific Americans*. For a revised version of Hofstadter's book, see Richard Hofstadter: *Social Darwinism in American Thought*. Boston: Beacon 1992.

62 Robert H. MacDonald: The Revolt Against Instinct. The Animal Stories of Seton and Roberts. In: *Canadian Literature* 84 (1980), pp. 18–29.

period. Morgan's book on *The American Beaver and His Works* (1868), which at first glance might seem somewhat out of place between his early ethnographical studies of the Iroquois and his later work on systems of kinship and social evolution, is arguably as much a study of the lifeways of the industrious rodent as it is a detailed rebuttal of contemporary arguments against animal intelligence. This becomes all the more evident when we read his book alongside an article he published more than 20 years earlier in *The Knickerbocker* under the pseudonym "Aquarius," an article that anticipates many of the arguments of his later monograph. Discussing the various capacities of "the principle called instinct"[63] – which, he argues, is obfuscating, because what it refers to is in fact nothing other than mind – Morgan claims that animals "have a language by which they apprehend each other" and without which "[c]oncert of action and division of labor would be impossible," that they "exhibit the exercise of memory and abstraction,"[64] and that phenomena such as the beaver's dam must be understood as the material result of "deliberative reasoning process[es]."[65] While today's ethology might have a word or two to say about the examples and anecdotes he uses to support his arguments,[66] Morgan's critique of instinct, "a designation that prohibits inquiry, because it pretends to furnish an explanation of itself,"[67] is remarkably incisive in how it alludes to instinct's role not merely as a vaguely defined category that lacks scientific value but as a conceptual device in discourses of human exceptionalism. This insight is formulated most pointedly in his chapter on "Animal Psychology" in the *American Beaver*, where he implies an almost strategic function to instinct as "an invention of the metaphysicians to assert and maintain a fundamental distinction between the mental principle of the human species and that of the inferior animals."[68]

63 Lewis Henry Morgan: Mind or Instinct. An Inquiry Concerning the Manifestation of Mind by the Lower Orders of Animals. In: *The Knickerbocker* 22,5–6 (1843), pp. 414–420, 507–515, here p. 417.

64 Ibid., p. 508.

65 Ibid., p. 509.

66 See, however, James L. Gould / Carol Grant Gould: *Animal Architects. Building and the Evolution of Intelligence*. New York: Basic Books 2007, who are among the supporters of Morgan's arguments and conclusions about beaver intelligence.

67 Morgan: Mind or Instinct, p. 514.

68 Lewis Henry Morgan: *The American Beaver and His Works*. Philadelphia: Lippincott 1868, pp. 275–276.

Though Morgan did not live to witness the 'nature fakers' controversy, Burroughs, for whom animals were beings devoid of any kind of complex interiority and "almost as much under the dominion of absolute nature [...] as are the plants and trees,"[69] would probably have been a viable target for his critique. For Burroughs, the problem with 'nature fakery' was not only that "the line between fact and fiction [was] repeatedly crossed" but that "a deliberate attempt [was] made to induce the reader to cross, too, and to work such a spell upon him that he shall not know that he has crossed and is in the land of make-believe."[70] In a similar vein, zoologist and conservationist William T. Hornaday warned his readers in *The Minds and Manners of Wild Animals* that the 'nature faker' "is always on the alert to see wonderful phenomena in wild life, about which to write; and by preference he places the most strained and marvelous interpretation upon the animal act. Beware of the man who always sees marvelous things in animals, for he is a dangerous guide."[71] While Seton never directly participated in the public controversy, Long – whose animal books, to the dismay of the likes of Burroughs, were also used in American schools – did not stay quiet. Defending his portrayals of animals in the *North American Review*, Long questioned the authority of science as the sole arbiter of truth about animal life, claiming that

> the study of Nature is a vastly different thing from the study of Science; they are no more alike than Psychology and History. Above and beyond the world of facts and law, with which alone Science concerns itself, is an immense and almost unknown world of suggestion and freedom and inspiration, in which the individual, whether animal or man, must struggle against fact and law to develop or keep his own individuality. It is a world of *appreciation* [...] rather than a world of *description*. It is a world that must be interpreted rather than catalogued, for you cannot catalogue or classify the individuality for which all things are struggling.[72]

Long critiqued what he understood to be the 'de-animating' tendencies of the scientific gaze, which, by supposedly reducing individual

69 John Burroughs: *Ways of Nature*. Boston: Houghton Mifflin 1905, pp. 77–78.

70 John Burroughs: Real and Sham Natural History. In: *Atlantic Monthly*, 03/1903, pp. 298–309, here p. 300.

71 William T. Hornaday: *The Minds and Manners of Wild Animals. A Book of Personal Observations*. New York: C. Scribner's Sons 1922, p. 6.

72 William J. Long: The Modern School of Nature-Study and Its Critics. In: *North American Review* 176,558 (May 1903), pp. 688–698, here p. 688, original emphases.

animals to rigid exemplars of a set of species characteristics, may well be more 'exact' with regard to their adherence to the requirements of scientific practice, but this did not necessarily make them more 'true'.[73] In Long's view, scientists indeed committed a kind of *bêtise*: while they divided 'the animal' into a variety of different species, they nonetheless tended to neglect the many forms of *intra*specific difference that manifested themselves in expressions of animal individuality. And, for Long, a true appreciation of animal individuality could not rely on a scientific preoccupation with descriptive objectivity but, quite to the contrary, required an imaginative and affective investment – it required "not only sight but vision; not simply eyes and ears and a note-book; but insight, imagination, and, above all, an intense human sympathy, by which alone the inner life of an animal becomes luminous."[74] Almost a century before the 'nature fakers' were dragged into the national spotlight, Henry David Thoreau anticipated the kind of skepticism voiced by Long and his likeminded contemporaries about science's ability to adequately convey the true meaning and significance of animal life. Thoreau's relationship with science was complex and far from antagonistic,[75] and so he questioned not so much science itself but the rigid classifying practices of (post-)Enlightenment natural history in a way that echoes Long's defense of his animal stories. In his journal entries dated February 17 and 18, 1860, Thoreau reflects in some detail on the "very lively and lifelike descriptions of some of the old naturalists,"[76] reserving particular admiration for Conrad Gessner's five-volume *Historia Animalium* (1551–1558) and Edward Topsell's *Historie of Foure-footed Beastes* (1607), which relies heavily on, and in large parts is an English translation of, Gessner's earlier work. For Thoreau, the writing of naturalists like Gessner showed that they "sympathize with the creatures which they describe."[77] Commenting on the mythozoological character of these works, whose pages are populated by a colorful ensemble of

73 Ibid.

74 Ibid., pp. 692–693.

75 For an excellent study of the relationship between Thoreau's transcendentalism and his engagement with contemporary science, see Laura Dassow Walls: *Seeing New World. Henry David Thoreau and Nineteenth-Century Natural Science*. Madison: University of Wisconsin Press 1995.

76 Thoreau: *The Journal*, p. 603.

77 Ibid.

real and fantastical creatures in the tradition of the medieval bestiary, Thoreau writes that, though some of the animals presented there only roamed the wilderness of the imagination, these writers nonetheless had "a livelier conception of an animal which has no existence, or of an action which was never performed, than most naturalists have of what passes before their eyes."[78] They had "an adequate idea of a beast, or what a beast should be [...], and in their descriptions and drawings they did not always fail when they *surpassed* nature."[79] Most importantly, Thoreau laments the inability or unwillingness of his scientific contemporaries to capture and convey an idea of a creature's "*anima*, its vital spirit, on which is based its character and all the peculiarities by which it most concerns us."

> If you have undertaken to write the biography of an animal, you will have to present to us the living creature, *i. e.*, a result which no man can understand, but only in his degree report the impression made on him. Science in many departments of natural history does not pretend to go beyond the shell; *i. e.*, it does not get to animated nature at all. A history of animated nature must itself be animated.[80]

What should we make of these nineteenth- and turn-of-the-twentieth-century debates about the interpretation and representation of animal life? And what, more specifically, should we think of the sometimes rather extravagant claims and anecdotes presented by 'nature fakers' like Long and Seton? It is not too hard to imagine why, for Burroughs, Seton's claim that in composing his animal stories he "freely translate[d]" from the 'animal' into the English language and in fact "*repeat[ed] nothing that they did not say*"[81] was either the result of an excessive imagination or, even worse, consciously misleading (hence the accusation of 'fakery'). But perhaps, I would like to suggest, we ought to look at Seton's and Long's animal stories from a different angle, one that resonates to an extent with some of the central issues with which animal studies and animal historiography still grapple today, issues such as representation and perspective, subjectivity and agency. These are, of course, neither 'animal-specific' nor exclusively associated with historiography, but they nonetheless bring into particular focus the limitations of both

78 Thoreau: *The Journal*, p. 605.

79 Ibid., pp. 604–605, original emphasis.

80 Ibid., pp. 605–606.

81 Seton: *Wild Animals I Have Known*, p. 94, original emphasis.

the anthropocentric practices of historical writing and of the kinds of materials their truth claims are necessarily based on: How can we say anything about the past lives of nonhuman creatures given the fact that the sources we commonly (have to) rely on are both human-made and human-centered? Do we, perhaps, need to complicate the very idea that these human sources *are* in fact always solely and purely human? Can we identify animal presences or expressions of animal agency in the documents of the past that have been written by human hands? Is there a particular disciplinary approach, mode of thinking, genre of writing that allows us to make more reliable claims about historical animal lives? And so on.

When Seton laments the "fragmentary nature of the records"[82] and tells his readers about how he "gathered, in a hundred different ways, the little bits of proof and scraps of truth that at length enabled me to write this history,"[83] he seems to identify with the work and the troubles of the historian. Similarly, in order to legitimize the historicity of his narratives and their protagonists, Seton frequently establishes a factual frame of reference for his stories, as is the case with the notorious wolf Lobo, who lived "from 1889 to 1894 in the Currumpaw region, as the ranchmen know too well, and died, precisely as related, on January 31, 1894."[84] Elsewhere, however, even though he doesn't address historiography directly, he questions the unthinking anthropocentrism which also informs (and constrains) the established forms of historical practice. "Those of you who would divide the world into human emotion and (on a far lower plane) animal impulse, have not dipped deep into the wells of truth," he writes, but "barely skimmed those stagnant ponds, those abysms of ignorance, called dictionaries and encyclopedias," comparing the impoverished conceptions of animal life prevalent among his contemporaries to the dogmatic ignorance of the sixteenth-century "church folk" who condemned the "blasphemous truths" of Copernicus.[85] "These stories are true," Seton claims in *Wild Animals I Have Known*, and although he admits to have "left the strict line of historical

82 Ibid., p. 10.

83 Ibid., p. 93.

84 Ibid., p. 10.

85 Ernest Thompson Seton: *Great Historic Animals; Mainly about Wolves*. New York: C. Scribner's Sons 1937, pp. x–xi.

truth in many places, the animals in this book were all real characters."[86] Seton's reference to the "strict line of historical truth" is perhaps as much an acknowledgment of the imaginative nature of his animal stories and the way in which they clash with the conventions of historiography as it is a critique of the historical method as such; the "strict line of historical truth," that is, functions perhaps not only as a reference to the epistemic techniques used to separate historical truth from fiction but also as a critique of the dubious metaphysical threshold that *always already* disallows nonhuman beings from entering the domain of a historical – as opposed to a merely 'natural' – life. If Seton insists that his animals were indeed "real characters" in the sense that they actually existed and acted somewhere in space and time, his animals were also allowed to *become* "real characters" because his animal (re)imaginings endowed them with the very parameters – of subjectivity, intentionality, (rational) agency – that enable them to appear as such.

These remarks about Seton are obviously not intended as an implicit call to abandon all historiographical accountability and plausibility in favor of a mode of 'wild thinking' that loses itself in limitless animal imaginings. Rather, I want to suggest that we might also read Seton's stories as a kind of 're-imaginative historiography' that uses the subversive potential inherent to the question of the animal to challenge the boundaries of the historical imagination as such, and that it is in this sense that his stories (as well as the controversy surrounding them) might have some implications for our current forms of "trying to write" animal histories. While it is unlikely that Collingwood's 'challenge' to (future) historians was indeed intended as one, we might argue that the kind of animal-oriented postanthropocentric historiography that has by now passed its formative period and managed to establish itself as a viable field of scholarly inquiry is, in a way, still being practiced in the mode of a "trying to write." Perhaps, that is, postanthropocentric historiography is something that is already actively being written and something that we still need to figure out how to write; something that is already 'here' yet still on the horizon. And perhaps it is something that we should (try to) write *while* arguing about how it can, or should, be written – which is not only a methodological but also a political and ethical question, one that, I think, is nicely captured by the subtitle of Hilda Kean's article on

86 Seton: *Wild Animals I Have Known*, p. 9.

the challenges of animal history: "What Is Really Enough?"[87] For Seton, a collection of animal histories like those presented in *Wild Animals I Have Known* "naturally suggests a common thought" in that they served to emphasize "a moral as old as Scripture—we and the beasts are kin."[88] And yet, perhaps such an idea of creaturely kinship is not only a moral that can be extracted *from* his stories but also, or even more so, their very precondition – a *stance* that enabled him to (try to) write their histories in the first place.

As has been pointed out by others, even though our shared species identity with past humans may allow us to make more plausible claims about their lives and experiences, the often very different realities – social, cultural, political, but also environmental, biological and corporeal – they lived and inhabited still require us to fundamentally rely on the use of our imagination. That is, even though they wandered the earth as members of our own species, it would be foolish to assume that we can have 'access' to their truths in any unmediated and *unimagined* way. The question of truth is, of course, a perennial problem in its own right, a discussion of which is very much beyond the scope of this essay. But I agree with Beverley Southgate's assessment in her 2007 'manifesto' for history that, the reception of poststructuralist-postmodernist critique notwithstanding, "there remains a widespread belief in the unitary nature of 'truth' about the past."[89] With regard to historical animal studies, the quest to recover the 'truth(s)' of animal lives is perhaps most often understood as an interdisciplinary endeavor that involves a more varied set of perspectives and methodologies, incorporating, for example, the insights of non-humanities disciplines such as ethology. Emphasizing this aspect, Cary Wolfe reminds us of the "daunting interdisciplinarity" that has accompanied the "very genesis"[90] of animal studies and points to the ways in which the "internal disciplinarity of history or literary studies or philosophy is unsettled when the animal is taken seriously

87 Hilda Kean: Challenges for Historians Writing Animal-Human History. What Is Really Enough? In: *Anthrozoös: A Multidisciplinary Journal of the Interactions of People & Animals* 25,3 (2012), pp. 57–72.

88 Seton: *Wild Animals I Have Known*, p. 12.

89 Beverley Southgate: "Humani Nil Alienum". The Quest for "Human Nature". In: Keith Jenkins / Sue Morgan / Alun Munslow (eds): *Manifestos for History*. London: Routledge 2007, pp. 67–76, here p. 70.

90 Cary Wolfe: Human, All Too Human. "Animal Studies" and the Humanities. In: *PMLA* 124,2 (2009), pp. 564–575, here p. 565.

not just as another topic or object of study among many but as one with unique demands."[91] With regard to the specifics of historiographical practice, however, it is important to remember that what this focus on interdisciplinarity does is allow us to articulate not so much the historical truths of animals but more informed, more educated, more elaborate historical imaginings that more seriously take into account the irreducible complexity of human and animal ways of being.[92]

The Scope and Structure of This Volume

The present volume understands itself as a contribution to a post-anthropocentric reappraisal of the genesis of the modern United States over the course of the American 'long nineteenth century,'[93] from the revolutionary birth pangs of the nation as such to the momentous social, political and economic transformations of the Progressive Era, which, as Stanley Corkin argues, marked "the birth of the *modern* United States"[94] and its emergence on the world stage as a fully-fledged capitalist industrial power. Particularly in view of the extensive historical timeframe in which the contributions collected here are situated – and given the vagaries that perhaps always accompany the process of putting together a collection of academic essays such as this one –, it is hardly worth mentioning that many topics, developments and contexts that fall within this timeframe remain un(der)addressed. Nor do the contributors necessarily share a joint philosophy on why and

91 Wolfe: Human, All Too Human, pp. 566–567.

92 As Éric Baratay argues, "a link must be made with the imagination, in as controlled a way as possible, so that we come out of ourselves, our condition, so that we decenter ourselves and move to the animal side, even into the animal, in order to make ourselves (in part) animal," without, however, losing sight of the fact that "our reconstitutions of animal lives remain human." (Éric Baratay: Building an Animal History. In: Louisa Mackenzie / Stephanie Posthumus (eds): *French Thinking About Animals*. East Lansing: Michigan State UP 2015, pp. 3–14, here p. 12.) For Vinciane Despret such a kind of decentering also means taking the risk of speculating about the interiority of animals: "how did animals understand and experience what humans offered them or forced on them?" (Vinciane Despret: From Secret Agents to Interagency. In: *History and Theory* 52,4 (2013), pp. 29–44, here p. 32.)

93 The term is, of course, British historian Eric Hobsbawm's, who uses it as an analytic framework for his discussion of European developments from the time of the French Revolution to World War I.

94 Stanley Corkin: *Realism and the Birth of the Modern United States. Cinema, Literature, and Culture.* Athens: University of Georgia Press 1996, emphasis added.

how to write animal history. What they do share, however, is the conviction that an adequate historical understanding of the 'human' past requires a critical and sustained engagement with its more-than-human dimensions. Accordingly, the contributions collected here offer various insights into the wide relevance of animality and human-animal relations as aspects that have always penetrated all areas of American society and culture and also crucially shaped the relations (of power) between different groups of humans. The long-nineteenth-century perspective of this volume pays tribute to the fundamental changes in the relations between humans and animals throughout the nineteenth century – both in the spheres of discourse and imagination and with regard to material practices and spaces of encounter and interaction –, while acknowledging that these changes must be understood in their pre- and post-nineteenth-century connections and continuities.

The contributions to the first section of the volume are centered on the significance of human-animal relations in the development of American modernity and on forms of human-animal relations that can be understood as expressions *of* modernity. Focusing on the profound transformations wrought by the ensemble of phenomena associated with this term, such as urbanization, industrialization, consumer culture and advances in science and technology, they also exemplify the complex and often contradictory status of animals in modernity. For example, while the nineteenth century saw the development of a modern sensibility that resulted in a stronger ethical consideration of animal life – especially with regard to working animals (such as draft horses), stray animals, and the variety of pets living in human households –, in the United States and elsewhere the nineteenth century also ushered in what Derrida describes as the "*unprecedented* proportions of [the] subjection of the animal" by the operations of industrial capitalism.[95] Grappling with the role of animals in American modernity requires us to

95 Derrida: *The Animal That Therefore I Am*, p. 26, original emphasis. For the role of the horse in American modernity, see, for example, Clay McShane / Joel Tarr: *The Horse in the City. Living Machines in the Nineteenth Century*. Baltimore: Johns Hopkins UP 2007; Ann Norton Greene: *Horses at Work. Harnessing Power in Industrial America*. Cambridge: Harvard UP 2008. For the development of American pet culture, see Katherine C. Grier: *Pets in America. A History*. Chapel Hill: University of North Carolina Press 2006. Of course, the status of modern animals becomes less ambivalent if we focus not so much on 'animals' but on different animal species and their respective roles in modern societies.

take into account not only quantitative and qualitative changes in representations of animals against the background of a growing print culture and the emergence of new representational technologies such as photography and early film but also the development of specifically modern practices and institutions of human-animal relations, among the darker manifestations of which is no doubt the mechanized animal death of the slaughterhouse.

The first chapter, by *Katherine C. Grier*, addresses the nineteenth-century rise of an American pet culture and industry with a focus on the development of the American trade in songbirds. Grier traces the activities of a number of German immigrant bird dealers who played a pioneering role in the establishment of the bird trade in the United States and whose biographies serve to illuminate the growth and diversification of the culture of pet keeping over the course of the century. While the two brothers Charles and Henry Reiche established a successful business in New York City that was centered on the importation of canaries (but also imported 'exotic' animals as large as elephants), the commercial efforts of another German immigrant, Henry Bishop – also known as 'Bishop, the Bird Man' – were concentrated on Baltimore. Besides running a successful mail-order trade and (like the Reiches) promoting his expertise in pets in the form of advice books, Bishop also advertised the business of fellow immigrant Otto Lindemann, who specialized in cage making and protected his various innovations in the construction of bird cages with patents. Besides serving as testimony to the growing demand in the animals themselves, the biographies of these German immigrants offer some remarkable insight into "the emerging world of pet supplies and equipment" and the increasing professionalization of the pet trade as an expression of American modernity.

Focusing on the specific role of literary fiction and the functions of literary animals, *Roman Bartosch* discusses the ways in which the factual or perceived absence of wild animal life in an urbanizing American society correlated with fictional expressions of an animal presence and agency that was characterized by a "supposedly wild, untamed realness." While, over the course of the nineteenth century, the lived realities of human-animal relations were increasingly shaped by the interactions between humans and domesticated animal species in built environments, Bartosch's discussion of Herman Melville's *Moby Dick* (1851) and Jack London's *The Call of the Wild* (1903) demonstrates how these ever more urban realities provided the "affective and experiential foundation" for contemporary imaginings of wild animality and their fictional narrativization. Literary animals, Bartosch argues, populate these narratives in the guise of "ciferae" – a concept he takes from Tom Tyler –, as "real, if absent, creatures of flesh and blood" who also function as "markers of desire, affect, and symbolism" and whose peculiar textual agency remains inseparable from the historical context of their literary creation.

Olaf Stieglitz' chapter deals with the cultural emergence of animal 'star athletes' in the context of American horse racing. As his chapter shows, this phenomenon was strongly interwoven with – if not indeed dependent on – the representational possibilities opened up by both the technology of photography as such and by its increasing importance in the growing, highly receptive media environment of the Progressive Era. Photographic visualizations of equine athletes such as Man o' War were of a more than merely illustrative character and of crucial importance for the popularity of horse racing as a spectator sport. While the "dense photographic dispositive" of American horse racing was characterized by an arrangement of human gazes and by the desire of those humans invested in the sport (such as owners, jockeys or betting spectators) to gain information about the qualities and capacities of the respective horses, horse racing photography also portrayed the animals as individual and even exceptional beings whose strong visual(ized) presence at times overshadowed the importance and achievements of their human partners. As Stieglitz shows, horse racing photography thus both allowed for and relied on a distinct animal presence – the nonhuman athlete – at the heart of its modern narratives of competition and performance.

Completing the first section of the volume, *Michael Malay*'s discussion of Upton Sinclair's *The Jungle* (1906) demonstrates that the famous muckraking novel's account of the horrid working conditions in the turn-of-the-century Chicago meatpacking industry invites a reading that not only highlights in unsparing detail the suffering of animal bodies in the Chicago stockyards but points to the interwovenness of a socialist and an 'animal' dimension in Sinclair's critique of industrial capitalism. Sinclair, who spent seven weeks in the stockyards district prior to writing *The Jungle* and hoped that it would induce Americans to voice their outrage regarding the exploitation and mistreatment of immigrant workers, refuted the idea that his novel was concerned with the "moral claims of dying hogs." But, as Malay demonstrates convincingly, beyond or even in conflict with Sinclair's intentions, such a transspecies perspective on the interconnected exploitation of both immigrant *and* animal bodies is in fact suggested by the narrative itself. Even though the novel "has mostly been read as a tale of humanity's soul under capitalism" in which suffering and dying animals function as metaphors for the plight of the proletariat, this metaphoricity is challenged by the way in which Sinclair's writing is suffused with – perhaps haunted by – the disturbing materialities of industrial-scale animal death he himself had witnessed. As Malay argues, Sinclair's novel thus also serves as powerful testimony to the new (commoditizing) modes of seeing nonhuman creatures brought about by industrial modernity's modes of production.

In the way it illuminates both the transformative effects of American modernity on the lives of animals and the interplay between human-animal relations and the social relations of power and inequality that shape *human* life in American society, Malay's contribution functions as a bridge to the second section of the volume. The essays in this section are interested in how ideas about both the figure of 'the animal' and the specifics of different animal species have been co-constitutive of human social categories such as race, gender and class and how particular forms of human-animal relations have shaped interhuman relations in often problematic ways. From the infamous suggestion of sexual relations between black women and apes in Thomas Jefferson's *Notes on the State of Virginia* (1785) to the animalization of black humans under slavery to the post-emancipation atrocities of lynching which, as an article quoted by anti-lynching activist Ida B. Wells claims, was seen as an appropriate response to the "beastial [*sic*] propensities"[96] of African Americans no longer 'kept in check' by slavery – the history of white epistemic and physical violence against black people offers ample testimony to the discursive intertwinings of animality (or species) with race,

96 Ida B. Wells: Southern Horrors. Lynch Law in All Its Phases. In: Ead.: *Southern Horrors and Other Writings. The Anti-Lynching Campaign of Ida B. Wells, 1892–1900*, ed. by Jacqueline Jones Royster. 2nd ed. Boston: Bedford / St. Martin's 2016, pp. 46–68, here p. 59. For the intersections of animality and race, also see Mark S. Roberts: *The Mark of the Beast. Animality and Human Oppression*. West Lafayette: Purdue UP 2008; Christopher Peterson: *Bestial Traces. Race, Sexuality, Animality*. New York: Fordham UP 2013; Lundblad: *The Birth of a Jungle*.

sex and other categories that shaped (though in different ways) Euro-American perceptions of, and relationships with, non-white and indigenous peoples both in American society and on the North American continent more broadly. However, while animalized humans were usually relegated to a precarious position outside the hegemonic domain of Man, we shouldn't limit ourselves to a historical analysis and critique of this concept but also ask, as Alexander Weheliye does, "what different modalities of the human come to light if we do not take the liberal humanist figure of Man as the master-subject but focus on how humanity has been imagined and lived by those subjects excluded from this domain?"[97] In a similar vein, given that the material practices of human-animal relations often figured prominently in differential constructions of the human – for instance, as markers of 'civilizational status' or gender difference –, we need to focus on these material practices not only with regard to the ways in which they informed dominative intersectional constructions of animality but also how they might have challenged or eluded them. This includes taking into account the role of nonhuman animals in these contexts not as passive objects of human knowledge production, hegemonic or otherwise, but as beings whose corporeal presence and agency could actively (re)shape human imaginings and discourses.

As *Brigitte Fielder* shows in the first chapter of the section, the dehumanizing institution and practices of chattel slavery as well as the rhetoric employed both in its defense and in its condemnation require careful attention with regard to the interplay and intersections of race and species. Focusing on dogs and their relationships with enslaved people as it was portrayed by antislavery writers, Fielder's insightful analysis of Harriet Beecher Stowe's abolitionist novel *Uncle Tom's Cabin* (1852) demonstrates that taking into account the complexity and ambivalence of the relationships between enslaved people and animals allows us to draw a more complex picture of "how both oppression and resistance occurred in a landscape of not just human, but also human-animal relations." In the context of slavery, the dog had a polymorphous discursive and material existence, functioning as a racist rhetorical figure employed to relegate black people to the status of inferior beings (and

97 Alexander G. Weheliye: *Habeas Viscus. Racializing Assemblages, Biopolitics, and Black Feminist Theories of the Human*. Durham: Duke UP 2014, p. 8.

to justify their being physically treated as such – 'like dogs') and as creatures of flesh and blood with whom they could have both antagonistic and affectionate relationships. While dogs often figured in abolitionist writing in the form of bloodhounds, instruments of terror used to violently re-enslave escaped black people and to prevent others from trying the same, they were also shown as companions of the enslaved, a potentially subversive relationship that was particularly dangerous in its suggestion that the canine allies of the slave system could also become friends with the enslaved.

Keridiana Chez illuminates the gendered politics of pet preference at the turn of the twentieth century by focusing on changing ideas about (the 'character' of) dogs and cats as well as the beneficial or detrimental effects of human relations with these species. While dogs were traditionally represented as masculine and associated with favorable qualities such as loyalty, honesty and obedience, the apparent unpredictability of cats, their insistence on bodily autonomy and seeming lack of affection for their human 'masters,' became part of a discourse of unruly or 'pathological' femininity-felinity in which the "interspecies pair" of woman and cat formed an "unhealthy affective economy." As Chez argues, however, in the context of fin-de-siècle anxieties and concomitant shifts in the construction of gender, dominant representations of dogs and cats underwent a similar change: while, despite some more favorable and complex representations by fiction writers, the negative image of the cat persisted as a metaphor for the disruptive effects of modernity, the animal's reviled independence and its lack of domesticability was appropriated for the construction of a different kind of dog – one that was more self-assertive and could function as the animal equivalent of a type of masculinity that successfully resisted the emasculating effects of 'overcivilization.' Chez article not only underlines the "entangled evolution" of discourses of gender and animality (in this case caninity and felinity) but also shows that in processes of "the gendering of the nonhuman" animals were never simply passive objects but "influenced human constructions [...], displacing narratives inscribed unto them back on human bodies."

Concluding the second section of the volume, *Aimee Swenson* focuses on the significance of the Navajo-Churro sheep in the cultural life of the Navajo people of the American Southwest and their central role in the conflict between the Navajo and an expanding American settler society.

Originating from the Iberian Churra sheep introduced by sixteenth-century Spanish conquistadors, the sheep were quickly integrated into Navajo culture, ushering in a transition of the Navajo from a hunter-gatherer to a pastoral society. An adequate understanding of the breed's vital role in Navajo society requires us to consider not only the animal's sociocultural and economic centrality but also its genetic and anatomical composition as a unique embodiment of the "reciprocal, interdependent histories" of the Navajo and their sheep. The Navajo-Churro breed, Swenson argues, thus functions as a "historical witness" in that it reflects a specific biophysical historical existence of human-ovine partnership "in which human and animal continuously affect and co-shape each other." As a result of Navajo resistance to increasingly aggressive white encroachment, a violent 1860s military campaign led by Army colonel Kit Carson during which thousands of the Navajo's sheep were killed, and a failed attempt at imposing a sedentary farming lifestyle on them, they were finally forced onto reservations, with their remaining sheep today still being the target of forced stock reduction programs. Beyond its specific historical focus, Swenson's chapter thus also offers important insight into the role of animals and human-animal relations in conflicts between white settlers and indigenous peoples in settler colonial contexts.

The contributions that make up the final section of the volume address the significance of animality and human-animal relations in the history of American exploration and territorial expansion. With the rise of Enlightenment natural history in the eighteenth century, scientifically minded Americans like Jefferson became increasingly interested in exploring and classifying the natural and animal 'productions' (as they were frequently called, reflecting the predominantly utilitarian attitudes of the time) of the national domain as well as those regions of the continent that would or could become a part of it. Exploration was, of course, never an 'innocent' activity but in fact accompanied by at times excessive violence against nonhuman nature and animal life (not to mention its colonialist impetus). The famous ornithologist John James Audubon, for example, still widely regarded as a trailblazer for American conservationism, killed thousands of birds for the drawings and descriptions that make up his multi-volume *Birds of America* (1827–1838) and

Ornithological Biography (1831–1839).[98] Like those of his fellow naturalists, Audubon's expeditions and studies were dependent on animal death. Beginning in the early nineteenth century, the focus of explorers and naturalists gradually shifted to the regions west of the Mississippi, and, whether they were aware of it or not, their individual expeditions, travels and adventures became part of a broader national (and nation-building) process with immense consequences. The concept of Manifest Destiny, coined by New York journalist John L. O'Sullivan in an 1845 article in the *Democratic Review* dealing with and encouraging the possible annexation of Texas by the United States, reframed earlier conceptions of American exceptionalism dating back to the colonial period in a more specifically territorial expansionist vein. While Manifest Destiny – especially in combination with an increasingly virulent 'Anglo-Saxonist' racism – no doubt represented its most aggressive articulation, American visions of a divinely preordained continental expansion 'from sea to shining sea' had already been anticipated by a host of earlier commentators in Jeffersonian times.[99] In combination with the dominant perception of a continental wilderness populated by wild beasts and 'savage' humans, none of whom had a justifiable claim to land that was awaiting its 'improvement' by white civilization, the relentlessness of territorial expansion had catastrophic consequences both for indigenous species and ecologies and the lifeways of indigenous societies.[100]

98 For a recent critique of Audubon's status as conservationist icon, see the editor's introduction in John James Audubon: *The Missouri River Journals of John James Audubon*, ed. by Daniel Patterson. Lincoln: University of Nebraska Press 2016. As Christoph Irmscher argues, Audubon's texts were often "tension-packed stories [...] in which Audubon himself appears alternately as the killer and the savior, the destroyer and the preserver of birds." (Christoph Irmscher: *The Poetics of Natural History. From John Bartram to William James*. New Brunswick: Rutgers UP 1999, p. xxiv.)

99 For the history of American 'Anglo-Saxonism,' see Reginald Horsman: *Race and Manifest Destiny. The Origins of American Racial Anglo-Saxonism*. Cambridge: Harvard UP 1981. For expansionism in the Jeffersonian era, see Frank Lawrence Owsley / Gene A. Smith: *Filibusters and Expansionists. Jeffersonian Manifest Destiny, 1800–1821*. Tuscaloosa: University of Alabama Press 1997.

100 It was only with the emergence of the New Western history in the 1980s that the history of westward expansion was more seriously considered with regard to non-white, non-male, indigenous and environmental perspectives. See, for example, Patricia Nelson Limerick: *The Legacy of Conquest. The Unbroken Past of the American West*. New York: Norton 1987; ead. / Clyde A. Milner / Charles E. Rankin (eds): *Trails. Toward a New Western History*. Lawrence: UP of Kansas 1991.

Neill Matheson's chapter focuses on naturalist William Bartram and the influential account of his late-eighteenth-century travels in the American Southeast. While a significant amount of scholarly work has discussed the significance of Bartram as an early American nature writer and proto-environmentalist with a remarkably nonanthropocentric worldview, Matheson brings into view the more specific and hitherto mostly neglected question of Bartram's attitudes towards nonhuman animals. As Matheson shows in his discussion of Bartram's *Travels* and his lesser known essay on "The Dignity of Human Nature," the naturalist's writing is haunted by a tension between his frequently articulated concern for animal life and his inability to prevent animal death and suffering at the hands of his contemporaries in the context of a dominant cultural tradition in which nonhuman beings for the most part remained outside the sphere of ethical consideration. While Bartram laments the pervasiveness of violence as such – that is, among human as well as nonhuman beings –, it is his sympathy for the plight of animals who suffer human acts of violence and cruelty that distinguishes and isolates him from his contemporaries. As Matheson argues, it is precisely his helplessness and impotence in the face of this violence which also underpins his interspecies ethics.

With a focus on the antebellum period, my own contribution discusses the role of trans-Mississippi Western geographies in what I term the 'zooanthropological imaginary' of nineteenth-century American culture. Beginning in the early decades of the century, the environments west of the Mississippi and the forms of human and animal life associated with them became the focus of American imaginings of animality and humanity in a period in which traditional ideas about the boundaries between them were increasingly becoming unsettled. My chapter argues that contemporaries perceived and experienced Western bioregions as 'animal geographies' that were characterized by an exceptional animal presence and agency and that imposed, or encouraged, modes of human-animal relations that could differ significantly from the experiences in built or rural Eastern American environments. While for some contemporaries Western animal and human life (including the relations between whites and 'Indians') embodied the already popular idea of a relentless struggle for existence from which white, civilized Man would, or was supposed to, emerge victorious, for others the experience of the West instead highlighted the reality of the human being as a living creature among others, with ethical implications sometimes acknowledged, sometimes denied. Antebellum Western environments thus functioned as imaginary and material spaces of ontological speculation and experimentation that played a significant role in pre- or proto-Darwinian conceptions of animality and humanity and the ethics of both human and interspecies relations.

Concluding the volume, *Andrew Howe* delves into the tragic history of the passenger pigeon, one of the irremediable casualties of territorial expansion and its often disastrous environmental consequences. While the American bison is the species that usually comes to mind in this context, unlike the pigeon the bison – an example of 'charismatic megafauna' that became nostalgically associated with the nation's frontier past – was rescued from the brink of extinction and today is no longer listed as an endangered species. The existence of the passenger pigeon, in contrast, found its definite end in 1914 in the Cincinnati Zoo with the death of Martha, the last known living member of the species. Howe's contribution illuminates the context and causes of the pigeon's extinction as well as early responses to and attempts at explaining the rapid decline of a species which had numbered in the billions at the beginning of the nineteenth century. The history of the pigeon also sheds some light on American engagements with the possibility of a permanent disappearance of species (that is, with the concept of extinction), an idea that was only seriously considered by a minority of authors prior to the nineteenth century, because it "violated deeply held views about the overall stability and perfection of the natural world."[101] The passenger pigeon, Howe argues, functioned as a "flexible symbol, representing immigrants, settlers, and indigenous groups," and the attention garnered in 2014 by the 100th anniversary of Martha's death as well as the variety of writings about the pigeon – including a number of songs – seem to underline that its extinction, as Howe puts it, "continues to trouble the American consciousness."

101 Mark V. Barrow: *Nature's Ghosts. Confronting Extinction from the Age of Jefferson to the Age of Ecology*. Chicago: University of Chicago Press 2009, p. 2.

I

Animal Lives and the Contours of American Modernity

"To the Admirers of the Feathered Creation"

The Birth of the Pet Industry and the Trade in Songbirds in Nineteenth-Century America

Katherine C. Grier

In February 1921, *Printer's Ink*, a new magazine directed to the growing advertising business, published a feature article on "Selling Pets." Readers learned that "hundreds of thousands – perhaps millions – of dollars" changed hands in animal sales every year, yet it was "impossible to tell just how old the traffic is, or precisely when it started, or how [...]."[1] Obscurity is still the condition for much of the history of the United States' 60 billion dollar trade in animals, supplies, equipment and services.[2] This essay explores one of the most lively and innovative parts of the early pet trade: the business of providing, selling, and caring for cage birds during the long nineteenth century up to the time of the *Printer's Ink* article.

Recovering the complicated – and not wholly systematized – relationships among the many businesses associated with the gradual commercialization of pet keeping is a challenge. Unfortunately, no business

1 Harold Perlin: Selling Pets. How Advertising Has Helped in the Development of an Unusual Business. *Printer's Ink* 2,3 (1921), pp. 46, 49–50, 53, here p. 46.

2 For spending statistics of the American pet industry, see http://www.americanpetproducts.org/press_industrytrends.asp.

records from nineteenth-century American firms selling pet animals and their equipage are known to survive at present. Thus the research requires examining an unusually wide array of primary sources, from merchants' advertisements in newspapers to the business cards and catalogs handed out by pet stores in the last quarter of the century. Magazine features, credit reports, patent records, popular printed images, photographs and surviving artifacts also provide glimpses into the circumstances of both pet salesmanship and pet ownership. Even by the 1920s, however, the word 'industry' wasn't suitable for the loose networks of wholesale and retail businesses associated with Americans' growing interests in having pets.

A Brief Timeline for the American Pet Trade

My research on the history of pet keeping suggests the following general timeline for the development of the pet trade in the United States.[3] In the eighteenth century, Americans mostly acquired cats and dogs with each other casually – picking up a kitten from a neighbor, for example, when a mouser was needed. City docks seem to have been lively with animals; exotic birds and animals, and unusual dogs were traded by seamen to individuals or small shopkeepers. People of means sometimes corresponded with Europeans and imported dogs, or received them as gifts. The routine sale of wild songbirds and small animals began in outdoor city markets where rural people sold captured creatures as a source of extra money.

By the early nineteenth century, however, cage birds appeared for sale as an occasional sideline in barbershops, stationers and taverns. A few short-lived bird stores appeared in big cities. By the 1820s, florists and horticultural warehouses kept goldfish in their cisterns and canaries in their greenhouses; they also sold imported birdseed. As they had in the eighteenth century, general merchants imported European birdcages as a small part of housewares. Ironmongers and wireworkers made and sold animal cages alongside rattraps, kitchen whisks and wire baskets. By the 1840s, specialized bird stores began to appear in larger cities, selling the first packaged pet foods and medicines. Around the same time, an American literature of advice on bird keeping appeared, although the authors often plagiarized English texts heavily. By the 1870s, dog

3 This timeline is based on Katherine C. Grier: *Pets in America. A History*. Chapel Hill: University of North Carolina Press 2006.

owners with money to spend could also purchase packaged pet food, imported dry biscuits baked by the same companies that made hard tack for maritime use. Specialist dog dealers also appeared in cities, offering both imported and American 'purebred' canines.

By the 1880s, the decade when the American Kennel Club appeared and the owners of 'purebred' dogs organized clubs with pedigree registries, competitive exhibitions for dogs, cats and other small animals, dubbed 'pet stock,' also began to take place in cities. Around that time, some traditional 'bird stores' evolved into full-service pet stores, adding 'purebred' dogs and pet stock such as rabbits and guinea pigs and exotics such as monkeys to the traditional stock of cage birds. Dog and cat owners could now purchase food, beds, collars and harnesses, packaged flea soaps and over-the-counter medicines. And, taking advantage of the flourishing railroad express business of the late nineteenth century, some of these small businesses grew by developing a mail-order trade in animals, especially canaries and other birds, and their supplies that paralleled the rise of mail-order shopping for other consumer goods. By the turn of the twentieth century, small animal veterinary practices, boarding kennels and even commercial pet cemeteries presaged the array of services used by American pet owners in the twenty-first century. American-made dog food, and more rarely cat food, was widely advertised, and canned food, mainly horse meat from unwanted livestock, began to appear in pet stores and grocery stores. While all these businesses certainly constituted a lively sector of the growing world of consumer goods, the collar makers, dog biscuit bakers and neighborhood bird-store keepers did not constitute a self-identified community of commercial interest until the 1920s, when the Pet Shop Owners National Association and the Pet Dealers Association were organized. The latter published *The Pet Dealer*, a monthly that began publication in 1927. The American Pet Products Manufacturing Association, the current umbrella professional association for the pet industry, was not organized until 1958.

Against this general background of the emergence of the American pet trade, this chapter specifically focuses on the trade in songbirds and their accouterments. The American enthusiasm for cage birds drove the pet trade throughout the nineteenth century. The birth of organized, rather than opportunistic, importation of cage birds for wholesaling began in the 1840s. The most famous of these enterprising bird dealers were Charles and Henry Reiche, German immigrants who became the largest importers of canaries from their homeland by the 1850s. Retail bird sellers also demonstrated considerable ingenuity in their methods. Another German immigrant, Henry Bishop, 'Bishop, The Bird Man' of Baltimore, Maryland, provides a case study of a pet enthusiast who became an enterprising pet shop owner in 1874 and created a successful mail-order business in cage birds and goldfish including a brand of foods and remedies that survived through the 1920s. The Reiches and Bishop both promoted their businesses and sold themselves to the public as experts by publishing inexpensive or free books of advice. Bishop took the next step, however, when he developed a namesake line of foods and remedies for cage birds by the late 1870s. Bishop's business also introduces us to the growth of cage production as a large scale and specialized trade rather than a sideline of wire working and furniture making. And here again, the small group of cage manufacturers included a number of German immigrants including Otto Lindemann, who advertised his stylish cages in Henry Bishop's self-published advice book on pet care. Lindemann and his rivals competed on the basis of patents, a potent marketing device at the time, and on the fashionable appearance, as much as on their price. They made a point of offering cages loaded with an array of special features for fussy owners and cherished pets.

The Bird Trade and the Birth of Business in Pets

Caged songbirds are a niche market in the pet industry today, but they were commonplace in American households beginning in the eighteenth century. The reason for their popularity was simple: they provided the background music to daily life, a source of cheer to children and invalids and company to women alone at their housework. While American native birds, especially mockingbirds and 'red birds' (American cardinals) were caged as pets until the early twentieth century, when state bird protection laws took effect, the most desired bird was always the canary, which had been raised in Europe since the seventeenth century, was relatively hardy, and bred easily in captivity. While it is likely that uncounted numbers of birds succumbed to the rigors of transport, household drafts or poor food, it seems that women in particular developed a considerable amount of expertise in the care of their musical pets. Mockingbirds, for example, required that owners provide soft food – live insects or homemade mixtures of egg and bread.

The first glimpses of American shopkeepers buying and selling birds appear in the mid-eighteenth century, when occasional advertisements appear in colonial city newspapers for canaries, the most expensive cage birds but considered the best singers and the most likely to 'thrive' in cages. In the *New-York Gazette* of January 14, 1760, for example, innkeeper James Barnard, advertised a "large Collection of Canary Birds, in full Plumage and song."[4] The source of these animals is unknown, but given the rigors of sailing-ship transport in the cold of the Atlantic Ocean, it is possible that these birds came via a British colonial Caribbean source or were even the result of Barnard's own breeding efforts. It is also possible that they weren't canaries at all but American goldfinches. Notices advertising birdseed appear more frequently, suggesting how common cage birds were. In 1769, New York shopkeeper Samuel Deall placed a notice for his wide assortment of vegetable seeds and groceries including "canary, and rape seeds for birds" imported from London.[5] Seed also showed up for sale in the shops of bookstore and grocers and horticultural suppliers.[6]

Actual 'bird stores' occasionally appear in advertisements in the first years of the nineteenth century, several decades earlier than my previous research suggested. H.J. Hassey advertised in *The New-York Evening Post* on 30 December 1802:

> *To the Admirers of the Feathered Creation*: H.J. HASSEY, No. 72 Wall-street, near the Tontine Coffee-House, begs leave to inform the public, that he has been at a vast deal of trouble and expence [*sic*] to procure the following collection of beautiful SINGING BIRDS, which cannot be equaled in this city, viz – *Canaries, different colors, Robbins* [*sic*], *Blue Jays, Doves, Pigeons, Quails, Mocking Birds, Yellow Birds, Parrots, and A tropical, remarkable for its plumage and note.*[7]

With his location so close to the wharves, Hassey also offered to provide "any Bird and Beasts that this country produces" to masters of vessels

4 Advertisement for James Barnard, innkeeper. In: *New-York Gazette*, January 14, 1760, p. 2.

5 Advertisement. In: *The New-York Gazette, and the Weekly Mercury*, January 30, 1769, p. 4.

6 *The New-York Gazette, and the Weekly Mercury*, June 26, 1769, p. 3: "Fresh Canary Bird Seed" offered by James Rivingston, Bookseller, "at the lower end of Wall-street." Supplement to *Rivington's New-York Gazetteer*, June 10, 1773, p. 3: "JOHN AMIEL, jun. Has just received by the Sampson, Capt. Coupar, and has for Sale at his store in Smith-Street" a variety of grocery items including "Canary and all kinds of bird seeds."

7 Advertisement. In: *The New-York Evening Post*, December 30, 1802, p. 1.

and others: "Foxes, Rabbits, Squirrels, Monkeys, &c."[8] In 1804 and 1805, a series of advertisements appeared in Philadelphia newspapers promoting a "Canary Bird Shop" at 101 Cherry Street, 3rd Floor. The notices offered cages, seeds, fountains (water dishes) along with single birds for one to three dollars apiece and pairs for four.[9] The short duration of these kinds of advertisements – none appears for more than a few months – suggests the ephemeral nature of most of these shops, which probably reflected the seasonal availability of the birds themselves.

The international trade in birds changed forever with the arrival of transatlantic steamship travel. Prior to this, a sea voyage under sail was hard enough on human beings; it must have been extraordinarily difficult to keep alive birds of any kind, and undoubtedly fatalities outweighed successful arrivals on either side of the Atlantic. At first, transatlantic voyages via steam power took a bit over two weeks. A small advertisement in the *New York Herald*, dated 6 May 1848, suggests the small-scale, even casual nature of the traditional trade in birds: "CANARY BIRDS – A FEW OF THE FIRST QUALITY, long breed, mottled and yellow Canary Birds, just arrived from Belgium, per ship Shakespeare, for sale at L.H. EMBREE'S. No. 134 Bowery."[10] However, another notice, in the same paper, suggests the future of the trade and the impact of steamships:

> SINGING BIRDS FROM GERMANY – CHARLES Reiche has just arrived in the b[a]rk Johann Friederch [*sic*], from Bremen, with the following collection of birds: – Nightingales, Wood Larks, Black Caps, White throats, Piping Bullfinches, Thrushes, Blackbirds, and 700 Canary Birds, all in full song and perfect health. For sale at 162 William Street.[11]

700 canaries! This was an unprecedented scale for shipping these fragile creatures, and along with the new speed of travel, it suggests other new methods.

This advertisement introduces a pair of German immigrant bird dealers, Charles and Henry Reiche, who built an organized and large-scale international trade in cage-birds to the United States. Today the Reiche

8 Advertisement. In: *The New-York Evening Post*, December 30, 1802, p. 1.

9 The first advertisement for the "Canary Bird Shop" appeared in the *Aurora General Advertiser*, January 24, 1804, p. 2; the final one appeared in *Poulson's American Daily Advertiser*, February 1, 1806, p. 1. Eighteen advertisements for the Canary Bird Store appeared during this period.

10 Advertisement. In: *New York Herald*, May 6, 1848, p. 3.

11 Ibid.

brothers are best known among historians of circuses and zoos for their importance as dealers in exotic animals beginning around 1870; Henry Reiche's 1887 obituary noted that the firm had done an estimated 300,000 dollars of business with the showman and circus pioneer P.T. Barnum.[12] The date of their arrival is unknown, as is their home, although Henry Reiche's death notice in 1887 reported that he would be buried in the resort town of Grünenplan in lower Saxony.[13] If this is the brothers' birthplace, they were natives of the Harz Mountain region, where rearing canaries was a source of additional income in a region that had suffered from the impact of deforestation. The brothers may have raised canaries themselves, and they certainly knew where to find them.

Charles, born in 1827, wrote in 1853 that he had been in America for almost ten years, and that he had already imported almost 20,000 birds by that time. However, the first newspaper advertisements for his New York business don't appear until the notice of May 1848 quoted above, and later advertisements for the firm list 1847 as its founding year. Charles Reiche and Brother announced their ambitions to bird-loving readers when they placed a full-page advertisement in the 1851 second printing of Daniel J. Browne's *The American Bird Fancier*. Browne was a writer who also produced volumes on gardening, poultry and composting for the *American Agriculturalist*. The Reiche brothers' advertisement notes that their business provided canaries at prices from two to ten dollars each, and only between the months of November and May: "During the warmer months of the year, we visit Europe for the purpose of replenishing our stock."[14] Perhaps realizing that becoming a recognized authority through publication was one way to gain potential customers, Charles Reiche published his own advice guide in 1853, *The Bird Fancier's Companion*. It is unlikely that the text is wholly Reiche's, since most volumes in the genre borrow heavily from one another, but the book was popular enough that it appeared in four editions between 1853 and 1871.

12 A third Frederick Reiche, who sold canaries and cage birds in Baltimore and Boston in 1843 and 1844, may be another member of the family, but he does not appear in accounts of the business. See *Baltimore Sun*, May 18, 1843, p. 3.

13 Death Notice for Henry Reiche. In: *New York Times*, June 17, 1887, p. 5.

14 Advertisement for Charles Reiche & Bro. In: Daniel J. Browne: *The American Bird Fancier*. New York: Orange Judd 1850 (Second printing, 1851), n. p.

The Reiches were both ambitious and peripatetic. There is evidence that they travelled between New York and Germany regularly, arranging for and accompanying shipments of birds and, eventually, animals. In 1856, however, Henry Reiche appears not in New York, where his brother was now well established in trade, but 3,500 miles away in San Francisco. Beginning November 8, "H. Reiche & Co.," as Henry called his business, advertised that 800 German canaries, "just imported from the HARZ MOUNTAIN [*sic*]" had arrived "in full song and perfect health" via the private mail steamer *Sonora*, which plied a route between San Francisco and Panama City. Henry Reiche had probably carried the birds from New York to Panama by steamer, then overland to the *Sonora*; they had already survived the trip from Germany. He also offered "English" starlings (probably the European starling, now an infamous urban denizen in the United States), Linnets (finches) and Nonpareils (painted buntings), probably gathered on a stop at the southern port of New Orleans.[15] In a December 20 advertisement for canaries as Christmas gifts, Reiche noted that his European birds were only sold in the store, and not sent "round in the streets," suggesting the presence of street hawkers selling local captives.[16] By February 1857, Henry Reiche sold off his remaining stock and apparently returned to New York.[17]

This was not the end of his efforts at selling animals away from the East Coast, however. He was back in San Francisco by April 1858, arriving by the steamer *John L. Stephens* with a "superior quality" stock including "VERY FINE SINGING CANARIES," eastern goldfinches, mockingbirds, and even one African Gray Parrot. All stock came from the "house of Charles Reiche & Brother, in Germany and New York."[18] The experiment of selling birds in California ended with this trip, but Henry Reiche arrived in New Orleans the next January, floating downriver from Cincinnati, Ohio (which he had presumably reached by train) with a much more varied cargo including "a large lot of Newfoundland and many other different species of Dogs, Hong-Kong

15 Advertisement. In: *San Francisco Daily Evening Bulletin*, November 7, 1856, p. 2.

16 Advertisement. In: *San Francisco Daily Evening Bulletin*, December 20, 1856, p. 4.

17 Advertisement. In: *San Francisco Daily Evening Bulletin*, January 28, and February 5, 1857, p. 3: "SELLING OFF. GERMAN CANARIES. At $ 6 each – Warranted to be Good Singers. THE OWNER WILL CLOSE HIS STORE in a few days, as he is going home by the next steamer."

18 Advertisement. In: *San Francisco Daily Evening Bulletin*, April 10, 1858, p. 2.

Geese; Poland Ducks; Poland Chickens and Gold Pheasant Chickens, also twelve different pairs of assorted Pigeons."[19]

By the 1860s, steamships had iron hulls and screw propulsion, reducing travel time for bird shipments to eight or nine days. By then, the Reiche Brothers had built an import business in both cage birds and exotic animals that was based in New York City (with a depot for receiving animals in nearby Hoboken, New Jersey) and Bremen. Henry's experimentation with peddling birds and other animals in the American West had ended; the 1860 United States Census shows him, with the occupation of "bird fancier," aged 28 and married to an American-born woman, Louise, with a one-year-old daughter.[20] The Reiche business was located on Chatham Street, a lively commercial district serving middle-class and prosperous working-class shoppers. Several views of the street from the 1850s, including a daguerreotype and an 1858 "General View of Chatham Street" show a streetscape of two-to-six-story wooden and brick buildings, with canvas canopies covering the sidewalk to provide shade and shelter for shoppers and merchandise displayed on the street.[21]

Although canary importation for both wholesale and retail sales remained the reliable heart of the business, by 1863 the firm also advertised its "extensive connections abroad" which enabled it to "receive orders for all kinds of rare Animals, and Birds."[22] This was the beginning of the brothers' second identities, as importers and impresarios specializing in the display and sale of exotic animals as large as elephants. Charles seems to have returned to Germany for extended periods beginning in the late 1860s, and he died there in 1885. While the Reiche Brothers' trade in exotic animals is outside the scope of this essay, it is worth noting that by the 1890s, this side of the business, now led by Henry's only son Hermann, operated in direct competition with the more famous German animal importer Carl Hagenbeck.

19 Advertisement. In: *The Daily Picayune*, January 25, 1859, p. 4.

20 1860 United States Federal Census, New York Ward 4, District 3, p. 31.

21 The street was renamed Park Row in the late nineteenth century, and the buildings that the Reiches knew have long since been pulled down. The street now runs along City Hall Park.

22 Advertisement. In: *New York Herald*, February 15, 1863, p. 3: "Having extensive connections abroad in our line, we are prepared to receive orders for all kinds of rare Animals, and Birds, and are always ready to pay the highest cash prices for all kinds of rare Live Stock." On March 3, 1863, p. 5, the Reiches advertised that they had "500 pairs, in fine condition" of "LIVE PRAIRIE HENS."

By then, the organized bird trade was regarded as remarkable enough to warrant press coverage. The *New York Times* published a lengthy article on the subject on 18 December 1870, coinciding with the seasonal crop of young canaries. "The demand for these feathered pets," reported the paper, has led to "an extensive trade, involving the expenditure of considerable capital, and the exercise of immense labor on the part of those interested therein."[23] Parrots still arrived mostly as a sideline of tropical steamship travel. An estimated 10,000 captive mocking birds arrived in northeastern cities from Virginia and North Carolina: "As soon as the fledglings are well-covered with plumage they are seized and sent in large cages to the North, being carefully fed on the way with prepared food."[24] However, the imported household canary was the real story. Almost all of the 40,000 birds reported to be arriving in America were bred in the dwellings of "peasants in the Hartz [*sic*] Mountains and in Saxony," and the singing males were gathered by "collectors" for the wholesalers. They were

> imported to this country in small wooden cages, made of the fir tree [...]. These cages are made with a common clasp knife, by the carvers of wood and the ingenious wood-workers of Saxony, and afford employment to a large number of young persons. No metal is used in their construction, the framework being fastened with pegs, and the cages are very cheap.[25] (Fig. 1)

The canaries travelled via "fast-going steam-ships," cared for by a "special agent."[26] By 1870, the reported mortality rate was around two per cent, a figure that still held more than 30 years later. The article's importation figure of 40,000 per year may have come from the New York City Customs House, since German canaries were subject to a 20 percent duty.[27] It also mentioned that canaries were bred successfully in the United States but offered no details; this part of the bird trade remains mysterious. And German singing canaries, which underwent schooling from both mature male birds that were regarded as good singers

23 The Bird Trade. Where Song and Cage Birds Are Procured. In: *New York Times*, December 18, 1870, p. 6.

24 Ibid.

25 Ibid.

26 Ibid.

27 Law Reports. United States Circuit Court – Southern District of New York. In: *New York Times*, May 16, 1870, p. 2: "Charles Reiche and Henry Reiche vs. Henry A. Smythe, Collector, etc." This was an unsuccessful lawsuit to recover the 20 percent duty on canaries imported by the Reiches.

Fig. 1
Canary transportation cage, German or English, probably between 1890 and 1920.

and 'bird organs' that repeated desired trills, were always considered the best. An 1892 American consular report on "The Canary-Bird Industry in Germany" noted that it was "almost exclusively a house industry of the poorest classes": "For more than a century canary-breeding has rendered bare existence a possibility to many poor people in Germany, while to others it has brought hope and comfort."[28] At the time the Reiches were active in the trade, when German canaries finally reached retail bird stores, they were small luxuries, costing from four to six dollars at a time when American wages for a skilled worker such as a furniture maker or a carpenter were typically around two dollars per day, while a comfortable middle-class income started at around 1,200 dollars per year.

By 1872, the Reiches were recognized as international animal dealers and operated an important attraction, the New York Aquarium, which combined features of an aquarium, a zoo and, in time, a circus. *The Poultry Bulletin*, a monthly newspaper directed to both farmers and poultry fanciers, reported on their activities regularly. A December item on "Importations and Exportations" gives a sense of the scope of their trade.

28 The Canary-Bird Industry in Germany. Report by Consular Clerk Murphy of Berlin. In: *United State Consular Reports.* Washington, D.C.: United States Government Printing Office 1892, pp. 296–298, here p. 296.

> Messrs. Chas. Reiche & Bro., 55 Chatham St., New York, have received at various times during the past autumn 28000 German canaries; 5000 wild birds, consisting of Goldfinches, Linnets, Chaffinches, Bullfinches, Siskins, Black birds, Thrushes, Starlings, Blackcaps, English Robins, Nightingales, etc.; 2000 African Finches of various kinds, 1000 Australian and other Parrokeets, 300 Parrots; a large assortment of Golden, Silver and English Pheasants; Mandarin and Casaka Ducks, Black and White Swans, etc.; also one Rhinoceros, three Giraffes, one Tiger, one Ostrich, one Porcupine, one Wart Hog, eight Deers and Antelopes, four Kangaroos, and a large variety of Monkeys.[29]

The list of creatures wrenched from their homes is remarkable, and it is worth noting that the Reiche brothers probably bear some responsibility for the arrival of the European starling and the English sparrow in America. But the heart of the business was still singing cage birds, especially canaries. A 1907 report on the trade in cage birds by the U.S. Department of Agriculture illustrated the method for shipping canaries in large numbers; pallets of stacked canary cages, carefully wrapped in canvas to avoid drafts, were accompanied across the sea by trained attendants who fed, watered and monitored the condition of the birds for the duration.[30]

By 1882, Charles Reiche was, according to the *New York Times*, the "father of the bird trade" in America. He died in 1885, and Henry followed two years later. Charles had been a lifelong bachelor, but Henry's son Hermann continued in the business for several decades. By then, however, the trade in imported cage birds had expanded exponentially, and other animal dealers had entered the field. A widely reprinted article titled "Canaries by the Thousands" reported that 250,000 male canaries were produced in the Harz Mountains each year, with 80 percent exported to America. By 1909, wholesalers imported 375,000 canaries, making up four fifths of all birds imported to America.[31] By this time, there may have been substantial American commercial breeders, but they have not yet been identified. World War I cut off the supply of German canaries and probably stimulated American fanciers to go into large-scale production. Still, commercial canary breeding and importation from Germany began again in the 1920s.[32]

29 Importations and Exportations. In: *The Poultry Bulletin* 3,10 (1872), p. 164.

30 Henry Oldys: Cage-Bird Traffic of the United States. In: *Yearbook of the Department of Agriculture 1906* (1907), plate VIII.

31 Canaries by the Thousands. In: *Western Kansas World*, March 3, 1894, p. 8; Canaries Lead Bird Imports In: *New York Times*, May 24, 2010, p. 5.

32 *Illustrated Catalog, Max Geisler Bird Co.* New York / Omaha, NE: self-publishing 1928, p. 1.

Neighborhood Bird Stores and the Mail-Order Trade: Bishop, the Bird Man

While the Reiche brothers retained a storefront selling canaries and other cage birds on Chatham Street, most of the birds they imported were sold to small dealers with bird stores of their own. Henry J.M. Bishop of Baltimore may have been one of these. Bishop's two passport applications, dated 1882 and 1905, reveal that he was born in the municipality of Langwedel in Lower Saxony in 1846 and immigrated to the United States through Bremen in 1862. By 1868, he was a naturalized citizen who resided in the port city of Baltimore.[33] Bishop's bird store grew out of his personal enthusiasm for keeping pets. In a brief autobiography published in 1886, Bishop, who now called himself 'Bishop, the Bird Man,' recollected that, during a previous career as a hotel clerk and ship steward, he "had as much as two hundred dollars worth of birds and aquariums at one time, just for my private amusement."[34] While working for the famous showman P.T. Barnum, Bishop visited Baltimore in the early 1870s. Perhaps drawn by the sizable and sociable German immigrant community in the city, he moved his family there. On June 17, 1874, he turned his hobby into a business, opening a "little Bird Store No. 49 East Baltimore street, with but little cash no credit and no more knowledge of the business than that of an *enthusiastic* private bird fancier."[35] Bishop, his wife and his six children seem to have lived above the store. By the 1870s, American cities contained scores of small bird stores like his, probably providing a modest living at best to their owners.

Henry Bishop had bigger plans, however. By 1878, he had expanded his business to specialize in two kinds of household pet keeping, cage birds and aquaria, although he did also obtain and sell some furry animals. He published a broadside, its contents an earnest and even poetic dispatch on the "general management" of the balanced aquaria (where the proper proportions of fish and plants required only occasional intervention by the owner), the psychological benefits of pets, the reliability and

33 National Archives and Records Administration (NARA), Washington D.C. NARA Series: *Passport Applications, 1795–1905*, roll #: 245, vol. #: Roll 245 – 01 Jan 1882–28 Feb 1882.

34 Henry Bishop: *Bishop, the Bird Man's Book on the Care of Birds and Aquaria*. Baltimore: Bishop 1886, p. 3.

35 Ibid.

honesty of Bishop himself and the array of products offered in his shop, from a three-foot "jardinier [*sic*]" aquarium to "Bishop's Bird Health Restorer."[36] As his business grew, Bishop became an active inventor, receiving four patents between 1880 and 1884 for an improved aviary cage with a revolving perch and a weighted "awning" to protect caged birds from overheating in the sun.[37] He also developed a line of packaged products under his name, including his own seed mixtures, Bishop's Prepared Mocking Bird Food, Bird Dainties, packaged gravel, Orange Color Food, Bird Health Restorer and Bird Insect Powder that he distributed through grocers and druggists as well as via express services to individual customers.

By 1886, Henry Bishop had begun to market himself as 'Bishop, the Bird Man.' He self-published a book, *Bishop, the Bird Man's Book on the Care of Birds and Aquaria*, and distributed it for free. The title page promised advice on the management not only of pets, but "Your Home and Yourself," a promise that he kept with a lengthy discussion on "nervous dyspepsia," an ailment from which he too suffered, and information creating healthful interiors full of fresh air and sunshine.[38] A woodcut of the store exterior depicted show windows full of songbirds and parrots, a couple of monkeys, a small alligator, and fish in large aquaria on stands. (Fig. 2)

Bishop was a man with a mission, and the small paper-cover book reveals its extent. While assurances of honesty in dealing, concern for the welfare of the livestock, and compliments to prospective customers were routine in the advertisements, brochures and catalogs of late-nineteenth century pet businesses, Bishop believed that he served a "natural desire of the human race to have something to protect and care for."[39] Family happiness depended upon the presence of pets, a point he repeated in verses scattered throughout the text:

36 Henry Bishop: *Henry Bishop's Advice to his Patrons on the Care and General Management of the Aquarium*. Baltimore: Bishop 1878, broadside.

37 US Patents 228,438 (June 8, 1880) Aviary Cage; 230,993 (August 10, 1880) Revolving Perch; 290,838 A (December 25, 1883) Sunshade for Bird Cages, and 296,912 (April 15, 1884) Advertising Bird Cage. All patents specified in this chapter were accessed through Google Patents. https://patents.google.com (accessed August 1, 2016).

38 Bishop: *Bishop the Bird Man's Book*, p. 5.

39 Ibid., p. 43.

Fig. 2
"Bishop, the Bird Man's, Reliable Bird House."

Woodcut published in Henry Bishop: *Bishop, the Bird Man's Book on the Care and Management of Birds, Aquariums, Your Home and Yourself*, 1886.

> If you wish to make home cheerful,
> Buy a pretty singing bird;
> As you breakfast in the morning
> His welcome song is heard.
> He will sing for you at dinner,
> And warble sweet at night.
> He will be the children's treasure,
> Fill their hearts with delight.
> When your wife his thrilling song has heard,
> She will say, "I am happy now, we have a bird."
> We all love him and call him Pete –
> He was bought at BISHOP'S,
> 830 East Baltimore Street.[40]

Perhaps sensing the limits of the bird trade, Henry Bishop saw fresh opportunity in the humble goldfish. He suggested that his aquaria – simple containers containing fish, plants and an ornament or two – were not only attractive elements of interior décor but healthful for invalids, who "watch with delight the motions of animal life," while the water absorbed "impure air."[41] A 1890 newspaper ad from the *Baltimore Sun* informed readers that Bishop's "beautiful fishes and a bird to sing" offered "Great Joy at Small Expense."[42]

Bishop recognized that the key to success in goldfish rearing was scale; more space meant more fish, and more fish meant the potential for wider sales. At some point, he was even successful at convincing the Park Board of Baltimore to lease him the ponds of Druid Hill Park for propagating goldfish.[43] By 1900, the scale of his goldfish operation was the object of great public interest. On 1 November, the *Sun* reported on the "annual affair" of

> emptying the boat lake at Druid Hill Park and catching the 40,000 or more small fish in it, which was begun Monday by Mr. Henry Bishop [...]. A large number of persons witnessed the catching of the fish by 25 men employed by Mr. Bishop [...]. The water was drawn from the lake, the fish scooped up and put in barrels.[44]

40 Bishop: *Bishop the Bird Man's Book*, pp. 5, 43.

41 Ibid., p. 61.

42 Advertisement. In: *Baltimore Sun*, December 16, 1890, p. 1.

43 Mr. Bishop to Use the Park Ponds. His Lease Renewed by the Board on Former Terms – Other Matters Transacted. In: *Baltimore Sun*, March 6, 1903, p. 16. The terms were 700 dollars per year, along with 200 dollars in donated animals to the Druid Hill Park Zoo, which he helped to found. Bishop also provided goldfish to fountains throughout the city.

44 Emptying a Lake for Goldfish. In: *Baltimore Sun*, November 21, 1900, p. 10.

The spectacle of Bishop, who was short, portly and jolly, supervising 25 mud-covered men must have been great fun for the spectators. By the time of his death in 1907, most of his goldfish operation was now located in Lakeland, Maryland, on 35 acres of land with "four large lakes and one reserve pond." By then, goldfish, shipped around the United States via rail, seem to have been his most important income stream. His obituary reported that 80 per cent of his business was via mail.[45] In fact, after his death, a short obituary in the *New York Times* called him the "Gold Fish King."[46]

Bishop's business continued and seems to have thrived at least through the 1920s. His face and his advice lived on in *Bishop the Bird Man's Treatise on Birds and Aquaria*, a reprint of some of his earlier writing and a sales catalog that was updated periodically to reflect the appearance of new products and the changing nature of the pet business. The 1929 edition, for example, included advice on caring for cats and dogs and sold products created for them by Dr. A.C. Daniels Company, a well-known maker of veterinary remedies. The little book now cost 25 cents.

The Well-Furnished Bird Cage

Henry Bishop, a man with a mission, had provided his 1886 book for free, thanks to the extensive full-page advertisements throughout that not only reveal his Baltimore business network but his growing relationships with another group of businessmen, the wireworkers who made bird cages for sale. Between pages 8 and 9 of *Bishop the Bird Man's Book on the Care of Birds and Aquaria* is tipped in a full page advertisement for O. Lindemann & Co.'s "Perfection Fender Cage". (Fig. 3) While Bishop reported that the inexpensive cages in his shop were supplied by John D. Meyer of Cortlandt Street, New York, selling the advertising space to Lindemann, when almost all of the other advertising pages promoted Baltimore businesses, suggests that he knew the founder of the firm, a fellow German immigrant working in the bird trade, and probably sold his goods. Otto Lindemann does not ever seem to have sold birds himself; rather, he concentrated on a less fragile and probably

45 Mr. Bishop the Bird Man Dead. In: *Baltimore American*, November 4, 1907, p. 15.

46 Gold Fish King is Dead. Henry Bishop Established Big Lakes and Supplies Many Cities. In: *New York Times*, November 4, 1907, p. 9.

I JUSTLY claim that the above Cage is the prettiest, most complete, and, for the price, the best cage ever offered in the United States. The special merits of this Cage are as follows: The Cage has a high polish; the top of body has two rows of crimped wire, which prevents their spreading and allowing the bird to escape; the cups are closed at the top, so that sparrows, when the bird hangs out in summer, cannot eat the bird's food and otherwise annoy him; the bottom has an extra brim one third of an inch in height—this is to keep the fender in place and proper shape. I furnish my Perfection Fender Cage, with Bathing Dish, O. Lindemann & Co's. Patent Food Holder, Cuttle Bone and Holder, Brass Spring, Spring Bracket and Fender, complete, at $3.50.

This Cage, and many other beautifully designed and practical Cages sold at my store, are manufactured by

O. LINDEMANN & CO.

252, 254 & 256 Pearl Street,

NEW YORK.

Fig. 3
"My Perfection Fender Cage."
Advertisement for O. Lindemann & Co., New York.

Woodcut published in Henry Bishop: *Bishop, the Bird Man's Book on the Care and Management of Birds, Aquariums, Your Home and Yourself*, 1886.

more profitable part of the pet trade: providing housing for family pets. He operated at a scale and a level of specialization that was relatively new to the business of making cages for birds.

In the eighteenth and early nineteenth centuries, bird cages were sometimes imported from England and Germany as part of shipments of other luxury goods.[47] However, some American wireworkers saw cage making as a profitable sideline. In 1802, James Babb of New York City advertised that he not only sold bird cages "made in the London fashion" but had an assortment of canaries on hand, too. Babb's cages were probably similar to the "Mahogany framed BIRD CAGES" offered for sale by James Poultney at his "Ironmongery" in Philadelphia in 1803.[48] Because wire was rather expensive, cages of the eighteenth and early nineteenth century usually took the form of wooden frames with three sides made of wire bars. Made of common woods, they were often designed to hang from nails on walls. Some cages were made entirely of wood, but tinsmiths also produced decorative cages, using thick steel wire or rolled tubes of metal for the bars. By the mid-nineteenth century, fancy painted tin cages, made with wooden finials for hanging and feet for sitting on tabletops, were popular. In fact, soon after Henry Reiche arrived in San Francisco, this advertisement appeared for New Year's Presents, just arrived on the steamer *Fleetwing*: "100 fancy pattern Tin Bird Cages; 1000 lb. Canary, Hemp, Rape and Millet Seed. For sale by BRADSHAW & Co."[49] These were what were later called 'japanned' cages, with paint and lacquer over tinplate.

Of course, as the bird trade expanded, so did demand for suitable housing for the family pet. While animal cages today are usually not particularly stylish, they are easy to clean and safe for the occupants. Cage makers in the past had different goals. Their products had to be

47 Philadelphian John Jacob Sommer, No. 61 Race Street, for example, published a notice that he had on hand a variety of goods imported directly from Hamburg, including three dozen bird cages and three casks of canary seed. See *Poulsen's American Daily Advertiser*, September 17, 1802, p. 3.

48 "JAMES BABB, Cage-maker & Wire-worker, No 4 Broad-street – Begs leave to inform his friends and the public in general that he carries on the above business in its fullest extent, and that he has on hand a variety of bird cages, made in the London fashion." (Selling Cages and Birds. In: *Mercantile Advertiser*, March 20, 1802, p. 4.) James Poultney's ad was published in *Poulson's American Daily Advertiser*. Specialist Cages for Different Species. In: *Poulson's American Daily Advertiser*, March 26, 1803, p. 1.

49 Advertisement. In: *San Francisco Daily Evening Bulletin*, December 20, 1856, n. p.

successful at keeping occupants inside but the variety of birds available meant that bird owners also expected to be able to purchase cages designed specifically for mockingbirds, cardinals, imported bullfinches, and canaries, among others. Further, cages had to be stylish, to a degree that makes them highly prized among collectors today. Nineteenth-century birdcages were important elements in room décor, just as their occupants provided both company and a soundtrack for daily life.

The trades of wire drawing and working with wire changed dramatically during the second half of the nineteenth century; industrial needs for wire cable and, in time, wire for electrical use dominated the business. However, a segment of wirework, which made consumer goods from rug beaters to egg baskets, still relied on craft skill. Birdcages were a special subset of consumer goods within wirework. Fine 'bright' or 'spring' brass wire produced as part of the growing brass industry in Waterbury, Connecticut and probably in smaller quantities in a handful of New York brass factories, became the material of choice for high quality bird cages.

One sign that the trade in birdcages was growing and becoming more competitive is the development of an array of patents. These patents not only represent efforts to improve production. They also represent efforts among cage makers both to expand their customer bases and to differentiate themselves from their competitors, since American consumers enjoyed owning patented objects and seem to have sought them out. Before Henry Bishop patented a handful of innovations in cage construction in the early 1880s, Otto Lindemann took out patents for such improvements as metallic mats for cage floors (1872), improved fountain cups (1874 and 1877) and one-piece cage bottoms that would not harbor insects or require the use of solder (1871). Julius Hepp, an immigrant tinsmith and metal spinner originally from Baden who probably worked for Lindemann, also assigned to the company a patent that improved the process of making decorative round cage bottoms of brass.[50]

50 Original patents (as opposed to re-issues) by Otto Lindemann identified to date are US122,472 Improvement in Metallic Mats for Bird-Cages, issued January 2, 1872; US135,567 Improvement in Bird-Cages, issued February 4, 1873; and US196,684 Improvement in Fountain-cups for Animal Cages, issued October 30, 1877. Julius Hepp's US124,576 Improvement in the Manufacture of Bird Cages, issued March 12, 1872, was assigned to Lindemann in the application.

Otto Lindemann was born in Westphalia in 1836 and arrived in the U.S. in 1851, travelling from Antwerp. His education or training is unknown, but by 1863 he had started business in lower Manhattan as a "bird cage manufacturer." An 1873 listing in *Trow's New York Directory* describes his business as a maker of "japanned and bright metal [brass] bird cages, and importers of flower pots, fern cases and aquariums"[51] on Pearl Street. By 1880, the U.S. Census reveals that he was married to another German immigrant and had six children ranging in age from two years to thirteen.[52] Lindemann's short obituary in the January 6, 1926 issue of the *New York Times* points out that he always lived on Staten Island, which had a large German enclave. As he grew more prosperous, Lindemann was able to purchase, around 1883, a large Italianate house on St. Paul's Avenue, to which he added a three-story mansard addition. He became a director of the Staten Island Savings Bank and a founder of Stapleton's Lutheran Evangelical Church.[53] It is clear that birdcage manufacture was good business.

Two O. Lindemann & Co. wholesale trade catalogs, dated 1883 and 1920, survive in public collections and offer a sense of the wide range of cage types and styles that could be produced using the techniques of flexible batch production, where a variety of delicate preformed parts could be brought together to create cages with different profiles, stylistic details and of different sizes.[54] Around the time of Lindemann's first known catalog, Andrew B. Hendryx of Connecticut founded the company that was his biggest competitor. It too made birdcages, picture wire and, reflecting its owner's personal interests, brass fishing reels. Yet

51 Listing for O Lindemann & Co. In: *Trow's New York Directory*. New York: Trow 1873, p. 769.

52 Otto Lindemann, 1899 Passport Application National Archives and Records Administration (NARA). Washington D.C. NARA Series: *Passport Applications, 1795–1905*; roll #: 522, vol. #: Roll 522 – 01 Apr 1899–13 Apr 1899; U.S. Census. Year: 1880, Census Place: Staten Island, Richmond, New York, roll: 923, Family History Film: 1254923, Page: 167C, Enumeration District: 301, Image: 0339. In: *Trow's New York Directory*. New York: Trow 1872.

53 Gale Harris et al.: *St. Paul's Avenue-Stapleton Heights Historic District. Designation Report*. New York: New York City Landmarks Preservation Commission 2004, p. 19.

54 O. Lindemann & Co.: *Catalogue of Bird Cages*. New York: self-publishing 1883 (Collection of Metropolitan Museum of Art, Accession Number 51.636.4); O. Lindemann & Co.: *Catalogue No. 41 of Japanned, Brass and Tinner Wire Cages*. New York: self-publishing 1920 (Collection of Historic New England).

the interiors of both Andrew B. Hendryx Company and O. Lindemann & Co., along with the handful of other firms in the trade, remain mysterious. Unlike other consumer-goods businesses, they never illustrated their workrooms or even their showrooms in their sales literature. However, in 1918, a legal appeal by O. Lindemann & Co. to the Board of Standards and Appeals of the City of New York offers some detail about the size of his operation at its peak. In 1903, the company had purchased a five-story brick building, 35–37 Wooster Street, in lower Manhattan. The first floor was rented out for unknown commercial purposes. The second through fifth floors, each 4,500 square feet, housed an office and commercial show room, a stock room, and two floors devoted to manufacturing. 47 people worked for O. Lindemann & Co. Lindemann was one of the largest and longest surviving of the Victorian cage makers, but the entire business encompassed only 18,000 square feet.

But let's return to the advertisement for O. Lindemann & Co. in Henry Bishop's 1886 book. "My Perfection Fender Cage," it announces, representing the single voice of a presumed maker and suggesting Otto Lindemann's investment in the quality of the product. The lacquered brass cage is not an empty home for a beloved canary; it is sold furnished with a bathing dish, "O. Lindemann & Co.'s Patent Food Holder," and a cuttlebone with its holder. It is also presented ready for display, with a wall bracket and brass spring and a decorative fender, like a miniature fireplace fender, that prevents seed from spilling. (Although the advertisement does not mention it, the cage, like most of the era, is designed with a bottom that fastens to the top with several latches, allowing it to drop down for cleaning.) The 'Perfection Cage' also cost as much as one of Henry Bishop's guaranteed canaries. And that fact presaged the emerging world of pet supplies and equipment. The purchase of the animal – the original motivation for contacting Henry Bishop by mail or entering his bird shop – was only the first of many expenses over its lifetime. Cages could be, and were, reused of course, but it was the first purchase that represented the level of commitment on the part of the prospective pet owner.

Around the time of the deaths of Charles and Henry Reiche, another German immigrant, Max Geisler, began his own importation business in canaries. By the 1920s, Max Geisler Bird Company filled the niche once occupied by the brothers, importing animals for zoos and

Fig. 4
Cover, *Illustrated Catalog*,
Max Geisler Bird Co., ca. 1920.

show business but also handling 100,000 canaries a year.[55] Eventually, Geisler's became a brand name for a full array of nationally marketed pet supplies, including branded canaries called "Living Music Boxes" and parrots labeled "Human Talkers." (Fig. 4) While the story of Max Geisler extends beyond the timeline of this chapter (the company was in family hands until acquired by ConAgra in 1973), the 1928 catalog continues the practical and promotional tactics in the pet trade pioneered by the Reiches, Henry Bishop and Otto Lindemann. Building upon interests and skills that almost certainly grew from their young lives in Germany, taking full advantage of new technologies of transportation and industrial production, capitalizing upon an already-present yet underserved interest in cage birds and other pets, and using a variety of print media to promote their businesses, this small group of German immigrant entrepreneurs helped to shape the American pet trade over the course of the long nineteenth century.

55 Max Geisler Bird Co.: *Illustrated Catalog.* New York: self-publishing 1928.

Ciferae in the City

Roman Bartosch

Introduction to the Wild

"Animal studies," writes literary scholar Susan McHugh, "starts from the […] assumption that the presence of nonhumans is a cultural constant" in literary narrative.[1] While I certainly agree that the relevance of nonhuman agents is a perennial issue in cultural narratives of all sorts and thus can be traced in the writing of authors all over the world and throughout history, the important question of 'presence' deserves closer attention. In this chapter, I therefore want to engage with the fictional narrativization of animal others whose presence correlates with a specific absence in the lifeworlds of their writers and, perhaps more importantly, the readership affected by the forms of animal presence and agency portrayed in the stories. The animal presence I want to talk about here is one of supposedly wild, untamed realness which was perceived in stark contrast to the environmental experience of most late-nineteenth and early-twentieth-century American readers, for whom their "lived relations with animals" were based, as Jennifer Mason argues, on the experience of and interactions with "ostensibly civilized creatures in the built environment."[2] In her estimation, this means that

1 Susan McHugh: *Animal Farm*'s Lessons for Literary (and) Animal Studies. In: *Humanimalia* 1,1 (2009), pp. 24–39, here p. 24.

2 Jennifer Mason: *Civilized Creatures. Urban Animals, Sentimental Culture, and American Literature, 1850–1900.* Baltimore: Johns Hopkins UP 2005, p. 1.

in order to understand "the contests for power in the human social order played out in literary texts," we do not have to restrict our focus to textual representations of wild animals – or even to texts that are in any straightforward sense 'about' animals –, and she is certainly right in arguing that more subtle representations of domestic human-animal relations may be just as instructive.[3] However, despite Mason's emphasis on the importance of 'civilized' creatures for our cultural, literary and historical analyses, I will, once again, move "beyond the periphery of civilization"[4] to have a closer look at those imagined-yet-real presences of wild literary animal agents. It is my contention that the interplay between (not only) American imaginaries of wild animal agencies and the actual absence of these animals in the daily lives of authors and readers generates, or rather thrives on, an ambivalence inscribed into the animal motifs that can help us rethink the power of fiction in facilitating the task of what Erica Fudge terms "care-filled"[5] readings.

In a discussion of John Law and Donna Haraway's writing on human-animal relations, Fudge suggests "care-filled" as an attribute in contradistinction to the more conventional "careful," arguing that "it is possible to have careful relationships that are not full of the kind of care Law and Haraway outline."[6] While "care" in the first case is a marker of professionalism and diligence, the "care" in "care-filled" points to the realm of concern and caution, which is more difficult to describe accurately but nonetheless crucial for readings of human-animal "choreographies." While careful analytical readings are relevant for literary as well as historical investigations, they too often, and maybe too easily, endeavor to 'give voice back' to animals, for instance by pointing to historical analogies with 'other others', as Hilda Kean does:

> Both women's history and animal-human history were seen as path-breaking new fields. Both have attempted to look at new subjects of history who had been marginalized and have given to new historical theories. [...] This idea of "rescuing" marginalized groups and revealing their past role dominated much women's and social history. It resulted in knowledge of ignored people and events [...].[7]

3 Mason: *Civilized Creatures, p. 1.*

4 Ibid.

5 Erica Fudge: Farmyard Choreographies in Early Modern England. In: Joseph Campana / Scott Maisano (eds): *Renaissance Posthumanism*. New York: Fordham UP 2016, pp. 145–166, here p. 146.

6 Ibid.

7 Hilda Kean: Challenges for Historians Writing Animal-Human Histories. What Is Really Enough? In: *Anthrozoös* 25 (2012), pp. 57–72, here p. 58.

I wish to challenge this approach on two grounds. First, I want to argue that there remains a fundamental difference between the task of writing the histories of other animals and the task of writing the histories of "marginalized groups" of human beings – a difference that literary animal studies has to take into account, productively if possible.[8] Second, and on more general terms, I want to argue that literary scholars have to be careful about claims of 'knowledge' derived from fiction, with regard to both animals and 'other othered' groups, and must be alert to the fragile epistemological and limited ontological validity of their findings.

The first argument draws on the idea that, the important parallels between human and nonhuman animals and our increasing awareness of the porosity of species boundaries notwithstanding, there remains a fundamental difference between human and animal worlds which must not – and cannot – be overlooked in our engagement with writing about these worlds. The task of envisioning multispecies environments and histories lies not in a revision of traditional humanism, "supplementing it or rounding it out so as to include what was traditionally excluded."[9] On the other hand, this difference is not to be played out in terms of human exceptionalism or any hierarchical conception of animal inferiority – what I will call normative anthropocentrism – but on the basis of the limitations of human understanding, our (in)abilities to comprehend the phenomenological lifeworlds and communicative potential of animal others – what I, following Tom Tyler, will call epistemological anthropocentrism.[10] The question is thus, as Jacques Derrida puts it, never really one of giving voice (back) to animals:

8 For a philosophical discussion of this claim, particularly with regard to the question of 'speciecism,' see Anne Burkard: Wie sich die ungleiche Berücksichtigung von Menschen und Tieren nicht verteidigen lässt. In: *Zeitschrift für philosophische Forschung* 68,2 (2014), pp. 153–179, esp. pp. 170–172. Also see Simon Glendinning: From Animal Life to City Life. In: *Angelaki* 5,3 (2000), pp. 19–30. Glendinning describes the challenge of speaking of the animal as a "phenomenological enigma" (ibid., p. 19) and, drawing on Aristotle's concept of the *zoon politikon*, outlines a "democratically urban" vision of interspecies coexistence "open to another heading" (ibid., p. 27) without the "singular *telos*" of anthropocentric humanism or the simple inclusion of a "shared animality" (ibid., p. 22).

9 Ibid., p. 28.

10 Tom Tyler: *Ciferae. A Bestiary in Five Fingers.* Minneapolis: University of Minnesota Press 2012, pp. 4, 21.

> Things would be too simple altogether, the anthropo-theriomorphic reappropriation would already have begun, there would even be the risk that domestication has already come into effect, if I were to give in to my own melancholy. [...] If, in a word, I assigned to it [the animal before him] the words it has no need of [...].[11]

Resisting the need for words and epistemic domestication – how can this even be done in a scholarly context? I think that literature's aesthetic and expressive potential can at least show us a way, if not into the wilderness, then at least towards the wild of an emergent semiosphere.

Urban Shadow Populations

During the same period in which, in the nineteenth century, a massive transformation of human-animal networks and relations took place – one that resulted in the gradual removal from urban spaces of many species of livestock and the introduction of the pet cultures of cats, dogs, and birds[12] – the emotionalization of what came to be understood as relations of human-animal companionship was reinforced, if not engendered, by a cultural imaginary of the wild, the natural, and the untamable. Particularly in the United States, but elsewhere as well, literary writing, in the very moment in which it began to narrativize the relations between pets and human urban dwellers, also took to the frontier of human-animal encounters at the threshold of the nature/culture divide and its semiotic incarnation through storyworlds, both in order to spell out counter-models to urbanized social organization and to make strategic use of the ambiguity of the animal motif.

It is therefore fruitful to look at the engagement with nonhuman urban others in narrative, as numerous studies have recently done.[13] Such attention paid by animal studies to literary animals in nineteenth-century fictional texts which constitute our current academic canon reveals that, perhaps surprisingly, animals more often than not play notable parts in these narratives. However, I wish to point to the fact that, such findings

11 Jacques Derrida: *The Animal That Therefore I Am*, trans. from the French by David Wills. New York: Fordham UP 2008, p. 18.

12 See Katherine Grier's contribution to this volume.

13 See Deborah Denenholz Morse / Martin A. Danahay (eds): *Victorian Animal Dreams. Representations of Animals in Victorian Literature and Culture.* Aldershot: Ashgate 2007; Michael Lundblad: *The Birth of a Jungle. Animality in Progressive-Era U.S. American Literature and Culture.* Oxford: Oxford UP 2013; Mason: *Civilized Creatures*; Harriet Ritvo: *The Animal Estate. The English and Other Creatures During the Victorian Age.* Cambridge: Harvard UP 1989.

notwithstanding, animals' presence in fiction still remains somewhat marginal. Just as today, writers and readers may have focused on the occasional pet, livestock or 'wild' animal who was then quickly turned into a symbol that could be charged with different meanings. But in relation to the actual ubiquity of animals in urban spaces, as products for consumption and means of transportation for instance, their visibility and significance in the literary canon is remarkably small. Just like their counterparts in flesh, blood and fur, fictional animals seem to compose a "shadow population"[14] in the houses of fiction that form a city, but this plays out differently in both contexts. While the absence of visible animals in cities was and is for the most part a matter of urban planning and infrastructure as well as changing procedures of production and transportation, the (in)visibility of animals in literary narratives links with a changing attitude towards animality and the cultural functions of literary writing. In both cases, however, it is, and Derrida may forgive me for playing clumsily with his concepts, a remarkable "illusion of absence" that requires close scrutiny.[15] And, as I will argue here, this illusion of animal absence should be regarded as a productive imaginative moment within a more general, modern structure of feeling which constitutes the discursive and affective framework of specific animal representations.

Interrogating animal motifs not as mere elements of narrative but in the context of an analysis of such modern structures of feeling may also allow us to avoid some of the more problematic tendencies of animal representation in, for instance, fiction, which grounds in a fundamental and arguably violent hierarchical binary, since, as Philip Armstrong puts it, "the generic notion of 'the animal' has provided modernity with a term against which to define its most crucial categories: 'humanity', 'culture', 'reason', and so on."[16] Reading and thinking (about) animals is therefore never, or should never be (seen as), a one-way process. If we ask ourselves, "Why Look at Animals?" or, as Anat Pick has recently

14 Jennifer R. Wolch / Kathleen West / Thomas E. Gaines: Transspecies Urban Theory. In: *Environment and Planning D* 13,6 (1995), pp. 735–760, here p. 736.

15 Jacques Derrida. *Of Grammatology*, trans. from the French by Gayatri Chakravorty Spivak. Baltimore: John Hopkins UP 1998, pp. 139–140.

16 Philip Armstrong: *What Animals Mean in the Fiction of Modernity*. London: Routledge 2008, p. 1.

rephrased the question, "Why Not Look at Animals?,"[17] we have to make use of the inevitable relationality that includes – emerges from but also brings about – the human. Animal fiction is not an avenue for thinking about the animal represented alone – fiction does not show us animals but ani*mots*. "The animal, what a word" indeed – but one that is "good to think" with.[18] In this spirit, we may either look at the narrative engagements with domestic critters in an increasingly urban environment or take this environment as the affective and experiential foundation of contemporary fantasies of an unprecedented imaginary wilderness, and it is the latter which I am interested in here.

It is by turning away from the idea of giving speech or presence 'back' to the animal that I want to start exploring ways of reading literary texts in the Derridean spirit of a "thinking, however fabulous and chimerical it might be, that thinks the absence of the name and of the word otherwise, and as something other than a privation."[19] I will thus try to turn what could be seen as a problem – the relative invisibility of 'real' animals in fiction – into something productive by claiming that fictional negotiations of the illusions of animal absence in nineteenth-century literature allow for readings that focus less on particular animals but on transgressive moments in which *animality* emerges as an interpretive possibility. Accordingly, I will try to show how the alleged muteness of animals thrown into the half-life of literary existence has, during the nineteenth century and beyond, left traces of a peculiar form of agency. This agency is less obvious than the forms of animal agency shaping different real-life encounters because rather than leading to *action* in the more direct sense of the term, it has led to a subtle transformation of literary poetics and patterns. It is also a form of agency that is not inherent to particular animal individuals or groups; rather, it shows in a highly complex interplay between discursive formations and praxes during the nineteenth century and in readerly and writerly forms of understanding within the urban environments in which many of the texts produced during the time are set or, more precisely, with which they are

17 John Berger: Why Look at Animals? In: Id.: *About Looking*. New York: Pantheon 1980; Anat Pick: Why Not Look at Animals? In: *Necsus. European Journal of Media Studies* (Spring 2015). http://www.necsus-ejms.org/why-not-look-at-animals/ (accessed September 19, 2016).

18 Derrida: *The Animal That Therefore I Am*, p. 23. The other reference is, of course, to Claude Lévi-Strauss.

19 Ibid., p. 48.

concerned, by imagining ways of getting away from them. It is, in other words, not an agency originating in a particular agent, but an agency engendered by complex and historically specific relationalities.

I want to look at how dwelling in nineteenth-century cityscapes transformed narrative structures and patterns to a degree that human and animal subjects were rendered relational, beings characterized by a common creatureliness; it is, I will argue, in such urban fiction that what Anat Pick calls "creaturely poetics" had its start. When humans increasingly found themselves in built environments that in turn engendered a desire and longing for 'nature', they began to produce, through the motif of the animal, fictions that in particular ways partook in the "ultimate dismantling of the human-animal boundary" current debates in human-animal studies are concerned with, and they did so not by "produc[ing] arguments or truth claims" but by narrativizing the confusion and uncertainty of creaturely lives in literature.[20] In thinking both developments together – the changing attitudes towards animals and the changing environments in which humans found themselves – I will try to describe an event of emergence that today allows us to reread animality in fiction in ways that effectively cross species boundaries, if only in the imagination. Such an attempt at the literary history of animals acknowledges the wariness of early animal historiography concerning the limitations of such a project which, in Fudge's words, "is not the history of animals; such a thing is impossible. Rather, it is the history of human attitudes toward animals."[21] And yet, I want to emphasize here that literary fiction is more than just documents, its creatures more than mere words. Fiction can have a transfigurative effect on our perception of reality – it makes nothing happen directly, but it may change everything. Therefore, the kind of literary history I have in mind cannot be primarily interested in representations – of animals or human-animal relations – but needs to focus on *functions*: what does a text do? How does it change perception? How has human and especially nonhuman agency influenced narrative? And how does narrative, in turn, influence concepts such as agency, sentience, or consciousness?

I therefore propose to take into account and engage with those fleeting figures of animality, flocking and crowding at the margins of

20 Anat Pick: *Creaturely Poetics. Animality and Vulnerability in Literature and Film.* New York: Columbia UP 2011, here pp. 2, 5.

21 Erica Fudge: *Animal.* London: Reaktion 2002, p. 6.

presence and presentability, rather than the 'real' urban cohabitants of nineteenth-century cityscapes, for the former are loaded with a significance that feeds off their vagueness and elusiveness – a quite distinct form of agency, as it were. Just as Virginia Woolf has taught us not to forget "Shakespeare's sister,"[22] and just as Edward Said has redirected our attention to the colonial plantations that guaranteed familial wealth in Jane Austen's novels,[23] reading urban fictions might require us to leave the safe confines of parlors and cities for the sake of wilder, and less unanimous, semiotic and epistemic grounds.

The Creaturely Rhetoric of Literature

Some of the most popular examples of American literature make use of, and have generated ongoing interest through, their rhetorical employment of markers of undecidability. Hubert Zapf makes this point convincingly in his discussion of the cultural-ecological functions of canonical American novels such as Nathaniel Hawthorne's *The Scarlet Letter*. Arguing from a perspective of cultural ecology, he understands literary writing

> as an ecological force-field within culture, a subversive yet regenerative semiotic energy which, though emerging from and responding to a given sociohistorical situation, still gains relative independence as it unfolds the counter-discursive potential of the imagination in the symbolic act of reconnecting abstract cultural realities to concrete life processes.[24]

Zapf therefore focuses less on the representational verisimilitude of fiction but on "[i]ts aestheticising transgression of immediate referentiality."[25] Not only the novel as a complex literary composition but the very symbol of the scarlet letter exemplifies this excess of meaning that can, then, indeed be read as a semiotic force field, as, for instance, Franco Moretti has shown:

22 Virginia Woolf: *A Room of One's Own*, ed. by David Bradshaw / Stuart N. Clarke. Malden: Wiley-Blackwell 2015, p. 37.

23 Edward Said: *Culture and Imperialism*. New York: Knopf 1993, pp. 62–97.

24 Hubert Zapf: Literature as Cultural Ecology. Notes Towards a Functional Theory of Imaginative Texts with Examples from American Literature. In: Herbert Grabes (ed.): *Literary History/Cultural History. Force-Fields and Tensions*. Tübingen: Narr 2001, pp. 85–99, here p. 88.

25 Ibid.

> At first, Hester Prynne's "A" is the sign of a condemnation—indeed, it is the condemnation itself turned into a sign. In the second chapter of the book, Hester can leave the prison with the heavy oak door that stands on the market square, because in reality she continues to carry it with her, pinned to her breast: it is so weighty a semiotic chain [...] that there is never any need (not even once, in the entire novel!) to make explicit the link between the signifier "A" and the signified "adulteress." [...] A univocal, inflexible sign, defining and labelling once and for all.[26]

In contrast, Zapf contends that "the letter 'A' in the course of the novel [...] becomes a polysemic sign whose semiotic power *transforms* the cultural system by which it was initially defined."[27] This excess of meaning, according to his understanding, not only leaves meaning suspended in a realm of undecidability, but it brings about change in the ways meaning itself is determined and distributed.

What about the animal, then? Could the "A" be taken to lead to the ostracized animal, especially in the urban contexts not of the novel's setting but of its production? Indeed, it has been argued that the scarlet letter takes on qualities of wildness through the excess of its unending semiotic transformation: "The scarlet letter is eventually transformed from a constitutive element of the public sphere into a private 'legend': stratified, mutable, different depending on the person and place—and, basically, no longer in anyone's interest to control."[28] Thus, the shifts of meaning present "*a neutral semantic drift of the allegorical sign*, which passes from one univocity not merely to another with the signs reversed [...], but to the polysemy of multiple paths basically equivalent to each other."[29] I propose the animal figure as another "A"; red, too, and in many cases so in tooth and claw – but also laden with desire and affect, and a longing for what lies beyond the disciplined realms of human organization and social systems. And it is this polysemic excess that can, and should, be recognized as the most important contribution of literary writing of and about animality both in the urban and nonurban wilderness.

This has important implications for the readings and remarks to follow. A care-filled reading of the engagements with animality in fiction might

26 Franco Moretti: *Modern Epic. The World System from Goethe to Garcia Marquez.* London: Verso 1996, p. 86.

27 Zapf: Cultural Ecology, p. 95, emphasis added.

28 Moretti: *Modern Epic*, p. 86.

29 Ibid.

indeed bring about an animal presence and thus serve to bridge the 'abyssal gap' between human and nonhuman animals noted by Derrida and others. But the semiotic excess of literary representation, which has most often been regarded as an enrichment, also means that instead of knowledge and understanding, readers are left with an openness and undecidability of how to read in a care-filled way. Between the abyss of linguistic meaning and the relative certainty of human-animal communication described, for instance, by Donna Haraway and Vicky Hearne, lies dormant the knowledge of fiction about animals. The latter is, in fact, never simply 'about' the animal but charges its motifs with surplus meanings, political, social, and affective. This, in turn, is never something to do away with but the very contribution of literature to the debates at hand: care-filled readings must bring together absences and excesses of meaning, and outline the functions of this kind of writing. In the readings to follow, I therefore concentrate on canonical texts in which animals are center stage and yet remain bound to their ambivalent role of formulating, in Sacvan Bercovitch's words, a "cultural dialectic" of a "social reality [...] at once volatile and malleable, and thus susceptible to radical transformation through the agencies of art."[30]

Ciferae from the City: Melville's *Moby-Dick* (1851) and London's *Call of the Wild* (1903)

"Call me Ishmael": despite its remarkable – and remarkably anthropocentric – opening, Herman Melville's *Moby-Dick* in both its structural composition and plot development undermines the human-bound perspective of 'man's' struggle with nature represented by the hunt for the White Whale. Before Ishmael, in the chapter suggestively entitled "Loomings," begins his homodiegetic account of his voyage and adventure, the book has already confronted us with a plethora of information about whales, setting the tone as it were, by highlighting, through etymologies and numerous quotations from Scripture, natural philosophy and contemporary science, the constructed nature of knowledge about whales and their ubiquity in human imaginaries. By thus stressing the enduring cross-cultural interest in whales while at the same time maintaining that "these extracts are solely valuable or entertaining, as

30 Sacvan Bercovitch: The Problem of Ideology in American Literary History. In: *Critical Inquiry* 12 (1986), pp. 631–653, here pp. 639–640.

affording a glancing bird's eye view of what has been promiscuously said, thought, fancied, and sung of Leviathan,"[31] the book begins on the premise of ambivalence and instability as regards the cultural knowledge of its core theme.

And indeed, the narrative is concerned not with 'whales' or 'the whale' in any cetological sense, but with 'The Whale,' a creature that is at the same time a full-fledged protagonist, as worthy of attention as the next man, and a blank screen for the projection of various human constructions of cultural and personal knowledges and affects. The fact that both functions are insuperable and inextricable is what makes the text an effective commentary on both nonhuman agency and a human desire for imagining animality as a counter-discursive means to get away from the modern urban lifeworld – which must not be mistaken for a desire to be or become animal – stemming from the increasingly urban realities of the time. As the narrator recalls, sailing and seeing "the watery part of the world" is a means of "driving off the spleen, and regulating the circulation":

> Whenever I find myself growing grim about the mouth; whenever I find myself involuntarily pausing before coffin warehouses [...]; and especially whenever my hypos [hypochondrias] get such an upper hand of me, that it requires a strong moral principle to prevent me from deliberately stepping into the street, and methodologically knocking people's hats off—then, I account it high time to get to sea as soon as I can.[32]

The voyage into the watery wilderness is "a substitute for pistol and ball," and Moby-Dick is thus conceptualized as both an antidote to the detrimental aspects of civilization and the object of Ahab's megalomaniacal desire for death and revenge. Together with the natural-scientific information framing the narrative, the stage is set for an inescapably culture-bound and rhetorically framed oceanic drama in which, after Ishmael "quietly take[s] to the ship,"[33] protagonists and readers have to learn to make sense of various encounters between humans and other humans, humans and other animals, and naturecultures and semiospheres. Zapf reads *Moby-Dick* as "a response to the aggressive political

31 Herman Melville: *Moby-Dick; or, The Whale*, ed. by Hershel Parker / Harrison Hayford. New York: Norton 2002, p. 8.

32 Ibid., p. 18.

33 Ibid.

and economic expansionism of American culture in its time"[34]; yet, while it is certainly possible to see the novel's concern with the whaling industry as an exemplification of this critique, 'The Whale' resists such metaphorization. It is true that it can be seen as an index of "the nonhuman, precivilisatory world that resists the civilisatory will-to-power personified, in monomaniacal absoluteness, by Captain Ahab."[35] But it is – does – much more.

Together with the crew, readers now and then enter an ambivalent naturalcultural space when they take to Melville's ocean, a space, as Armstrong argues, in which the "contending currents" of emergent global imperialism and economic modernization "met and mingled."[36] And just as he notes the significance of urbanization in this process of shifting imaginaries, he also concludes that it comes as no surprise that "animals, dead or alive, should figure at the centre of these historical and economic shifts."[37] They are liminal figures, dwelling in the wilderness of an urbanized imagination and incarnating, on the level of diegesis as well as rhetorically, an imagined hybridity of atavistic nature and emergent modernity. Just like the whalers, who retreat to the ocean in search for wild nature away from modern, urbanized environments yet construe their temporary naval home and its surroundings in terms of human forms of social organization, this naturalcultural take on animality shows how, as cultural beings, literary wild animals cannot escape the influence of urban modernity. As Carol Colatrella notes in this context, "characters and plots in Melville's narratives" always seem to "allude to class, gender, and racial or ethnic inequalities arising from urbanization,"[38] and this includes, and complicates, the notion of wilderness.

As "Melville's whales become sites for precisely this kind of translation"[39] between nonhuman and human domains, they create experiences of uncertainty and unreadability through their being culturally framed, for instance by ubiquitous metaphors drawing on urban and domestic

34 Zapf: Cultural Ecology, p. 97.

35 Ibid.

36 Armstrong: *What Animals Mean*, p. 99.

37 Ibid., p. 100.

38 Carol Colatrella: Urbanization, Class Struggle, and Reform. In: Wyn Kelley (ed.): *A Companion to Herman Melville*. Malden: Blackwell, pp. 165–180, here p. 165.

39 Armstrong: *What Animals Mean*, p. 126.

fields, or on the whaling economy. Yet, "[j]ust as it eludes the nets of scientific taxonomy, and the canvases of other media used in attempts to capture its likeness artistically, the whale cannot be rendered by enumerating its various parts in their cut and commodified forms," Armstrong avers and adds that, "as a result [...], *Moby-Dick* fractures the orthodox nineteenth-century model of agency into a profusion of agentic effects."[40] These networks of agentic effects not only includes the set of characters, human and nonhuman, but also comprise, and are built on, the structure of the narrative and moments of its readerly realization.

In the famous "The Grand Armada" chapter, for instance, readers have to follow a complex path through different semiotic environments if they seek to understand Melville's rendering of the whaling experience and the animals' behavior: After "several hours of pulling," the whalers "almost disposed to renounce the chase, when a general pausing commotion among the whales gave animating token that they were now at last under the influence of that strange perplexity of inert irresolution, which, when the fishermen perceive it in the whale, they say he is *gallied.*"[41] While readers may find it difficult to judge whether whalers actually use this term, a footnote Melville adds to the novel's proofs from which the English edition was to be set informs us that the term "gallied" is now "completely obsolete" but occurs "once in Shakspere [*sic*]." There, it refers to the fear of "wanderers of the dark"; that is: humans, framed by the cultural environment of Shakespearean verse.[42] And the passage goes on:

> [...] like King Porus' elephants in the Indian battle with Alexander, they seemed going mad with consternation. [...] Had these leviathans been but a flock of simple sheep, pursued over the pasture by three fierce wolves, they could not possibly have evinced such excessive dismay. But this occasional timidity is characteristic of almost all herding creatures. [...] Witness, too, all human beings, how when herded together in the sheepfold of a theatre's pit, they will, at the slightest alarm of fire, rush helter-skelter for the outlets, crowding, trampling, jamming, and remorselessly dashing each other to death.[43]

40 Ibid., p. 119.

41 Melville: *Moby-Dick*, p. 300, original emphasis.

42 Ibid., p. 300, fn. 3.

43 Ibid.

Here, Melville's proto-environmental vision, which Elizabeth Schultz has described as one of inscrutability,[44] is in fact created by an excess of references: to Alexander's victory over Porus in the battle of Hydaspes, to the more mundane experiences of domestic sheep, only to ultimately bring in human, in fact creaturely, behavior in the face of distress and mortal fear. The novel's "radical redefinition of the relation between human and animal"[45] is thus an effect of its narrative and rhetorical composition which, by emphasizing the very relationality and inscrutability of creaturely existence, creates a space of ambiguity and semantic overload.

In terms of novelistic composition, this is underlined by the structure of the 135 chapters that follow the encyclopedic opening quoted above and which almost always oscillate between the narrative aboard the Pequod and diverse explanations of and references to whale lives, their "schools" and ways of existence. "The Whiteness of the Whale" is analyzed against the background of cultural codes of color and is used to emphasize the animal's "mystical and well nigh ineffable" nature[46] – which in turn leads back into the realm of human civilization because the implications of such musing on skin color could not have gone unnoticed by contemporary readers, one of whom scathingly decries Melville's work for its "moral obtuseness."[47] In another instance, the behavior of male whales is described as "cavalier attendance upon the school of females": "this gentleman is a luxurious Ottoman, [...] surroundingly accompanied by all the solaces and endearments of the harem."[48] Orientalizing the orient as well as the ocean allows for an ambivalent semiotic space in which whales adhere to American standards of beauty and the French tongue is used to describe them: "it cannot be denied, that upon the whole they are hereditarily entitled to *en bon point.*"[49] Whales in this novel exist in constant tension between cultural readability and a kind of enigmatic agency thriving on these cultural references, and this is not a coincidental ambivalence but the heart of the matter. The knowledge to be derived from this semiotic polyvalence is neither factual nor

44 Elizabeth Schultz: Melville's Environmental Vision in *Moby-Dick*. In: *Interdisciplinary Studies in Literature and Environment* 7 (2000), pp. 97–113.

45 Armstrong: *What Animals Mean*, p. 119.

46 Melville: *Moby-Dick*, p. 159.

47 Anonymous: Melville's Moral Obtuseness. In: Melville: *Moby-Dick*, p. 478.

48 Melville: *Moby-Dick*, p. 305.

49 Ibid.

definite, since it cannot eradicate ambivalence – it does not give in to the illusion that this were even possible, to the "melancholy" of semiotic domestication or the "anthropo-theriomorphic reappropriation" mentioned by Derrida, but instead thrives on a kind of polysemantic excess which becomes the governing structural principle of the whole narrative. As Tyler characterizes the knowledge derived from our modern bestiaries: "We are left with no answer or definition, to be sure, and we attain no stable body of knowledge that can tell us what an animal is. Such a body would be an inflexible corpus, a rigidifying *corpse* of knowledge, no better than the inanimate ciphers. The death of the Animal leaves no such carcass or cadaver."[50] What we are left with, then, is a sense of the relationality and uncertainty – as well as the possibilities! – of meaning to be derived from literary fiction.

With regard to human knowledge about animals and the agency of literary animals, Tyler speaks of, and suggests to read the latter as, *Ciferae*. Originating in Sanskrit, translated into Arabic and later adopted by Europeans, *cipher* denotes "nought" or "zero," and when the zero was included in systems of calculation, "the whole system came to be known by its name, 'cipher.' The process of calculating by means of the new system was, by extension, 'ciphering.'" The term then came to refer to something or someone filling a place, a "nonentity," to secret or disguised meanings, and, eventually, to "Egyptian hieroglyphs [...] that frequently took the forms of animals. Here the creatures, of no consequence in their own rights, filled a place in the script so that a meaning might be conveyed."[51] For Tyler as well as for me, the point about *Ciferae* is to accept – and take full advantage of – the always already excessive layers of meaning that envelop any such type of (literary) animal. Doing away with it would also strip the cipher off its ferality, which is why we have to learn, as Tyler puts it, "Deciphering Deciphering."[52] In other words, we have to read in a care-filled way, with an attentiveness both towards the 'thisness' and individuality of animal others and the unruly instability of their narrative and cultural constructions, for "[i]nside any Ciferae, [...] we find untamed Ferae, just as within every *Canis familiaris* there remains an ancestral *Canis lupus*."[53]

50 Tyler: *Ciferae*, p. 50.
51 Ibid., p. 23.
52 Ibid., p. 22.
53 Ibid., p. 41.

Tyler avers that "[i]t is only with their [the Ciferae's] assistance that we will be able to eradicate both the vacantly obfuscating ciphers and the monstrously misleading Animal that have plagued philosophy,"[54] and it is exactly this textual agency I think literature helps best to explore and experience. But neither ciphers nor their specific feralities are stable or ideal entities; they are, rather, historically contingent, politically as well as aesthetically charged, leading a virtual existence brought about by the interplay of their polysemic nature and care-filled readerly engagements with this literary agency. A careful reading would duly identify anthropomorphism. Care-filled readings may help to understand that the novel's concept of wilderness and ambivalence, which allows for the specific 'ciferal' agency to unfold, can directly be related to the real and imaginative topographies of the historical situation of the novel's creation: neither without the increasing urbanization, the effect of which was a profound shift in human-animal relations of many sorts, nor without the scientific grasp of the animal species in question could the text have employed its animal figuration and conceptualized it as an antidote and challenge to its contemporary realities. I believe that proof of this cannot easily be extracted from 'real' historical facts, since it is the question of reality as such that comes to be redistributed; it is on the level of novelistic form that such agencies can be felt. And it is in this context that Zapf writes,

> the white whale is not only guiding the action as a full-fledged protagonist and powerful antagonist to Captain Ahab [...] but also [as] the counterpart of Ishmael the narrator. [...] Meeting the other that is the whale means also a transcendence of the narrator function as an individual, anthropocentric figure, an "intra-action" in Kate Barad's terms.[55]

It is, in other words, on the level of textual conventions and patterning that ciferal agency can be felt and understood.

Another brief case study, of the reception but also the conception of Jack London's *Call of the Wild*, will serve as a second example before I conclude by outlining what I think are the three lessons to be derived from encountering 'Ciferae in the City.' The question of knowledge and literariness is at the heart of the most controversial debates over

54 Tyler: *Ciferae*, p. 45.

55 Hubert Zapf: Metamorphosen des Helden. Menschliche und nichtmenschliche Akteure in der amerikanischen Literatur. In: *Komparatistik Online* 2 (2015), pp. 13–25, here p. 18, transl. R. B.

London's most popular and successful novel. Most influential and interesting in terms of aesthetic knowledge production is surely the 'nature fakers' controversy, which involved, besides London himself, such well-known contemporary writers as William J. Long, Ernest Thompson Seton and Charles G.D. Roberts as well as John Burroughs and Theodore Roosevelt on the opposing side. At the heart of the debate was the conflict between scientific accounts of animals and the poetic license of nature writing and literary fiction: was 'naturalist' fiction about animals and animal consciousness in line with scientific knowledge – or ignorance – of these matters? And was literary speculation especially about the interior lives of animals more than affective fallacy and 'sham' history?[56] Despite London's prolonged silence on the matters discussed and argued about, his text, like many others of the time, "illustrates the extent to which constructions of animality were in flux in the popular imagination, as well as the power of written texts to shape that imagination,"[57] as Michael Lundblad writes. Starting from the claim that the nature fakers debate can be understood as a paradigmatic case "of contested constructions of animality and their cultural implications at the turn of the century,"[58] Lundblad convincingly shows how exactly discourses of race, sexuality and animality work and intersect but also how they are destabilized. His particular focus on sexuality leads him to describe, for instance, how homosexuality is seen as a perversion that links homosexuals with beasts (populating a culturally construed 'jungle') while, at the same time, heterosexuality is conceived of as 'natural' and 'instinctive' – both arguments in fact draw their ideological energy from references to 'nature', making it impossible to understand the 'natural' wilderness as something untouched by heavy cultural construction.[59]

With regard to the uneasy and contested place of nature in this ambiguous discourse, it is helpful to look at the *Ciferae* let loose by London. It is not only in the context of what Greg Garrard dubs London's

56 For a detailed, book-length engagement with this debate, see Ralph H. Lutts: *The Nature Fakers. Wildlife, Science and Sentiment.* Charlottesville: University of Virginia Press 2001.

57 Michael Lundblad: *The Birth of a Jungle. Animality in Progressive-Era U. S. Literature and Culture.* Oxford: Oxford UP 2013, p. 20.

58 Ibid., p. 21.

59 Also see William Cronon: The Trouble with Wilderness; or, Getting Back to the Wrong Nature. In: Id. (ed.): *Uncommon Ground: Toward Reinventing Nature.* New York: Norton 1995, pp. 69–90.

"half-mournful, half-thrilled Spencerian Darwinism,"[60] however, that a word of caution about the celebration of ciphers' ferality is in order: the agentic force of literary animal figures does not mean that this energy is always politically subversive or straightforwardly anti-hegemonic in the sense welcome to most critics and scholars. Rather, while it can be understood as an open-ended counter-discursive movement, it is ultimately impossible to cancel out the Social Darwinist subtext of much of London's writing. In fact, as Garrard concludes, "Buck's feral power makes him an *Uberhund*, beyond good and evil," which underwrites the Nietzschean idea of the end of morality and renders Buck "a potent denizen of London's intensely moralized domain of 'wild' amorality."[61] It is thus less a matter of celebrating the subversive potential of ferality in fiction as it is a return to a 'natural' wilderness now strongly framed in Darwinian terms – as Garrard argues, "if the return of the repressed is bad psychology, the return of the wild is even worse ecology."[62] Still, Lundblad has it right when he states that "London might have thought of himself as a Darwinian, but his texts reflect and produce broader cultural anxieties and alternatives [...], whether he is conscious of them or not."[63] In light of what has been said above, it is both a question of reading London's *Ciferae* in the context of their creation – affective creatures of desire, emerging from, and yet determined to escape, their modern urban environments by virtue of their potentiality for creating moments of semiotic undecidability – and an attempt to explore the enduring textual agency of the animal figures at hand.

If we move from creator to creature and look at the ways in which this 'ciferality' plays out in the story, we again find a certain unease, evident in the constant oscillation between two opposing trajectories. One is the "Spencerian Darwinism" of the *Uberhund*; the other is constituted in the less clearly demarcated realm of "half-mourning" and "half-thrill" that I understand as a bow to the ambivalence and polysemantics of literary animals more generally. Both are crucial for the text's meaning since, as Garrard puts it, "London promotes us to a peculiar sort of divine condition: weak, edible creatures made by evolution to

60 Greg Garrard: Ferality Tales. In: Id. (ed.): *The Oxford Handbook of Ecocriticism*. Oxford: Oxford UP 2014, pp. 241–259, here p. 249.

61 Ibid., p. 250.

62 Ibid., p. 244.

63 Lundblad: *Birth of a Jungle*, p. 8.

transcend, and ultimately to direct, evolution."[64] And both aspects are also discernible on the formal level of the novel, which, as Alex Kershaw maintains, "took naturalism into uncharted territory."[65] In his own praise of the text, Jonathan Auerbach underlines the importance of textual composition and the resulting ambivalence, arguing that, while the narrative follows "the standard naturalist plot of decivilization" and its trajectory from culture to nature, it also moves, "in a more troubled but also more passionate manner, toward self-transcendence that cannot be fully contained by the conventional naturalist model."[66] This narrative double move opens up new possibilities of expression and narration that are closely linked to the focalizing, ciferal creature Buck. The cross between a St. Bernhard and a Scotch shepherd who eventually heeds the call of the wild is, on the one hand, clearly described as a "sated,"[67] saturated animal to whom the stereotypes usually reserved for the landed gentry seem to apply. Buck's "decivilization," which Auerbach calls the "standard naturalist plot," is established by his being kidnapped and having to work for several masters and by learning about "the law of club and fang," one of the numerous lessons that are part of Buck's unsentimental education.[68] Buck's strategy of survival relies on adaptation, and the implications of this will surely have been obvious to the eyes of contemporary readers, possibly trained in or at least familiar with Darwinist thought.

But the roles of heredity and milieu are in fact diluted inasmuch as the events connected with Buck's supra-individual past (i. e. his affiliation to the species of dogs) are part of a clever combination of hereditary determinism (under whose stark rule other animals and people perish) and the idea of a collective unconscious. It is in the moments when

64 Garrard: Ferality Tales, p. 247.

65 Alex Kershaw: *Jack London. A Life*. London: HarperCollins 1997, p. 125. The following part of the chapter has mostly been taken from an article in which I discuss the narratological and ethical implications of this tension-filled structure in more detail and with regard to Lawrence Buell's and Hubert Zapf's respective notions of the ethics of fiction. See Roman Bartosch: *Call of the Wild* and the Ethics of Narrative Strategies. In: *Ecozon@* 1,2 (2010), pp. 87–96.

66 Jonathan Auerbach: *Male Call. Becoming Jack London*. Durham: Duke UP 1996, p. 92.

67 Jack London: The Call of the Wild. In: Id.: *The Call of the Wild, White Fang, and Other Stories*, ed. by Andrew Sinclair. London: Penguin 1993, pp. 39–140, here p. 45.

68 Ibid., pp. 55–64.

Buck listens to the song of the huskies, "one of the first songs of the younger world in a day when songs were sad," that the text transgresses its own naturalist boundaries.[69] Combining the poetic power of atavistic adventures and primitivist "songs of the pack"[70] with the naturalism of the major parts of his prose results in strong moments in the story when *Ciferae*, not animals, roam the diegetic Klondike as well as the readerly imagination – what contemporaries denounced as 'nature faking' comes, from this perspective on textual agency, closer to ciferal ambiguity than to any *Uberhund* ambiguity that the author might have imagined. In fact, these narrative devices contradict and transcend the blatant Social Darwinist aspects of London's fiction and stress both London's "abhorrence of cruelty" to animals and humans alike and the text's potential of being re-read as a modern environmental text.[71] Most importantly, the dialectics of *Ciferae* takes effect on two levels, which I will discuss in more detail below: the text presents its focalizer, Buck, as a ciferal character, and the narrative itself, its discursive structure (in the narratological sense), mirrors this ciferal ambiguity, which underwrites the creaturely appeal of the text.

There are many reasons why Buck can be identified with easily. Part of this is surely the narrative situation – despite the heterodiegetic narrative voice, focalization often tends towards the internal, and we see the world through Buck's eyes in ways that are often most endearing, in particular when Buck does not understand human concepts such as greed for gold. At the same time, his status as animal is subtly contested. When, in a later chapter, Buck reaches camp after hours of walking and toiling, the narrator relates: "All day he limped in agony, and camp once made, lay down like a dead dog."[72] Paradoxically, by using the image of a dog as a metaphor, in this scene Buck is humanized. Consequently, Buck's thoughts are referred to in terms of human cognition – Auerbach

69 London: Call of the Wild, p. 74.

70 Ibid., p. 140.

71 Jacqueline Tavernier-Courbin: The *Call of the Wild* and *The Jungle*: Jack London's and Upton Sinclair's Animal and Human Jungles. In: Donald Pizer (ed.): *The Cambridge Companion to American Realism and Naturalism. From Howells to London.* Cambridge: Cambridge UP 1995, pp. 236–262, here p. 239. For the influential concept of the modern environmental text, see Lawrence Buell: *The Environmental Imagination. Thoreau, Nature Writing, and the Formation of American Culture.* Cambridge: Belknap Press of Harvard UP 1995, p. 7.

72 London: Call of the Wild, p. 70.

mentions "to imagine," "to realize," and "to wonder," amongst others – and are only rarely relativized by phrases such as "dimly aware" or "feels vaguely."[73]

Interestingly, just as with *Moby-Dick*, this narrative strategy not only takes effect with single 'humanimal' characters but can also be found on the level of narrative discourse, which makes the narrative, rather than the focalizer, ciferal too. As mentioned above, the novel's naturalist character is challenged by strongly poetic, almost lyrical accounts of "songs of the younger world"[74] or the "nocturnal song" that helps Buck hark "back through the ages of fire."[75] The same can be said about the effects of the cliffhanger moments of each chapter ending, which seem to me like careful – care-filled, really – orchestrations of the power of *Ciferae*. Increasingly, Buck becomes both an addressee of readerly compassion and an icon of animal supremacy, and eventually, when he turns into the mysterious Ghost Dog, London models the story in ways "closely related to a folk motif recorded in an area close to where [he] gathered the material for his Alaskan stories," relating his own narrative to what he thought was a form of ancestral memory.[76] When Garrard remarks that, ultimately, "the transformation from anthropomorphized focalizer to lupomorphic enigma remains uncompleted,"[77] this openness of meaning should not be seen as a narrative flaw but as the defining feature of *Ciferae*.

This ambivalence is played out on various levels: homosociality and play with sexual innuendo create a sense of humanimal ambiguity, as is the case when Buck and Thornton's fondness for each other is described: "Buck seized Thornton's hand in his teeth. Thornton shook him back and forth. As though animated by a common impulse, the onlookers drew back to a respectful distance; nor were they again indiscreet enough to interrupt."[78] Or when Buck's emotional and cognitive abilities are stressed in ways that are clearly meant to build a direct relation with the likewise understanding reader: The chapter "Who has Won to

73 Auerbach: *Male Call*, p. 89.

74 London: Call of the Wild, p. 140.

75 Ibid., p. 74.

76 Lawrence Clayton: The Ghost Dog. A Motif in 'The Call of the Wild'. In: *Jack London Newsletter* 5 (1972), p. 158.

77 Garrard: Ferality Tales, p. 250.

78 London: Call of the Wild, p. 121.

Mastership" ends with the dog Dave finally being shot after a terrible struggle with his sickness, and the dogs are said to instantly understand the significance of the noise, although Dave is brought out of sight, and the men try to hide their killing of the dog. "A revolver shot rang out [...] [B]ut Buck knew, and every dog knew, what had taken place behind the belt of river trees."[79]

The chapter titled "The Dominant Primordial Beast," in contrast, does not end in that fashion. There is no emotional climax as such, but the language of the chapter's ending is nonetheless interesting. Buck has just won his fight with Spitz, the violent lead dog of the sled team, and the reader has learned that Buck, seemingly unlike the other dogs, possesses "imagination."[80] Spitz dies and Buck becomes the "dominant primordial beast": the narrator makes this statement as if from Buck's view, and continues: "Buck stood and looked on, the successful champion, the dominant primordial beast who had made his kill and found it good."[81] Buck is victorious and has achieved his end, and he looks on his work and finds it good – the biblical connotations are easy to grasp. They add an almost ceremonial tone to the otherwise brutal event and anticipate Buck's final apotheosis. Although the emotional quality is not similar to the other examples, the language, both its biblical phrasing and rhythm, achieves a comparable effect. While London's narratives of the North are often regarded as stories set in a "metaphysical arena in which natural selection and the survival of the fittest are enacted unendingly"[82] and the wilderness is understood as devoid of human traces and, hence, empty, the metaphor of song as well as the many other cultural echoes suggest differently: It is a humming, singing world, and the alleged lack of human signification is but the preliminary condition of a semiosis of the more-than-human world. The creatures populating this world – word creatures all, and *Ciferae* – are characteristically polyvalent, and so are the literary discourses and readerly imaginaries in which they exist.

79 London: Call of the Wild, p. 90.

80 Ibid., p. 79.

81 Ibid., p. 80.

82 James Dickey: Introduction. In: London: *Call of the Wild*, pp. 7–16, here p. 10.

Conclusion: Three Lessons for Care-Filled Interpretation

I have started by speculating about the role of urban environments in literary fictions that turn to animals in ways that support their presence and agency as *Ciferae*: they are understood as real, if absent, creatures of flesh and blood and are, likewise, markers of desire, affect, and symbolism. *Ciferae* are thus *in* the city only in the sense that they are being invoked, read and felt in the environments of urban modernity; as arbiters of creaturely ambiguity, they hail *from* the city and are meant to return there with tales of the more-than-human word. This isn't a typo: since this magic is done by language, *Ciferae* are not a critique of language-bound human ways of cognition but take full advantage of what the linguistic turn has taught us. They do not stand for the critique of the general singular that is the 'animal' but celebrate the richness and unending semiosis of *animot(s)/animaux*. All that is necessary for this, I think, are care-filled readings, so let me conclude this chapter by pointing to such ways of reading and 'deciphering deciphering' in the form of three lessons for care-filled interpretation.

The first lesson is one of relationality: In contradistinction to the ideal of factuality in other areas of knowledge production, the forms of knowing of aesthetic discourses are realized in relations, not in discrete data. What we can learn from reading fiction, in other words, is not facts or truth-claims about humans, animals and everything in-between but rather how an experience of creaturely poetics creates a sense of uncertainty and connectivity that eventually takes effect in a stance of wonder and, perhaps, care, or supports what Matthew Calarco has described as an "agnostic animal ethics."[83] This is the case in literary fiction more generally, but *Ciferae* of and in literature may well be the most prominent and instructive case in point. Theirs is a smoothness of signifying processes, and a mediating power between two worlds of meaning, from which we as readers can learn a lot. We are, to again invoke Tyler, indeed "left with no answer or definition" and "attain no stable body of knowledge that can tell us what an animal is"[84] – but getting a sense of the relationalities through which such alter-epistemologies are enacted means getting a lot right already. This is not the "epistemological

83 Matthew Calarco: Toward an Agnostic Animal Ethics. In: Paola Cavalieri (ed.): *The Death of the Animal. A Dialogue.* New York: Columbia UP, pp. 73–84.

84 Tyler: *Ciferae*, p. 50.

sin" of which Lorraine Daston writes when she traces the history of anthropomorphism.[85] As Tyler remarks, "[s]imply by employing the term *anthropomorphism* one has already adopted a set of unexamined assumptions about human beings."[86] It is rather a cautious engagement with our epistemological anthropocentrism, "both useful and healthy for the speculative enquiry just so long as we remember that we are not seeking to verify postulated characteristics or attributes but are, rather, using this strategy as an explanatory investigative tool."[87] It is by means of this investigative tool that we may learn, through narratives such as Melville's and London's, that "[n]either a creature nor its influences are entirely discrete and self-compelling,"[88] and that we may be able to experience, by way of our being drawn into the mode of semiotic excess in distinct and individual ways, what Michael Rowe calls "a modification of the subject" in terms of its "creaturely situation" that not only changes our view of the existence of animals but also does not leave untouched our understanding of human subjectivity.[89] This holds true for the literary animals I have engaged with here, but perhaps it begins to dawn on us that it may hold true for subjects outside the diegesis as well.

A second lesson, one that is closely connected with the potential of speculation, is the question of the kinds of worlds or environments peopled by *Ciferae*. Again, their presence is most acutely felt in the creaturely narratives outlined above, but these findings can easily be transferred to other texts and textures. While, perhaps surprisingly, early ecocriticism and animal studies have focused on specific environments and their representational verisimilitude – in the spirit of regionalist interest, with a sense of mimetic appreciation or for other reasons –, it becomes clear that the ecologies of *Ciferae* are always explicitly 'made-up,' part imagination and part empirical reality, and quite comfortably at home in their naturalcultural domain. The ocean exists, the Klondike

85 Lorraine Daston: Intelligences. Angelic, Animal, Human. In: Ead./Gregg Mitman (eds): *Thinking with Animals. New Perspectives on Anthropomorphism*. New York: Columbia UP 2005, pp. 37–58, here p. 39.

86 Tyler: *Ciferae*, p. 59.

87 Ibid., p. 57.

88 Michael H. Rowe: Jack London's Wolf Cubs, Michel Serres's Burning Ship and the Creaturely Situation. In: *European Journal of English Studies* 19,1 (2015), pp. 55–65, here p. 56.

89 Ibid.

exists, but the landscapes Moby Dick or Buck roam are always also landscapes of the mind, of affect, and of longing. If we understand that instead of actual environments, readers encounter and explore *possible* worlds, it becomes easier to see that literature is more than and different from a representational machine – a producer of "ideas of ideas" in Plato's famous, derisive remark – but a generator and actant in processes of creaturely meaning making and the making of homes in both world- and wordscape. Describing this in terms of a "Kantian 'as-if'" and from the perspective of a "dynamics of interdependence," Serenella Iovino states that "the text and the world are a complex information unit" through which feedback loops can be generated that allow the text to have a direct effect on its surrounding world.[90] While the notion of 'information,' indebted as it is to cybernetics and systems theory, can in my view not fully grasp what affect and agency encompass, I nonetheless subscribe to the new materialist impetus to take seriously the agentic material force of the written wor(l)d.

The third and, for the moment, last lesson from this lies in understanding the spaces of possibility opened up by *Ciferae* and the reader-as-critter in the context of inter- or transdisciplinary engagements with ecology and animality. I have quoted above Hilda Kean's conviction that animal histories can be written in the same ways as the histories of other othered groups, and I have expressed certain reservations about this. While I am certainly not qualified to decide on these matters, I suggest, in the meantime, that fictional literature can be understood, *qua* its polysemic nature, as a tool for guided and sensitive speculation, a complex zooanthropological machine through which other discourses – the sciences in particular – can be and have always been challenged. Again, the animal case is particularly insightful, since the revision of age-old ideas of the inferiority of animals vis-à-vis human beings seems to me to be largely a result of literary and sentimental education. From a scientific side, the question of the 'automatic' nature of animals had been answered long ago, but it was the enduring power *Ciferae* have had, and continue to have, on the imagination that led us to where we are now: in the midst of a teeming and buzzing relational world of creatures made of flesh, blood, and words.

90 Serenella Iovino: Ecocriticism, Ecology of Mind, and Narrative Ethics. A Theoretical Ground for Ecocriticism as Educational Practice. In: *Interdisciplinary Studies in Literature and the Environment* 17,4 (2010), pp. 759–762, here p. 761.

Horses, Cameras, and a Multitude of Gazes

Visualizing Animal Athletes, 1890s–1930s

Olaf Stieglitz

For most newspapers all over the United States it was headline material, at least in their growing sports sections. On race day, November 1, 1938, the *Chicago Tribune* titled in excited anticipation: "At Last – War Admiral vs. Seabiscuit." Right after the event, the *New York Times* declared that "the better horse had won," thus elevating Seabiscuit into the ranks of racing legends who are still famous today.[1] Surely the 'Match of the Century' between the Triple Crown champion from the East (War Admiral) and the rising underdog from the West (Seabiscuit) was met with national enthusiasm, and the many forms of nostalgic memory it still evokes – novels, children's books, feature films, internet forums or YouTube clips – suggest that two heroic animal athletes delivered prime performances of truly larger than human proportions.[2]

1 *Chicago Tribune*, November 1, 1938, p. 23: "War Admiral and Seabiscuit to Race Today"; *New York Times*, November 2, 1938, p. 29: "40,000 Watch Seabiscuit Defeat War Admiral at Pimlico."

2 The most popular account of Seabiscuit is Laura Hillenbrand: *Seabiscuit. An American Legend*. New York: Random House 2001, on which the Academy Award nominated movie directed by Gary Ross (USA 2003) was based. For a brief but more scholarly treatment of the horse and his career, see Gerald R. Gems / Linda J. Borish / Gertrud Pfister: *Sports in American History. From Colonization to Globalization*. Champaign: Human Kinetics 2008, p. 262.

Before you get the wrong impression, let me insert a disclaimer: My chapter is not intended as yet another contribution to the Seabiscuit legend, nor does it discuss the many forms of symbolism that went along with its creation and dissemination – the inevitable story of the undersized, underrated and thus neglected stallion that came to signify the pride of ordinary Americans during the Great Depression. Instead, what I am interested in here is how it was possible at all that animals, thoroughbred race horses, could be addressed and identified as (star) athletes, as strikingly anthropomorphized characters with distinct traits, capacities, opportunities or handicaps that opened up the very possibility for such legend-building in the first place. As I am going to argue in this chapter, one important reason for identifying animals as athletes and comparing the athletic accomplishments of race horses[3] with those of human beings was the way those animals were depicted in a dense photographic dispositive. In order to understand both the enthusiasm aroused by events such as the November 1938 match race between two thoroughbreds and the way they were (and continue to be) charged with symbolic meaning, I want to outline how race horse photography from the 1890s onward contributed to the establishment and refinement of a particular human gaze that 'elevated' these (star) horses from a 'merely' animal into a closer-to-human status.

Both of the aforementioned articles and many more in dozens of contemporary newspapers reporting on the one-on-one race between the two star stallions, held at Pimlico Race Course in Baltimore, were richly illustrated by photographs. While the pre-race feature of the *Tribune* depicted the two competing thoroughbreds during training sessions, emphasizing careful preparation and a determination to win, the post-race *Times* article showed War Admiral and Seabiscuit speeding along the rails and approaching the finish line. Taken together, the images of these two newspapers alone add up to an almost classic iconography of horse racing: close-up shots in the stable area, at the paddock, or during warm-ups allowed for a detailed inspection of horses' bodies, especially their heads and muscular posture, while wide-angle shots allowed for the depiction of speed and showed (or suggested) the cooperation and resonance between horse and jockey. Embedded in articles that commented on the horses' 'character,' the physical 'shape' they were in, their

3 I focus on thoroughbred racing here, although a discussion of harness racing could be interesting as well, since it adds a machine-like component to the equation that makes a difference in the human-animal relationship.

race records and breeding heritage as well as other aspects which made them unique, these images served much more than a merely illustrative purpose. During a time when photography was still widely and self-evidently considered to reveal reality, essence, and truth,[4] pictures of race horses multiplied an arrangement of gazes already characteristic for horse racing as a spectator sport and facilitated the creation of animal athletes as indispensable (narrative) elements in the social environment of racing more generally.

As this brief outline already indicates, this chapter is located at the intersection of at least three scholarly fields. First, this chapter can in many regards be understood as part of a newer cultural history of sports that distances itself from a focus on events and teams, results and records, and asks not only for the social and political dimension of sports but is primarily interested in its cultural significance. Not only in the U.S. but also internationally sport history touches upon a large variety of cultural history subfields – from histories of bodies and sexuality to histories of emotions and violence to memory studies.[5] Recently, sports scholars have also become more sensitive towards a second important field of reference for this chapter, the growing interdisciplinary field of (human-)animal studies, which is currently making its entry into every significant discipline of the humanities and the social sciences, including the traditionally 'theory-cautious' field of historiography. In line with this trend, sports studies and history publications that deal seriously and sensitively with the presence and agency of animals and the significance of human-animal relations in sports become increasingly visible. As Michelle Gilbert and James Gillet point out in their introduction to a recent anthology, the fact that "more attention is being paid to the place of animals and interspecies relationships in a wide variety of contexts" evolved from a longer tradition of writing about animals in sports.[6] Besides studies on different blood sports that

4 For a social history of photography in the United States between the 1890s and World War II and the many ways it was discussed in relation to notions of evidence, see Mary Warner Marien: *Photography. A Cultural History*. London: King 2010, pp. 162–278; Miles Orvell: *American Photography*. Oxford: Oxford UP 2003, pp. 61–80.

5 Amy Bass: State of the Field. Sports History and the "Cultural Turn." In: *Journal of American History* 101,1 (2014), pp. 148–172; Susan K. Cahn: Turn, Turn, Turn. There Is a Reason (for Sports History). In: *Journal of American History* 101,1 (2014), pp. 181–183.

6 Michelle Gilbert / James Gillet: Sport, Animals, and Society. In: Iid. (eds): *Sport, Animals, and Society*. New York: Routledge 2014, pp. 3–11, here p. 3.

feature fighting animals such as bulls, roosters, bears, or dogs, there has been a particularly rich scholarship on equestrian sports in general and horse (but also dog) racing in particular.[7] The majority of these older studies are certainly not animal studies works in today's sense, since they were not primarily concerned with animals *as animals* or with the significance of interspecies relations. More recent contributions, however, are clearly inspired by the trend towards treating animals and human-animal relations as important aspects of academic inquiry with regard to, for instance, questions of identity formation and construction or animals' cultural roles in different societies – a perspective that is also crucial for my own chapter.[8] Finally, this chapter positions itself in the field of visual culture studies or, more precisely, in what is sometimes called visual history. Although specific approaches vary significantly, all of them share a commitment to taking visual materials seriously as sources in their own right. As historian Peter Burke summarizes the traditional attitude of historiography towards images: "In cases in which the images are discussed in the text, this evidence is often used to illustrate conclusions that the author has already reached by other means, rather than to give new answers or to ask new questions."[9] Much the same can be said about sports historians, as Mike Huggins und Mike O'Mahony argue in their introduction to a collection of articles they published with the intention of making scholars in this field more sensitive to the relevance of visual sources.[10] Nevertheless, cultural historians of sports are becoming increasingly aware of the abundance of visual material as a crucial element of modern sports since its very beginnings. Sports have always been part of a specific media environment that relied heavily on visual representation. Moreover, the emergence and growing popularity of spectator sports points not only

7 For a discussion of blood sports in the second half of the nineteenth century, see Steven A. Riess: *Sport in Industrial America, 1850–1920*. Wheeling: Harlan Davidson 1995, p. 17. On dog racing, see Gwyneth Anne Thayer: *Going to the Dogs. Greyhound Racing, Animal Activism, and American Popular Culture*. Lawrence: University of Kansas Press 2013.

8 E.g. Susan Nance: A Star Is Born to Buck. Animal Celebrity and the Marketing of Professional Rodeo. In: Gilbert / Gillet (eds): *Sport, Animals, and Society*, pp. 173–191.

9 Peter Burke: *Eyewitnessing. The Uses of Images as Historical Evidence*. London: Reaktion 2001, p. 10.

10 Mike Huggins / Mike O'Mahony (eds): *The Visual in Sport*. New York: Routledge 2012. Also see Gary Osmond: Reflecting Materiality. Reading Sport History through the Lens. In: *Rethinking History* 12,3 (2008), pp. 339–360.

to the fact that doing sports is an important part of the visual culture of every society but that sporting practices are almost always embedded in socially and culturally specific visual regimes of watching selves and others. In sports, athletes' bodies are displayed, gazed upon and thus ultimately established as subjects.[11]
In order to pursue my argument, the main part of this chapter discusses typical settings of race horse photography which are, in turn, tied to specific regimes of visibility: stable and paddock gazes on the one hand, racing and finishing gazes on the other. For each arrangement, I have selected a few examples, more or less at random, out of the huge mass of images available. I am going to offer interpretations that will underline the ultimate role these representations played in constructing race horses as identifiable athletes deserving a similar or, at times, even a greater amount of attention than their human partners. Before discussing this in more detail, however, the following section will offer some historical contextualization by outlining the history and relevance of horse racing in North America and discussing the prominence (and materiality) of photography in the visual dispositive of this particular sport.

I. The History, Relevance, and Materiality of Watching Horse Races in North America

Horse racing is one of the oldest sports in North America dating back to the colonial era and it has usually been as popular as it has been controversial.[12] From the beginning, the sport's development was clearly aligned along regional and sectional lines: From colonial times

11 For a general discussion, see the contributions in the anthology by Felix Axster / Jens Jäger / Kai Marcel Sicks / Markus Stauff (eds): *Mediensport. Strategien der Grenzziehung*. Munich: Fink 2009. On the important role of visibility in sports, see Olaf Stieglitz: Bewegungsbilder – Historische Sportfotografie und ihr Platz in der kulturwissenschaftlichen Sportforschung. In: Swen Körner / Volker Schürmann (eds): *Reflexive Sportwissenschaft – Konzepte und Fallanalysen*. Berlin: Lehmanns Media 2015, pp. 156–167. The rise of spectator sports is discussed in Rob Steen: *Floodlights and Touchlines. A History of Spectator Sport*. London: Bloomsbury 2014.

12 My description of the historical development of horse racing is based on these texts: William H. P. Robertson: *The History of Thoroughbred Racing in America*. Englewood Cliffs: Prentice-Hall 1964; Steven A. Riess: *The Sport of Kings and the Kings of Crime. Horse Racing, Politics, and Organized Crime in New York, 1865–1913*. Syracuse: Syracuse UP 2011; Id.: The Cyclical History of Horse Racing. The USA's Oldest and (Sometimes) Most Popular Spectator Sport. In: *International Journal of the History of Sport* 31,1–2 (2014), pp. 29–54.

through the Early Republic until the Civil War, horse racing was primarily a sport of the South. Especially around the late eighteenth century, plantation owners established the 'Sport of Kings' as part of an aristocratic Southern lifestyle displaying wealth, nobility, leadership and a certain understanding of masculine competence. Furthermore, owning, breeding, handling and racing carefully chosen horses was part of the clearly structured and rigorously patrolled social arrangement of the Old South, especially in Virginia, Maryland, South Carolina and somewhat later in Kentucky. While in earlier years owners used to ride their horses themselves during races in order to prove their masculinity and honor in almost duel-like competitions, later horse racing became a highly specialized and professionalized undertaking. Owners arranged for clubs, race tracks and events and increasingly handed over the daily horse routines as well as the actual racing to slaves, thus establishing a long tradition of African Americans as both capable and reliable stable crews and jockeys.[13] In contrast to the situation in the South, horse racing was generally illegal in all of New England for religious reasons, its association with aristocratic vice, and – primarily – because of its assumed connections to and involvements in gambling and the criminal underworld.[14] The situation was somewhat more liberal New York and Pennsylvania, where race tracks were established in New York City and Philadelphia. While they attracted large crowds of mostly better-off people, the race tracks occasionally triggered waves of moral outrage not only because of issues like gambling and corruption but also due to the growing sentiments of middle-class urbanites towards animal welfare and demands for a better treatment of working animals.[15]

Although many of the controversies surrounding the sport remained influential after the Civil War, and although reformers continued,

13 See, for instance, Susan Hamburger: Jimmy Winkfield. The "Black Maestro" of the Race Track. In: David K. Wiggins (ed.): *Out of the Shadows. A Biographical History of African American Athletes.* Fayetteville: University of Arkansas Press 2006, p. 619. Also see Katherine C. Mooney: *Race Horse Men. How Slavery and Freedom Were Made at the Racetrack.* Cambridge: Harvard UP 2014.

14 Richard O. Davies / Richard G. Abram: *Betting the Line. Sports Wagering in American Life.* Columbus: Ohio State UP 2001.

15 Karen Halttunen: Humanitarianism and the Pornography of Pain in Anglo-American Culture. In: *American Historical Review* 100,2 (1995), pp. 303–334; Diane L. Beers: *For the Prevention of Cruelty. The History and Legacy of Animal Rights Activism in the United States.* Athens: Ohio UP 2006, esp. ch. 2 and 3.

at times successfully, to demand more effective controls and firmer restrictions, horse racing became more and more important all over the United States. Around 1900, it was among the top three national sports and, similar to baseball and boxing, its increasing professionalization meant that making money was the core interest of those involved in race course action. While elite horse owners were able to build upon the established infrastructure, the racing community also consisted of breeding experts, coaches, stable crews, jockeys, journalists, underworld figures and, of course, betting spectators; together, these groups significantly raised the overall visibility of the sport. Proprietary tracks intended for a less affluent audience now opened in almost every larger city and betting became legal on- and off-site in an increasing number of states. During the 1920s, horse racing reached its peak in popularity and became an important part of the 'Golden Age of American Sports' saga – with owners, coaches, jockeys and famous horses stepping into the limelight of stardom.

The rise of thoroughbred racing was closely related to notions of visibility. In fact, even more so than other popular spectator sports of the time, it very much depended on the idea of producing a dense visual dispositive. This is because the success of all human agents in the world of horse racing fundamentally relied not only on the quality and agency of the individual horses and their performing bodies but also on the *visibility* and *visualization* of these aspects.[16] Gaining prize money (for owners and jockeys), holding a secure job within a racing outfit (for stable crews or veterinarians), and placing a promising bet (for the spectators) often rested on gaining reliable 'evidence' on a thoroughbred's qualities as a racer; qualities which were usually estimated based on heritage, physical appearance, race records and assumed 'character' traits. In particular, owners grounded their long-term planning and decisions in the 'science' of breeding and in the special charts and diagrams of pedigree, the genealogical tree of a race horse.[17] The race tracks themselves

16 For the importance of (corporeal) animal agency in the sport of horse racing, see, for example, Shelly R. Scott: The Racehorse as Protagonist. Agency, Independence, and Improvisation. In: Sarah E. McFarland / Ryan Hediger (eds.): *Animals and Agency. An Interdisciplinary Exploration*. Leiden: Brill 2009, pp. 45–65.

17 On the importance of breeding for horse racing, see Rebecca Cassidy: *The Sport of Kings. Kinship, Class and Thoroughbred Breeding in Newmarket*. Cambridge: Cambridge UP 2002; Simone Derix: Das Rennpferd. Historische Perspektiven auf Zucht und Führung seit dem 18. Jahrhundert. In: *Body Politics* 2,4 (2014), pp. 397–429.

were constructed to allow both experts and ordinary spectators a close examination of the horses before, during and after the race – with an open view pathway from paddock or stable to an inspection ring which allowed for a final look at the animals before they entered the actual oval course, around which high-rise stands as well as the interior infield made it possible to watch the race (in the best case) from start to finish, if necessary with the help of binoculars. In addition, live commentators used to 'visualize' every phase of the race by using a highly picturesque language. To this arrangement of gazes, photography added an important extra dimension.[18]

Despite the limitations imposed by lengthy exposure times, photographic representations of animals were created as soon as the 1840s.[19] The genre of equestrian photography was early on closely related to portraits and their specific artistic conventions, thus allowing for a visualization of either the notion of a horse's individuality or a certain relationship between animal and owner. Adrian Alban Tournachon's images dating from the mid-nineteenth century might serve as well-known examples for both forms of representation. The rising fascination with horse racing, a growing desire for further scientific inquiry into animal locomotion, and experiments in the technical enhancement of photography all added up to produce those groundbreaking studies that ultimately formed the basis for photography's crucial role in the visual dispositive of horse racing. The motion studies of Étienne-Jules Marey, Eadweard Muybridge, Ottomar Anschütz and others not only laid the foundation for the depiction of rapidly moving animals, humans or objects in motion (and thus prefigured film), in their special attention to race horses they also created an important relationship between the visualization of horses' performances and discussions of their capabilities, qualities, and identities.[20] The horse on Muybridge's first plates, shot with twelve lined-up cameras in the 1870s, had both

18 Film in many ways served a similar role, of course. I nevertheless do not discuss motion pictures in this chapter because I would argue that their role in creating animal star identities was not a crucial one before the 1920s or 1930s, in particular because film was still much too underdeveloped to appropriately capture the movements of charging thoroughbreds in a way that was visibly superior to photography.

19 Arpad Kovacs: *Animals in Photographs*. Los Angeles: Getty 2015, pp. 6–16.

20 Marta Braun: *Picturing Time. The Work of Étienne-Jules Marey*. Chicago: University of Chicago Press 1992; Gerald Lang / Lee Marks: *The Horse. Photographic Images, 1839 to the Present*. New York: Abrams 1991.

a distinguished owner, railroad tycoon Leland Stanford, and an individual name, Occident – important criteria which underpinned these plates' status as prototypes for the formation of a visual relationship between social arrangements and animal performances (a wealthy man owning a very special horse) and a linkage between animal performances and animal identities (only horses capable of extraordinary performances are worthy of a name one remembers).[21]

Whereas these early developments oscillated between technological progress, scientific interest, and art, much of what followed in race horse photography was designed with a view to the specific interests of the different human actors who had a stake in the sport. Photographic images of horses 'working' on race tracks became increasingly omnipresent and achieved a wide distribution. They were printed in breeding manuals and auction catalogues, in general newspapers and magazines as well as in specialized racing papers for the betting community, on the highly popular collectors cards distributed by (for example) tobacco companies and thus specifically addressed to adults, on advertising posters and billboards, on postcards particularly made for spectators who wanted to demonstrate both their experiences at the race track and their expertise in horse racing.[22] Taken together, the estimated tens of thousands of photographic images of race horses taken by both professional and amateur photographers in the U.S. alone between the 1890s and the 1930s created a quantity and quality of representations that not merely *illustrated* the sport but *actively participated* in its whole setting. Any given race meeting was necessarily embedded in a dense series of images, depicting training and preparation, the race's start, progression, and finish, the celebrations afterwards, and the winners and losers in the entire social setting they were part of. The animals and their specific identities were highly relevant in this regard because they constituted a decisive element in the creation of meaningful – and, in a sense, 'more-than-human' – narratives of competition. While the visual dispositive of horse racing rested (and still rests) on the individual horses and their

21 Shawn Michelle Smith: *At the Edge of Sight. Photography and the Unseen*. Durham: Duke UP 2014, esp. ch. 3.

22 Robert Bogdan / Todd Weseloh: *Real Photo Postcard Guide. The People's Photography*. Syracuse: Syracuse UP 2006; Philip von Borries: *RaceLens. Vintage Thoroughbred Racing Images*. Gretna: Pelican 2014; Erin C. Garcia: *Photography and Play*. Los Angeles: Getty 2012.

accomplishments, race track photography was also a crucial means of highlighting the knowledge and expertise required to race a horse, to ride a horse, to train (with) a horse, but also to bet on a horse. In order to achieve this, a core canon of more or less unchanging visual representations can be identified: first, the portrait photographs of horses, alone or with owners or stable crew, usually taken at a stable, a paddock, or in the inspection ring; second, the training shot, displaying the dedication and cooperation of a team consisting of horse and jockey plus crew helpers; and, third, the racing image, showing the successful coordination of jockey and animal in a setting accentuating speed and movement. By way of a closer analysis of examples of such photographs, I will argue that one particular result of these conventionalized representations was the creation of animal star athletes.

II. The Making of Animal Star Athletes

In a nutshell, the early example of a collectors card from Great Britain depicted above prefigures many crucial aspects characteristic for horse racing iconography and the making of animal athletes. (Fig. 1) Created on behalf of F. & J. Smith's Cigarettes company during the 1880s and distributed as a gift included in cigarette packs, it found its way over the Atlantic into the collection of a North American horse aficionado. Collectors cards were an important medium during the late nineteenth and early twentieth centuries used by many manufacturers of cigarettes or cigars, chocolate, or breakfast cereals to attract (not only younger) customers to their products. Companies specialized in creating hundreds of different series of cards and sports motifs were prominent among the mass of cards produced. For professional photographers they offered reliable commissions and an opportunity for marketing their studios on a national level.[23]

23 For a discussion of photographers and the actual production of such cards, see Harry Katz / Frank Ceresi / Phil Michel / Wilson McBee / Susan Reyburn: *Baseball Americana. Treasures from the Library of Congress.* New York: Harper Collins 2009, pp. 87–109. There is a rich literature on the history of collectors cards, but most of it is addressed to the fans and collectors of today and written in an at best semi-scholarly fashion. As far as I know, there is no actual academic history of this medium in general. Nevertheless, recently many historians have begun to integrate the analysis of collectors cards into their individual projects. This is particularly true for scholars working in the fields of (post)colonial history who are trying to demonstrate how the marketing of colonial products such as tobacco, chocolate or coffee was framed in racial images.

Fig. 1: "Melton", collectors card, UK 1880s.

The front page of the card I have chosen displays three images, but it does so in an uneven composition: The center contains the portrait of Melton, an English thoroughbred stallion. It is a full-figure photography, the horse is facing left, with its head slightly turned towards the camera, almost as if trying to catch the eye of the beholder. The image is clearly embedded in the conventions of earlier equestrian art and photography. It evokes the genre of the portrait and thus, together with the stallion's name in the lower right corner of the card, already places the horse into a position of human-like individual identity (in contrast to the reduction of animals to their species designation or their utilitarian purpose, in this case the animal's status as a race horse). The image certainly depicts a 'special' horse, different from the millions of working horses still very much present in both British and North American societies at that point in time. To the left and somewhat lower than Melton's head, the facial portrait of Lord Hastings, the horse's owner, is displayed. Looking only at the front page of the card, one can merely assume Hastings' relationship to the animal. It is not actually explained, but most contemporaries were probably aware of the crucial role aristocrats played with regard to horse racing. Much the same is true for the third photograph on the card's front page. To the right and somewhat above the horse it depicts F. Archer, Melton's regular jockey, also in the form of a facial portrait and sporting an easily identifiable jockey outfit.

The front page alone already illustrates the social arrangement of horse racing not only in Great Britain but also in the United States: a wealthy owner and a prominent jockey, both well-known if not famous, but nevertheless in many regards less important than the animal actor in the setting. The star on the card is Melton, and turning it around makes obvious why this is the case. Melton, we learn here, has not only won the Derby but also "the St. Leger and many other good races"; he is an extraordinarily successful horse within the already special class of thoroughbreds. The back page of the collectors card contains text which adds to and enriches the information and impression conveyed by the front page. The social arrangement is now part of a thicker narrative that serves to 'ennoble' Melton even further: "He was a horse of superb quality, and a favourite of his owner."

As the example of this early collectors card suggests, the whole setting of horse racing, or at least its representation for a wider public, was leaning towards an emphasis on the animal actor.[24] The card still relied on a very rich and detailed relationship between image and accompanying text. Although collectors cards with horse racing depictions remained popular for years to come, other photographs now printed in newspapers and magazines or on posters and postcards substituted them both quantitatively and qualitatively. Despite these changes, the established social arrangements of human-animal relations remained stable, as is demonstrated by another photograph I would like to discuss in more detail. (Fig. 2) It was taken in 1904 by an unknown photographer of the *Chicago Daily News* staff, a newspaper that at that time already relied very much on the use of photography to enrich their articles.[25] The image shows a similar composition to the card discussed above: It depicts a race horse, Highball, in its center, and although he is not shown in his entirety he still dominates the picture. To Highball's left, we see a white man in suit, tie and hat, a person introduced by the image's caption as Bud May, "horseman." Again, one cannot be exactly sure about the relationship between human and horse, but given that the image was most likely taken during a training session or at an early

24 I am stressing the public image here because I am aware of the highly unequal status of human and nonhuman actors in the horse racing setting. Even thoroughbreds were usually treated harshly if not cruelly, and 'working' as a race horse was rarely accompanied by respect or sensitivity towards the species.

25 Its huge archive of published and unpublished photographs can be accessed at the Chicago History Museum, and large parts are also available online. See http://www.chicagohistory.org/research/resources/online-resources/online (accessed October 14, 2015).

Fig. 2: Horseman, Bud May, facing racehorse, Highball, with African American jockey mounted, standing on racetrack, close view, 1904.

stage of preparation for a race, one can assume that Bud May was a coach. Also depicted is an unnamed African American riding Highball, probably a stable boy because he is neither wearing a jockey's dress nor any professional equipment (including riding boots).[26] While May is looking at Highball's head, the rider is facing the camera, as is the horse. Again, the photograph accomplishes at least two important objectives. On the one hand, it visualizes a very specific social arrangement within the world of horse racing, a setting of precise roles and relationships in which white men and black men were not equal but nonetheless had to cooperate in order to ensure the horse's competitive success on the race track. On the other hand, the photograph also 'elevates' the horse, and the print chosen here even further accentuates this aspect by highlighting Highball's head within an added frame. The photographer and/or the reporter using the image thus established an even clearer and more explicit focus on the horse, with horseman and

26 While the image's caption (fig. 2) refers to him as a jockey, it is likely that the person who created the caption did not pay much attention to whether or not he actually was one and simply assumed so because he was mounted on a race horse.

stable boy becoming even less prominent than they had already been in the picture's original composition. The close-up of Highball's head, of his face looking at the camera, clearly not only stresses relevance, it also underlines particularly human notions of personality, character, and identity. It opens both gazes, that of the horse and that of the beholder, for a recognition of mutual subjectivity. And although it does so in a very much medialized form, in some remarkable ways the visual dispositive of horse racing is not entirely one-dimensional and unidirectional.[27] Although the visual regime was structured asymmetrically and thus always entailed a marginalization and exploitation of nonhuman others, the world of horse races was also about *exchanging* gazes. Horsemen (and -women) in different capacities inspected, evaluated and certainly admired the animals performing on race tracks – but, at least at times, horses also became visible in their abilities to *look back*, to return the gaze as subjects in their own right.[28] The influential discussions by John Berger and Jacques Derrida elaborate on the significance of animal gazes, underscoring their often unsettling or uncanny qualities.[29] It is this elusive yet tangible uneasiness evoked by the encounter or confrontation with the animal gaze that is uniquely captured and preserved by means of photographic technology.

Photography increased race horses' visibility as nonhuman subjects endowed with a certain amount of agency, a quality that became especially evident in another recurring feature of thoroughbred iconography: the racing shot. In this 'subgenre,' horses were depicted while galloping on a race track, either along the rails during the race or moving towards or across the finish line. At first glance, these images

27 The importance of the face for an attribution of human-like subjectivity to animals is discussed in Rolf F. Nohr: Tarzans Gesicht und die "letzte Differenz." In: Maren Möhring / Massimo Perinelli / Olaf Stieglitz (eds): *Tiere im Film. Eine Menschheitsgeschichte der Moderne*. Cologne: Böhlau 2009, pp. 29–45. For the general role of faces in processes of subjectivation, see Hans Belting: *Faces. Eine Geschichte des Gesichts*. Munich: Beck 2013.

28 Although discussing a different context, a similar argument is made by Wendy Woodward: *The Animal Gaze. Animal Subjectivities in Southern African Narratives*. Johannesburg: Wits UP 2008, pp. 1–18.

29 John Berger: Why Look at Animals? In: Id.: *About Looking*. New York: Pantheon 1980, pp. 1–28; Jacques Derrida: *The Animal That Therefore I Am*, trans. from the French by David Wills. New York: Fordham UP 2008. Also see Philip Armstrong: The Gaze of Animals. In: Nik Taylor / Tania Signal (eds.): *Theorizing Animals. Rethinking Humananimal Relations*. Leiden: Brill 2011, pp. 175–199.

seem to primarily emphasize the skills of the jockey or the success of jockey-horse cooperation, but I would like to argue that it is ultimately the horse who plays the leading role. As Simone Derix convincingly demonstrates, the dispositive of horse racing is clearly defined by human control over horses supposedly in constant need of guidance by a (rational) human actor in order to perform successfully – a specifically masculine narrative of dominance that also informs other contexts of human-animal relations.[30] Nevertheless, although horse racing is in many ways a highly unequal and exploitative relationship it also has to be understood in terms of partnership. This is because completely suppressing, ignoring or underestimating the animal's own agential capacities makes success on the race track next to impossible. To use German social historian Alf Lüdtke's term, the "Eigensinn" (roughly translated as 'self-will' or 'obstinacy') of the animal has to be taken into account. And this necessary compromise means that in the context of horse racing a certain degree of animal agency not only has to be acknowledged or 'tolerated' but is, in fact, indispensable.[31]

A brief analysis of two further images might illustrate my point. American thoroughbred racing knows many animal legends, and among them Man o' War still looms large, not only because of his own record but also due to his role in breeding – among many other successful racers, Man o' War sired War Admiral and was the 'grandfather' of Seabiscuit. The horse is depicted here (fig. 3) with his regular jockey, Johnny Loftus, and although this print from the New York Public Library is not precisely dated or described in any more detail, other evidence suggests

30 Derix: Rennpferd, pp. 421–428. I am using the term 'dispositive' (also translated as 'apparatus') in its Foucauldian sense here, emphasizing power/knowledge dimensions in relation to the actual material practices which articulate them. See Michel Foucault: The Confession of the Flesh. In: Id.: *Power/Knowledge. Selected Interviews and Other Writings, 1972–1977*, ed. by Colin Gordon. New York: Pantheon 1980, pp. 194–228, esp. pp. 194–198. At other points in the text I use the term *visual* dispositive with a stronger emphasis on aspects of mediality.

31 Alf Lüdtke: *Eigen-Sinn. Fabrikalltag, Arbeitererfahrungen und Politik vom Kaiserreich bis in den Faschismus*. Hamburg: Ergebnisse 1993. In many regards, 'Eigensinn' is a term coined to describe the role of German workers during the late nineteenth and early twentieth centuries, that is, their being subject to control on the one hand and their capacity for actual political resistance on the other. In a more general sense, Eigensinn indicates the attempt to provide for a more nuanced reading of the concept of agency. Informed by the ideas of Michel Foucault and Antonio Gramsci, Eigensinn underscores the capacity for agency of marginalized or subaltern subjects without, however, neglecting its conditions of possibility and its many limitations and failures.

Fig. 3: "Man o' War", [1920].

that it was most likely taken at the Stuyvesant Handicap in 1920.[32] The photograph's perspective is almost classic: It shows a single race horse in full speed along the rails approaching the finish line; every larger muscle of the animal is visible and flexed; the head faces forward, seemingly focused, concentrated, determined; the legs are in the air, not touching the turf below. The weight of the jockey seems irrelevant; in fact, one might believe that Loftus has no part in the horse's accomplishment at all. He rests still, as does his whip, almost becoming a mere extension of the rapidly moving animal body. The photograph is obviously designed along the lines established by the images of Muybridge and other motion studies that accentuated the locomotion of galloping horses and were disinterested in the jockey's part in the racing endeavor. For contemporary racing experts though, this and many other photographs first of all demonstrated perfect interspecies coordination.[33] Par-

32 The Stuyvesant Handicap is an annual horse racing event held at Aqueduct Race Track in Queens, New York. The event has not been held since its cancellation due to lack of interest in 2009.

33 A huge amount of early twentieth-century racing literature is available in digitized form, from turf dictionaries to breeding and handling manuals to betting advice; see especially the HathiTrust digital library (www.hathitrust.org). The material can be subdivided into texts for experts (e.g. owners, coaches, jockeys) and texts for a general, usually betting, public. Without having conducted an in-depth, quantitative

adoxically, a jockey who almost disappeared was considered a jockey in command, a capable handler who had laid the foundation for such a performance over the course of many intense training sessions, subjecting the horse to (usually) his will. But, unfortunately for the jockeys and other 'true' experts, in the eyes of those who primarily consumed such photographs in print media or other outlets of visual culture, the emphasis on the handling competencies of professional jockeys was almost entirely eclipsed and substituted by the presence and corporeal agency of strong, powerful horses – the true athletes on the tracks – who ultimately ensured victory.

There are at least three reasons that support this point. First, photographs like this one underscore the broader visual dispositive of the race track of which they are an essential part. The gazes of spectators center on the horses, on their way from the paddock to the inspection ring to the actual track. All of the *human* efforts of owners, coaches or jockeys are relegated to the past or remain hidden in these moments and are of, at best, secondary importance. Visiting a race course is about betting on a winning thoroughbred, not a winning jockey, and the visual arrangement clearly foregrounds this aspect.

The sheer quantity of images such as the one of Man o' War and their interpictorial references to other representations constitute the second reason why the impression of animal athletes as the true stars of the sport becomes so convincing. Around 1900, horse racing developed into a mass-media spectacle and as such rivaled for attention with various forms of commercialized entertainment – other popular sports, the cinema, show business. As many historians have argued, these new forms of entertainment both created and were dependent upon a star system that centered on identifiable, memorable characters and the human interest and emotional (as well as financial) investments they were able to evoke.[34] In order to compete in this fiercely contested field of entertainment spectacle, horse racing had to rely on the dramatic

investigation, it appears to be the case that the more a publication addressed a general, non-professional audience, the more it favored the horses over jockeys and coaches (and, by extension, animal over human agency) to explain success in horse racing.

34 A still highly useful discussion of the emergence of commercialized entertainment in the United States is Gary Cross: *Time and Money. The Making of Consumer Culture*. London: Routledge 1993. For the role of the visual in this context, see Elspeth H. Brown: *The Corporate Eye. Photography and the Rationalization of American Commercial Culture, 1884–1929*. Baltimore: Johns Hopkins UP 2005.

appeal of the powerful horse outperforming its rivals and the superior strength and determination embodied by the animal's fighting spirit. This aspect had to be visualized over and over again despite the fact that in doing so the human (f)actors in the sport became increasingly marginalized. Phrased differently, the American public demanded all the qualities of an athlete consolidated in and epitomized by the body and 'character' of an individual animal. And although they were bred, trained and handled by expert humans, only the animal actors in horse racing were in a position to satisfy this desire.

The third and final reason for the relative insignificance of the jockey in race horse iconography was the importance of the notion of *speed* within the discursive and imaginary framework of modernity. The reliance on a visualization of speed inevitably devalued the achievements of the jockey and usually also his visibility, as is evident in a final photograph which closes my argumentation in this chapter. The advocates of modernity celebrated speed in many areas as characteristic of societies' progress,[35] and visualizing speed had also been an important objective of race horse photography since the early motion studies of the 1870s. The racing context itself allowed for ample possibilities to visualize speed in a way that resonated well with actual race course experiences and the feeling of watching a race from the stands or from the infield. It also allowed for the 'freezing' of speed, making it consumable even when the action was already over. The wide-angle shot showing a group of thoroughbreds galloping in close formation towards the finish is a hallmark of horse racing iconography. It integrates the performance of the individual horse in a narrative of competition, of victories and defeats, which arguably lies at the heart of modern sport's mass attractiveness. In many ways, it functions as an extension of more individualized star-images like that of Man o' War discussed above: Whereas the individual racing shot establishes the 'star athlete,' the group racing shot relates individuality to an environment of competition in which the star's existence becomes truly meaningful – a star horse becomes a star athlete because of its ability to dominate a group of rivals. Over time, the race

35 The importance of notions of speed as emblematically modern is discussed in Hartmut Rosa / William E. Scheuerman (eds): *High-Speed Society. Social Acceleration, Power, and Modernity*. University Park: Pennsylvania State UP 2009. Also see Anson Rabinbach: *The Human Motor. Energy, Fatigue, and the Origins of Modernity*. New York: Basic 1990; Stephen Kern: *The Culture of Time & Space, 1880–1918*. Cambridge: Harvard UP 2003, pp. 109–130.

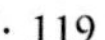

Fig. 4: Horse Racing, Derby Day, Washington Park Track, racehorses racing towards the camera during a race on the track, 1929.

shot of groups of horses became much more refined due to enhanced technological possibilities, as is evident in this photograph. (Fig. 4) Also taken by an anonymous *Chicago Daily News* photographer, it shows a scene from a race day at Chicago's Washington Park Race Track in the summer of 1929. In contrast to the earlier constraints of visual compositions, faster cameras and traps installed in or on the rails or in the turf now allowed for front and, in this particular case, up-from-below perspectives of galloping race horses moving towards the eye of the beholder. Only a couple of years later, photo-finish cameras were installed in a number of places, with the speed-freezing shot becoming an important element in the decision about a race's outcome.[36] And while from a sideways perspective the jockey tended to drop out of sight because the observers' gazes were absorbed by the animals, in frontal images the jockeys' human presence became even more tenuous and marginalized. As the example nicely demonstrates, it is the animals' heads that clearly move into the center of attention. One might argue that the intricacies of interspecies coordination as well as the complex physical appearance of the horse are lost or become irrelevant in this perspective, but the emphasis on the horses' heads more than

36 Riess: Cyclical History, p. 39.

compensates for this impression and also serves a more crucial purpose. This image, and many others created with the technological possibilities of the late 1920s and 1930s, were able to bring together and arrange the necessary stylistic ingredients for the visual emergence of animals as athletes. They combined elements of identification, subjectivity, and agency as well as a meaningful narration of individuality (or even personality) within a highly receptive social and cultural environment, and they did so in part by appealing to true and widely recognized markers of (Western) modernity such as competition, performative corporeality, and streamlined speed. The thoroughbred as animal athlete and non-human athletic subject emerged within the visual order of the sport of horse racing, and photographic representations were among the crucial conditions of possibility for this development.

III. A Multitude of Gazes

In what now counts as a seminal text in many fields of the humanities as well as in animal studies, the artist and critic John Berger asks: "Why Look at Animals?".[37] The essay begins with philosophical elaborations on humans and animals exchanging gazes and develops into a train of thought that leads Berger from Homer to Rousseau and Descartes and to a lengthy discussion of the display of animals in zoos. Perhaps somewhat unsurprisingly, horse racing is not mentioned in his essay, but as I have argued here, Berger's question might just as well be posed (and perhaps be answered) with regard to horse racing photography.

Very early in his essay, Berger states that the "animal has secrets which, unlike the secrets of caves, mountains, seas, are specifically addressed to man."[38] Similarly, and as far as the specific topic of this chapter is concerned, the entire visual arrangement of (modern) horse races is centered on uncovering the horses' secrets, or, and perhaps more appropriately, their hidden promises. The reason for looking at thoroughbred race horses lay (and still lies) in the immediate future, at the finish line of each race and in the windows of the bookmakers. While the many expectant gazes directed at the horses would in most cases result in disappointment, photography and the developing canon of race horse iconography offered a solution to the difficulty of interpreting animal

37 Berger: Why Look at Animals?

38 Ibid., p. 3.

bodies and their potentials to perform. If the animals had secrets, photography was believed to reveal them, to make them visible, to make them worth betting on. Photography offered closer, more reliable insights and perspectives that remained accessible beyond the immediate limitations of time and space. Photography promised an accurate, quasi-scientific perspective that allowed for a much more trustworthy estimate of a horse's strength, speed, endurance and general ability.

While the visual dispositive of the modern race course as it was established throughout the nineteenth century was clearly designed to suit the human racing community consisting of owners, coaches, stable crews, jockeys, journalists and betting spectators, it still allowed the animals to return the gaze and to display *Eigensinn*. As Berger argues, the objectifying power of the human gaze notwithstanding, "the animal – even if domesticated – can also surprise the man." And it is because of this capacity or potential inherent in an animal's gaze that "a power is ascribed to the animal."[39] Animal gazes were ephemeral and oftentimes remained unrecognized or unappreciated, and one might argue that in many ways photographic technology can be understood as just one more way of 'capturing' animals in order to satisfy human consumptive desires. But photography's role and the effects of its development and immense dissemination after 1880 and especially after 1900 were more ambivalent than this. In fixing the animals' gazes and in making their presence felt, photographic representations inevitably served to reinforce notions of animal subjectivity. They enabled thoroughbreds to become animal athletes, recognizable individual characters with (at least sometimes) star appeal and an actual influence on the shape of human-animal relations more generally. This visually enhanced (if not created) animal subjectivity 'elevated' an already special kind of non-human being, the thoroughbred race horse with a documented pedigree, to an even closer-to-human status. In fact, it even grouped the race horse with a very special kind of *human*, the modern athlete, a figuration that was itself closely associated with circulating ideas about modernity in the West.[40] Despite the fact that the implications of this

39 Ibid.

40 Christiane Eisenberg: Der Sportler. In: Ute Frevert / Heinz-Gerhard Haupt (eds): *Der Mensch des 20. Jahrhunderts*. Frankfurt am Main: Campus 1999, pp. 87–112; Michael Mackenzie: The Athlete as Machine. A Figure of Modernity in Weimar Germany. In: Michael Cowan / Kai Marcel Sicks (eds): *Leibhaftige Moderne. Körper in Kunst und Massenmedien, 1918–1933*. Bielefeld: Transcript 2005, pp. 48–62.

development for a reconceptualization and reimagining of the status of animals in human societies were never fully articulated and that race horses ultimately remained 'working' horses – objectified, exploited and often mistreated –, photography nevertheless opened up unique opportunities for acknowledgement and inclusion that were denied to many other nonhuman species.

Modes of Production, Modes of Seeing

Creaturely Suffering in Upton Sinclair's *The Jungle*

Michael Malay

When Upton Sinclair finished *The Jungle* in 1906, he hoped the novel would open American hearts and minds to the exploitation of workers in the Chicago stockyards. A chronicle of the life and times of Jurgis Rudkus, a migrant worker from Lithuania, the novel described, with unprecedented clarity and vividness, the harrowing nature of work in the industrial slaughterhouse, including the furious pace of the production line, the ill-treatment of laborers at the hands of managers, and the precariousness of working conditions: a laborer with ten hours of work one day might have no employment the next. The novel led to change, but not of the kind Sinclair wanted. Responding to the scandal caused by *The Jungle*, the Roosevelt administration passed two landmark policies that regulated, among other things, the handling and packaging of meat.[1] But the government's emphasis on improving sanitary conditions surprised and saddened Sinclair. He had wanted to see fundamental changes to how workers were treated under industrial capitalism, not policies which required more hygienic practices.

1 *The Federal Meat Inspection Act* and *The Pure Food and Drug Act*, 1906.

"I aimed for the public's heart," he famously wrote in his *Autobiography*, "and by accident I hit it in the stomach."[2]

A number of readers responded in the way Sinclair had hoped. *The Jungle* "will open countless ears that have been dead to socialism," Jack London remarked in 1906, and "plough the soil for the seed of our propaganda."[3] The novel, he said, was "the *Uncle Tom's Cabin* of wage slavery."[4] Another early reviewer, a young Winston Churchill, wrote that the book's portrait of the meat industry would pierce "the thickest skull and the most leathery heart."[5] *The Jungle* "forces people who never think about the foundations of society to pause and wonder."[6] Later critics were equally moved by Sinclair's novel even if they were more critical. The "author's psychology of character is indeed a simple one," remarked Walter Rideout, who complained that Sinclair's characters lost "their individuality" as the novel developed, "becoming instead any group of immigrants destroyed by the Beef Trust."[7] Similarly, Morris Dickstein felt that Sinclair's characters were rendered "without condescension" but also "without much human dimension." His figures, compared to Dreiser's or Zola's, were flatter and "more constrained."[8] However, for both Rideout and Dickstein, Sinclair's sensitivity to the fundamental meanness of the Chicago system, as well as his passionate portrait of life in the stockyard, meant that his novel partly survived its own demerits. "Hardly individuals," Sinclair's characters "nevertheless collectively achieve symbolic status"[9] Rideout concluded. Or, as Dickstein

2 Upton Sinclair: What Life Means to Me. In: *The Cosmopolitan. A Monthly Illustrated Magazine* 41 (October 1906), p. 594. As Sinclair added in *The Brass Check*: "I realized with bitterness that I had been made into a 'celebrity,' not because the public cared anything about the sufferings of these workers, but simply because the public did not want to eat tubercular beef." (Id.: *The Brass Check. A Study of American Journalism*. Champaign: University of Illinois Press 2003, p. 42.)

3 Jack London: What Jack London Says of *The Jungle*. In: Upton Sinclair: *The Jungle. A Norton Critical Edition*, ed. by Clare Virginia Eby. New York: Norton 2003, pp. 483–484, here p. 483. Henceforth page numbers from *The Jungle* will be cited in-text.

4 Ibid., p. 484.

5 Winston Churchill: The Chicago Scandals. The Novel Which is Making History. In: Sinclair: *The Jungle*, p. 489.

6 Ibid.

7 Walter Rideout: Jurgis' Conversion. In: *The Jungle*, pp. 491–492.

8 Morris Dickstein: Introduction to *The Jungle*. In: Harold Bloom (ed.): *Upton Sinclair's* The Jungle. New York: Chelsea House 2002, pp. 44–59, here p. 55.

9 Rideout: Jurgis' Conversion, p. 492.

observed, Sinclair's "great gift is his sense of fact."[10] *The Jungle* derives its power simply by recording, in an "endless deadpan flow of concrete details," the degrading conditions of the stockyard.[11]

The novel's critique of industrial capitalism remains compelling. For Harvey Swados, writing in the 1960s, Sinclair's Chicago spoke powerfully to the inequalities and oppressions of contemporary capitalism. "There is a close parallel," he writes, "between the payment in hunger, blood and agony of the peoples of the under developed world and that extracted from the immigrant builders of the American empire."[12] And, for Christopher Hitchens, similarly, *The Jungle* starkly reflects how "commodities deposed, and controlled, human beings." Sinclair's novel, he continues, "is the most successful attempt ever made to fictionalize the central passages of Marx's *Das Kapital*."[13] Something of Sinclair's legacy can also be gauged by the way *The Jungle* is repeatedly invoked by contemporary writers and journalists. When Eric Schlosser wrote *Fast Food Nation* in 2001, for example, his critique of the American food industry, Sinclair was very much in the background. "Nearly a century after the book's publication," Schlosser observed of *The Jungle*, "many descriptive passages still ring true."[14] Despite its fame, however, an important aspect of the novel continues to be underappreciated by most critics: Sinclair's descriptions of nonhuman others. This lack of critical attention is odd. At key stages of the novel, *The Jungle* describes the lives of cows and pigs in vivid detail, describing the cramped train journeys they take to the "packing district," the unsanitary conditions they inhabit, and the ruthless methods by which they are dispatched. As such, the book is full of disturbing details – bulls that accidently gore each other because of their proximity in freight cars, diseased carcasses being "dressed" up as tinned meat, men dumbly hacking away at swinging bodies – details which, on aggregate, offer an intense and garish picture of the stockyards. However, little has been said about the ethical and interspecies dimensions of these scenes. *The Jungle* has

10 Dickstein: Introduction, p. 43.

11 Ibid., p. 57.

12 Harvey Swados: The World of Upton Sinclair. In: *Atlantic Monthly*, 12/1961, pp. 96–102, here p. 102.

13 Christopher Hitchens: A Capitalist Primer. Upton Sinclair's Realism Got the Better of His Socialism. In: *Atlantic Monthly*, 07–08/2002, pp. 176–179, here p. 176.

14 Eric Schlosser: *Fast Food Nation. The Dark Side of the All-American Meal.* New York: Mariner 2012, p. 309.

mostly been read as a tale of humanity's soul under capitalism; in this dark story, animals are, at best, a side issue.

This critical view can partly be attributed to Sinclair himself. "For fifty-six years," he writes in his *Autobiography*, "I have been ridiculed for a passage in *The Jungle* that deals with the moral claims of dying hogs – which passage was intended as hilarious farce."[15] According to Sinclair, however, this is a mistaken interpretation. He was simply using animals to illuminate the novel's real subject: the plight of human workers. Indeed, as the narrator of *The Jungle* insists at one point, the stockyard animals are "metaphors of human destiny" (43) – nothing more and nothing less. The real moral deprivation of the stockyards, in other words, was not that it treated animals "like" animals but that it treated humans "like" animals. In this context, a focus on animal welfare missed the point. *The Jungle* was written to expose capitalism's treatment of the proletariat, tell stories about vulnerable migrant workers, and agitate for social reform. The novel ends, for instance, with a ringing appeal to "Organize! Organize! Organize!" so that "Chicago will be ours!" (327–328).

This essay offers an 'animal' reading of *The Jungle*. It reads *The Jungle*, that is, in precisely the terms Sinclair disavowed – as a novel that addresses the "moral claims of dying hogs." This 'address,' however, is not so much explicit as incidental – part of the novel's unwittig atmosphere. Sinclair may have used animals for sardonic purposes ("hilarious farce") or as symbols ("metaphors of human destiny"), but his designs were thwarted by the nature of his materials: to write about the stockyard necessarily involved close attention to the lives of real, breathing animals – and this included an awareness of the conditions under which they died. By proxy, then, and partly by accident, *The Jungle* ended up offering an exact and gruelling picture of the lives of animals under capitalism in early twentieth century America. The book's socialist message had a multispecies dimension.

The second part of this essay develops this reading of *The Jungle* by situating the novel in relation to historical developments that were unfolding in America in the late 1800s and early 1900s. In particular, it uses *The Jungle* as an occasion to think about three major developments that Sinclair directly or indirectly explores in his novel: the growth of factory farms and the consolidation of industrial farming practices; the

15 Upton Sinclair: *Autobiography*. New York: Harcourt & Brace 1962, p. 164.

particular effects these developments had on human and nonhuman animals; and the more general changes that factory farms inaugurated in modern American relationships with the natural world. How were animals 'seen' by Americans before the development of the modern slaughterhouse – and how did these ways of seeing change during and after the development of industrial slaughter?

Entering the Slaughterhouse

From 1860 to the early 1900s, Chicago was the meatpacking centre of North America, unrivalled in the scale, speed and the efficiency of its operations. Although there were precedents for industrial farming of this kind – particularly in Cincinnati (once known as "Porkopolis") – Chicago developed the stockyard model to its most extreme form. In its heyday it employed thousands of laborers, "processed" hundreds of animals per hour, and controlled markets from the Midwest to New England.

Before this rise, Chicago had been a busy but small meatpacking centre. While Chicago meatpackers had access to cities like Detroit, they were, for most of the 1830s and 1840s, conducting trade with local consumers. The arrival of the railroads in the 1850s, however, combined with a rapid influx of new settlers, changed everything. The industry began to grow tremendously and soon Chicago began competing with its Midwestern rivals. When Civil War broke out in 1861, leading to the Union blockade of the Confederate Port (an event which disrupted the use of the Mississippi for cities like Cincinnati), Chicago became the main supplier for the Union army, a client which "consumed over half a billion pounds of packed meat."[16] Within a matter of years, Chicago meatpackers suddenly found themselves at the centre of a vast hinterland, serviced by an extensive network of railroads, and with links to thousands of suppliers. In the 1861–62 packing season, the *Chicago Tribune* triumphantly reported, Chicago outstripped Cincinnati for the first time, slaughtering 514,118 hogs to Cincinnati's 483,000.[17]

Even so, the Chicago meat trade in the early 1860s was inefficient and disorganized. As Dominic Pacyga notes, stockyards were selling meat

16 William Cronon: *Nature's Metropolis. Chicago and the Great West*. New York: Norton 1991, p. 230.

17 Chicago Provision Trade. In: *The Chicago Tribune*, April 10, 1862, p.1, quoted in Theodore J. Karamanski / Eileen M. McMahon (eds): *Civil War Chicago. Eyewitness to History*. Athens: Ohio UP 2014, p. 174.

at different prices (causing confusion for buyers) and were dispersed across different locations around the city, a situation which "resulted in near chaos."[18] Recognizing the need for consolidation, the city's main traders proposed the Union Stock Yard in 1864, a 320-acre site which would bring all the major meatpackers into a single space. Opened the following year, the site was, by all accounts, a substantial feat of engineering. According to Pacyga, the stockyard could handle "21,000 cattle, 75,000 hogs, 22,000 sheep, and 200 horses" – a capacity which increased dramatically over the next two decades. By 1900, Pacyga writes, "the original 320-acre site grew to 475 acres with a pen capacity of 75,000 cattle, 50,000 sheep, 300,000 hogs, and 5,000 horses. In that year, 14,622,315 animals filled its vast array of pens and chutes."[19] In these years, too, the Union Stock Yard became truly national, sourcing animals from as far away as Colorado and Texas, and sending "packed" meat to consumers in New York and Philadelphia. The volume of slaughter was extraordinary. What would have taken a previous generation an entire week to slaughter, Pacyga notes, was completed in Chicago in a single day.[20]

The development of the stockyard is, in part, also the story of industrial modernity: it involved nothing less than a profound technological and material rearrangement in how humans experienced their societies and interacted with the world around them. In these circumstances, then, it was only natural that the stockyards engendered a range of powerful responses, from amazement, wonder and curiosity to horror, shock and disgust, and sometimes a confused combination of all these experiences at once. The stockyard makes for a "wonderful drama," remarked Count Harry Kessler in 1896, awed by the "huge cattle gates," "endless buildings" and "railroad lines" he saw there. But it also held "disgusting impressions for the eyes, nose and ears," he wrote.[21] Rudyard Kipling, who visited the Chicago stockyard in 1889, was equally repelled and fascinated. Acknowledging the ingenuity of the system, a "town-ship

18 Dominic Pacyga: *Chicago. A Biography*. Chicago: University of Chicago Press 2009, p. 60.

19 Ibid., p. 61.

20 *Chicago: City of the Century*, USA 2003, D: Austin Hoyt, PBS. Transcript: http://www.pbs.org/wgbh/amex/chicago/filmmore/pt.html (accessed September 29, 2016).

21 Count Harry Kessler: *Journey Into the Abyss. The Diaries of Count Harry Kessler, 1880–1918*, ed. and transl. from the German by Laird Easton. New York: Vintage 2003, p. 164.

of cattle pens cunningly divided into blocks," he also shirked at the stockyard's treatment of animals, noting the way pigs panicked in their pens.[22] The sound of "sharp hoofs and multitudinous yells," was deeply shocking, he wrote, as was the sight of men covered in "blood-red" from "bosom to heel."[23] "Once having seen" the stockyards, Kipling wrote, "you will never forget the sight."[24]

Sinclair's *The Jungle* begins with a similar sense of astonishment at the scale of industrial life in Chicago. Arriving at the city's outskirts, Jurgis and his family are startled by "rattling freight-cars," factories pouring out "immense volumes of smoke" and a "procession of dreary little buildings" (26). And, in an experience that was common enough for Chicago citizens, Jurgis can *smell* the stockyards before he can see them. It came "in whiffs," the narrator remarks – an "elemental odour, raw and crude; it was rich, almost rancid, sensual and strong" (27). These smells are soon followed by "a vague disturbance" in the background. The narrator explains: "It was only by an effort that one could realize that it was made by animals, that it was the distant lowing of ten thousand cattle, the distant grunting of ten thousand swine" (27). When Jurgis finally arrives at the stockyard, after weeks of looking for work in Chicago, the visual impression is no less astonishing:

> north and south as far as the eye can reach there stretches a sea of pens. And they were all filled—so many cattle no one had ever dreamed existed in the world. Red cattle, black, white, and yellow cattle; old cattle and young cattle; great bellowing bulls and little calves not an hour born; meek-eyed milch cows and fierce, long-horned Texas steers. The sound of them here was as of all the barnyards of the universe; and as for counting them—it would have taken all day simply to count the pens. (33)

Jurgis' first experience of the stockyard is figured in ambivalent terms. On the one hand, the Chicago system represents a rupture from traditional ways of life. Jurgis, we are told, "had dressed hogs himself in the forest of Lithuania", but he "had never expected to live to see one hog dressed by several hundred men" (38). Later in the novel, Jurgis will also be shocked when he witnesses men "literally" working "upon the run,"

22 Rudyard Kipling: How I Struck Chicago, and How Chicago Struck Me. In: Anselm L. Strauss (ed.): *The American City. A Source Book of Urban Imagery*. Chicago: Aldine 2007, pp. 41–48, here p. 45.

23 Ibid., p. 46.

24 Ibid., p. 45.

at a "pace with which there is nothing to be compared except a football game" (40). On the other hand, however, Jurgis is also impressed by the enormity and efficiency of the operation. The stockyards are "like a wonderful poem", a marvel of human ingenuity, something to which he must simply submit. "All that a mere man" like Jurgis could do, the narrator remarks, "was to take a thing like this as he found it, and do as he was told" (42).

This naiveté on Jurgis' part will later contrast with his utter degradation as a stockyard employee. He will witness countless accidents, feel the peril of uncertain labor conditions, and work until his own physical and spiritual exhaustion. After a few months, he will also learn that his wife, Ona, has been sexually exploited by one of the factory managers. Jurgis will also be swindled from his house, lose his son to an early death, and witness Ona's death (who dies after giving birth to a stillborn child). These psychological and physical traumas, powerfully rendered, remain among the most affecting scenes in the novel. But it is also clear we are meant to take Jurgis as a "type": his misfortunes, as individually realized as they are, also stand in for a more general experience. As with other immigrants, Jurgis is initially dazzled by the power of industrial modernity; and, as with the others, Jurgis will soon find himself at the mercy of the Chicago "jungle". The American promise conceals a sinister secret – a point Sinclair's narrator makes early on as readers are first introduced to the stockyards. "One could not stand and watch very long without becoming philosophical, without beginning to deal in symbols and similes, and to hear the hog squeal of the universe" (37).

The narrator's didactic intrusion could not be plainer: the "hog squeal of the universe" is really the cry of oppressed laborers. They "were so innocent," the narrator remarks of the hogs, and "so very human in their protests [...] Now and then a visitor wept, to be sure; but this slaughtering machine ran on, visitors or no visitors. It was like some horrible crime committed in a dungeon, all unseen and unheeded, buried out of sight and of memory" (36). For Sinclair, this "crime" in the "dungeon" is clearly the crime of unregulated capitalism. The narrator is using the image of dying hogs to draw attention to eastern Europeans who have been exploited by American captains of industry and who are being ignored by the American middle class. But one way of reading *The Jungle* is to think of Sinclair's metaphors as metaphors that fail – as "symbols and similes," that is, that do not entirely succeed, or which are charged with an extra-metaphorical resonance. This, for example, is the persuasive reading offered by Carol J. Adams in *The Sexual Politics of Meat*, who points out that Sinclair's attention to the material aspects of the stockyard is too vivid, too exact, to be ignored. "Butchering failed as a metaphor for the fate of the worker," Adams writes, "because the novel carried too much information on how the animal was violently killed."[25] Sinclair may have thought of his animals in figurative terms, in other words, but the mass of details he accumulated in *The Jungle* carried their own charge. The "crime committed in a dungeon," "unseen and unheeded," also spoke vividly of the nonhuman experience.

> The carcass hog was scooped out of the vat by machinery, and then it fell to the second floor, passing on the way through a wonderful machine with numerous scrapers, which adjusted themselves to the size and shape of the animal, and sent it out at the other end with nearly all of its bristles removed. It was then again strung up by machinery, and sent upon another trolley ride; this time passing between two lines of men, who sat upon a raised platform, each doing a certain single thing to the carcass as it came to him. (37)

It is hard to read this description as "hilarious farce": the attention paid to the hogs is too acute. It is also hard to read the hog's slaughter as a straightforward symbol for unchecked capitalism. Sinclair's language is filled with, not to say overwhelmed by, images which take their force from the material conditions of the slaughterhouse. At certain stages in the novel, the writing seems to take on a life of its own – metaphorical, perhaps, but also straightforwardly real, full of the horrible poetry of facts:

> [The hogs] climbed a long series of stairways outside of the building, to the top of its five or six stories. Here were the chute, with its river of hogs, all patiently toiling upward; there was a place for them to rest to cool off, and then through another passageway they went into a room from which there is no returning for hogs. (35)

Allegory or not, this passage cannot help but reveal the conditions under which animals lived and died in the stockyards – the hogs' uncomfortable crowding in the chutes, for instance, or the lack of places "for them to rest to cool off." Moreover, while "patience" is meant to establish a link with human workers (by introducing a moral term supposedly only applicable to humans) the description in fact highlights the cruelty of

25 Carol J. Adams: *The Sexual Politics of Meat. A Feminist-Vegetarian Critical Theory*. New York: Continuum 2010, pp. 78–79.

what is being done to these animals. The "patience" of the hogs stands in inverse relation to the rapacity of the stockyard system, built to kill as many animals as quickly as possible. The "hog squeal of the universe" might be the cry of human suffering, then, as the narrator intends us to hear it, but the cry might also be taken literally – as representing the discomforts of these particular hogs climbing this particular chute.

To be sure, the narrator of *The Jungle* does not consider the "moral claims" of these hogs in any sustained way. But there is a particular sense in which he is unable to. The whole effect of the slaughterhouse is to make creaturely subjects disappear – in the sense of physically "disassembling" animals, but also in the conceptual sense that animals can no longer be seen *as* subjects, as individual creatures. Indeed, the speed and intensity of the stockyard system – as in the following description of "cattle" being slaughtered – seems to preclude the very possibility of such acknowledgments occurring at all:

> The room echoed with the thuds in quick succession, and the stamping and kicking of the steers. The instant the animal had fallen, the "knocker" passed on to another; while a second man raised a lever, and the side of the pen was raised, and the animal, still kicking and struggling, slid out to the "killing-bed." Here a man put shackles about one leg, and pressed another lever, and the body was jerked up into the air. There were fifteen or twenty such pens, and it was a matter of only a couple of minutes to knock fifteen or twenty cattle and roll them out. (39–40)

The straightforward narration of this scene captures the chilling efficiency with which the whole process takes place. Creatures are killed *en masse* in a streamlined process which takes "only a couple of minutes." But such passages also reveal, perhaps even against Sinclair's knowledge, a form of relating to animals in which cruelty is not only formalized in our material relationships with them but also at the level of language. We are told, for instance, that workers who stun animals are called "knockers," that animal bodies are mechanically "jerked up into the air," and that animals that have been improperly stunned are still taken to the "killing-bed". The narrator's descriptions – tonally flat – not only reveal the indifference of industrial slaughter but the extent to which these animals are effaced through the grammar of description itself. In this system, "cattle" are "rolled" out in a ceaseless stream, anonymized by the efficiency of the production line and the bureaucratic culture which employs the workers and keeps the machines running. As for animals that die during train journeys, they are simply called "downers" (63).

Christopher Hitchens, in his review of *The Jungle,* makes the persuasive claim that the political ambitions of the novel (Sinclair believed his book would convert readers to socialism) were overwhelmed by the author's talents as a story-teller. "Sinclair's realism," Hitchens writes, "got in the way of his socialism."[26] Similarly, one might argue that Sinclair's description of nonhuman life in the stockyards got in the way of his 'metaphors'. By so clearly describing what Walter Rideout calls the "rich disorder of felt experience"[27] – from thirsty hogs to cows bruised from painful train journeys – Sinclair's socialist novel also became a novel 'about' nonhuman others, whose suffering he chronicled with almost excruciating detail. The result is that *The Jungle* went beyond the Chicago system as industrial and technological *spectacle*, and so beyond the superficial and sentimental responses of most visitors. As Pacyga points out, for instance, the stockyards were open to the public from the "day they opened", with tours even making their way to the "kill floors," but they were primarily seen as (and experienced as) a "tourist attraction".[28] Of course, like Kessler and Kipling, tourists might have been shocked and repulsed by what they witnessed; like Kessler and Kipling, however, their perspective was limited to the viewing platform. They could therefore never see beyond what Paula Young Lee calls "the dazzling cleverness of the machinery" in industrial slaughterhouses, part of whose effect is to gloss "over the ethical complexities raised by its activities."[29] Sinclair, on the other hand, who collected material for his novel by posing as a Chicago stockyard worker, was able to see beyond the slaughterhouse as "wonderful poem," and so reveal the messy and complicated internal dimensions hidden from public view. In short, he succeeded in what he never set out to do – making visible the pain of animals on the "killing-beds" and showing, with painful clarity, new forms of human cruelty that were emerging in the era of the stockyard.

26 Hitchens: Capitalist Primer, p. 177.

27 Rideout: Jurgis' Conversion, p. 492.

28 Dominic Pacyga: Chicago. Slaughterhouse to the World. In: Paula Young Lee (ed.): *Meat, Modernity and the Rise of the Slaughterhouse*. Lebanon: University of New Hampshire Press 2008, pp. 153–166, here p. 162.

29 Paula Young Lee: Introduction. Housing Slaughter. In: Ead. (ed.): *Meat, Modernity and the Rise of the Slaughterhouse*, pp. 1–12, here p. 7.

To advance an 'animal' reading of *The Jungle* is to trust the tale over the teller, restoring what Adams calls the "absent referent"[30] to full view. But an animal interpretation need not exclude a socialist reading. On the contrary, there are deep links between a society's oppression of marginalized workers and its treatment of nonhuman others. Indeed, as Jurgis realizes towards the conclusion of the novel, he is "one of the packer's hogs. What they wanted from a hog was all the profits they could be got out of him; and that was what they wanted from the working man" (299). This is an interesting if inchoate moment of creaturely recognition. Jurgis comes to make sense of his situation through analogy: he sees that the merciless forces that extract value from the hogs are the same forces that exploit him for his labor. But Jurgis' recognition never gets beyond this point, beyond the notion that his suffering is shared by nonhuman creatures in substantial ways. At the heart of his (and the narrator's) outrage is not the pervasiveness of violence against animals but the structural violence capitalism maintains over the working class. And yet, almost despite itself, *The Jungle* shows how the subjugation of human workers and nonhuman others are intricately related: animals are destroyed *en masse* by the new socio-economic arrangement that also damages human lives and bodies. The forms of exploitation are dialectically linked, a relationship borne out most strongly by Sinclair's description of the stockyards' division of labor:

> One [worker] scraped the outside of a leg; another scraped the inside of the same leg. One with a swift stroke cut the throat; another with two swift strokes severed the head, which fell to the floor and vanished through a hole. Another made a slit down the body; a second opened the body wider; a third with a saw cut the breastbone; a fourth loosened the entrails; a fifth pulled them out – and they also slid through a hole in the floor. There were men to scrape each side and men to scrape the back; there were men to clean the carcass inside, to trim it and wash it. Looking down this room, one saw, creeping slowly, a line of dangling hogs a hundred yards in length; and for every yard there was a man, working as if a demon were after him. (37–38)

The speed of the operation is a triumph of factory efficiency, a technical and bureaucratic feat. But it is also part of a system where human labor

30 The "absent referent" is a key concept in Adam's book, and one she takes from Margaret Homans: *Bearing the Word. Language and Female Experience in Nineteenth-Century Women's Writing.* Chicago: University of Chicago Press 1986. See Adams: *The Sexual Politics of Meat*, p. xxiv.

becomes increasingly specialized as well as uncreative and repetitive. As Jonathan Burt notes of the Chicago stockyards:

> [I]n 1884, 5 splitters handled 800 head of cattle in a ten-hour day, whereas a decade later 4 splitters would handle 1,200 a day. By the turn of the century, the single butcher had been replaced by a killing gang of 157 men divided into 78 different "trades".[31]

In practice, the specialization of "trades" meant that a "knocker" or a "splitter" could perform the same action hundreds of times over a ten-hour day (or longer). One's relations to 1,200 animals, in other words, could be confined to a single kind of activity. Over time, Burt argues, this led to profound changes for humans and nonhumans alike. The "scale of the picture and the fact that so many humans as well as animals are subject to brutalization erase each individual moment of death as it occurs hundreds of times an hour. One cannot see the animals for the industry."[32]

The specialization of work that Burt outlines above was linked to, and grew out of, new ways of valuing animals as commodities and so to the proliferation of animal 'products'. As the narrator remarks of the factory where Jurgis works: "No tiniest particle of organic matter was wasted" (41). Sinclair's narrator continues:

> Out of the horns of cattle they made combs, buttons, hair-pins, and imitation ivory; out of the shin bones and other big bones they cut knife and tooth-brush handles, and mouthpieces for pipes; out of the hoofs they cut hair-pins and buttons, before they made the rest into glue. [...] When there was nothing else to be done with a thing, they first put it into a tank and got out of it all the tallow and grease, and then they made it into fertilizer[.] (41)

The "they" in this passage refers, of course, to a huge army of specialized laborers, and the effect of such descriptions is to show that, in the same movement as human work becomes increasingly particular, the animal body is turned into ever smaller units of value. The growing alienation of the worker, in other words, goes hand in hand with the new use-values being extracted from the animal body. One consequence, as Burt argues, is that animal bodies could no longer be seen in their

31 Jonathan Burt: Conflicts around Slaughter in Modernity. In: The Animal Studies Group: *Killing Animals*. Urbana: University of Illinois Press 2006, pp. 120–144, here p. 122.

32 Ibid., pp. 121–122.

entirety – as whole living organisms – but as fragments of flesh which needed to be separated: legs, breast-bones, a clean carcass.

Clearly, developments within the stockyard cannot be seen in isolation from developments in the wider world. Changes in modes of production did not only follow the internal logic of efficiency, but were closely linked to technological developments, the play of market forces and the particular decisions and strategies pursued by management. As William Cronon revealingly points out, for instance, Jonathan Armour, one of the major Chicago meat-packers, actually countenanced huge economic losses in the early days of his business, partly because, in his desire to break into new markets, he sold meat at discount prices – a decision which forced him to look for new efficiencies at the point of production. Cronon writes:

> Armour estimated that a 1,260-pound steer purchased in Chicago for $40.95 would produce 710 pounds of dressed beef. When sold in New York [...] this beef would earn only $38.17 – a clear loss even without deducting production and transport costs. Only by selling by-products could the packers turn this losing transaction into a profitable one.[33]

Another way of putting this is that the imperatives of market-forces rebounded upon the animal: the bodies of hogs and cows were made to yield more kinds of value in direct relation to the costs associated with the industry's expansion into new markets. In declaring a "war on waste," Cronon writes, the packers "pushed the disassembly line toward its fullest possible development." Doing so, "they turned what had been a single creature – a hog or a steer – into dozens and then hundreds of commodities."[34]

Inevitably, these changing modes of production led to new forms of seeing, new ways of relating to animal life. In particular, the intensity and scale of the 'disassembly line' produced a different 'sense' of the animal other – one that was highly anonymized and – and which, in turn, allowed a new ethical configuration to emerge between the worker and his labor. Animal slaughter, formerly an operation of

33 Cronon: *Nature's Metropolis*, p. 251.

34 Ibid., p. 250. Jonathan Burt makes a related point: "The changing patterns over time of the transportation of beef from live cattle to carcasses to boxed beef and packaged cuts reflect not only the increasing distance between live animal and finished product but also the way in which the industry has increasingly sought to optimize every aspect of its process." (Burt: Conflicts around Slaughter, p. 123.)

multiple yet integrated steps, came to be subdivided into specialized 'roles,' a development which was related to, and which further enabled, an attitude in which animals were seen – increasingly a priori – as mere bodies to be dismantled into units of value. Thus, when the narrator of Sinclair's novel speaks of cows being "rolled" out, as though they were so much raw material to be worked upon, his language reflects some of the new material relations with animals that were taking shape in the industrial era.

In addition to these troubling ethical relationships, another feature of the dialectic was how the suffering of the animal other became invisible precisely in relation to the growing number of animals being slaughtered on a daily basis. "Processed" in such large masses, animals became harder to view as individuals, a development which shaped – emotionally, materially, conceptually – how animals were seen and treated in the stockyards. As Sinclair's narrator observes,

> [The workers] had chains which they fastened about the leg of the nearest hog, and the other end of the chain they hooked into one of the rings upon the wheel. So, as the wheel turned, a hog was suddenly jerked off his feet and borne aloft. At the same instant the ear was assailed by a most terrifying shriek; the visitors started in alarm, the women turned pale and shrank back [...]
> Meantime, heedless of all these things, the men upon the floor were going about their work. Neither squeals of hogs nor tears of visitors made any difference to them; one by one they hooked up the hogs, and one by one with a swift stroke they slit their throats. There was a long line of hogs, with squeals and life-blood ebbing away together; until at last each started again, and vanished with a splash into a huge vat of boiling water. It was all so very business-like that one watched it fascinated. It was pork-making by machinery, pork-making by applied mathematics. (36)

There is a touch of superciliousness in the narrator's attitude to the workers. The men are made to seem callous, "going about their work" with little regard for the "squeals of hogs" and the "tears of visitors." (Momentarily, the narrator's viewpoint echoes Kipling's, for whom the stockyard workers "did not seem to care"[35] about the act of killing.) Unlike Kipling, however, the narrator recognizes that the material conditions of the stockyard both produced and required this 'business-like' approach. In a factory where animals could no longer be treated as individuals (indeed, where the formal possibilities for that kind of

35 Kipling: How I Struck Chicago, p. 46.

recognition have, as it were, disappeared) the methods of the stockyard simply had to be adopted. As the narrator remarks of Elzbieta, for instance, a relation of Jurgis' who works in the "cannery":

> It was stupefying, brutalizing work; it left her no time to think, no strength for anything. She was part of the machine she tended, and every faculty that was not needed for the machine was doomed to be crushed out of existence. There was only one mercy about the cruel grind—that it gave her the gift of insensibility. (133)

To Kipling, what seems like an apparent lack of feeling is, to Sinclair's narrator, the result of labor conditions – conditions which placed onerous, difficult and unvarying tasks on its workers. Part of the force of *The Jungle*, in this context, is to make clear what tourists to the stockyards could not see, namely why Elzbieta's "gift of insensibility" is not so much a choice in this environment but a necessity. More generally, Sinclair also shows, in this passage as in others, why a 'business-like' approach to killing could not help but become standard practice as industrial stockyards became the norm in America. Within a few decades, the 'disassembly' of animals into dozens of units by hundreds of workers was simply part of the industrial process and no longer strange or unique. The rapidity with which these changes were accepted is registered, at the individual level, through Sinclair's portrait of Jurgis. Initially astonished by the scale of the stockyard – so different from his Lithuanian experience – Jurgis quickly adapts to the industrial methods. But there are, of course, no alternatives. One must either work at the speed set by the "pace-makers" – who are continually "speeding up the gang" – or find a different job (57).

As *The Jungle* progresses, there are fewer and fewer descriptions of work in the slaughterhouse. This is because the novel's action develops considerably once Jurgis leaves the stockyard after a series of catastrophic events: he becomes, for a while, a tramp in the countryside, a criminal operator in Chicago's underworld and then a worker in a steel factory, followed by one last brief stint in the stockyard as a "strike-breaker" (254). The book's attention focuses on other themes: wealth inequality in Chicago, the conflict between the union and the bosses, and the attractiveness of socialism as a form of resistance to capitalism. But although the stockyard fades from the foreground of the novel, there is a powerful sense in which it continues to pervade *The Jungle* at the level of language. Words and images that belong to the stockyard come to haunt, in subtle but persistent ways, the experiences of the novel's working-class characters. For example, Jurgis is described as a "dumb beast of burden" (138), while Ona, his wife, is seen as a "wounded animal" (137). And, towards the novel's conclusion, reflecting on his four years in the "wilderness" of Chicago, Jurgis thinks of the "beasts of prey" that had exploited him and his family in the city (299). The stockyard, the narrator colourfully adds, was "capitalism made flesh" – "the Great Butcher" of the city (300).

In an insightful reading of the concept of 'animality' in Progressive-Era literature, Michael Lundblad argues that notions of "the jungle" were intricately shaped by popular ideas derived from the work of Sigmund Freud and Charles Darwin, and particularly by the potent blend that emerged between these two thinkers towards the end of the nineteenth century.[36] Specifically, the mix of popularised notions of animal behaviour (derived from Darwin) and popularised notions of the human mind (derived from Freudian psychoanalysis), offered what Lundblad calls a "Darwinist-Freudian" paradigm – a powerful framework in which "animal instincts" could be situated in, and understood with reference to, the "human psyche."[37] As this model pervaded popular discourse, moreover, the "Darwinist-Freudian" paradigm came to offer a compelling framework for American culture to explain itself to itself, both producing and legitimizing, for example, "new constructions of animality as 'naturally' violent in the name of survival" or characterizing heterosexuality as normative "in the name of reproduction."[38] A diverse range of phenomena could now be explained, in effect, with the terms provided by Darwin and Freud, from competition between people (which could be seen as a 'natural' part of human societies) to the 'unnatural' impulses of homosexuality (which was seen to go against Darwinian reproduction), to the operations of the human mind and the desires of the body. These cultural narratives also began to influence, eventually, representations of class and society, shaping, for instance,

36 Michael Lundblad: *The Birth of a Jungle. Animality in Progressive-Era U.S. Literature and Culture*. New York: Oxford UP 2013. For another discussion on the "dialectic between Darwinism and Freudianism" in relation to the "discourse of species," see Carrie Rohman: *Stalking the Subject: Modernism and the Animal*. New York: Columbia UP 2009, p. 22.

37 Lundblad: *Birth of a Jungle*, p. 4.

38 Ibid., p. 2.

how the middle classes saw and understood the working class – the last of which, as Lundblad observes, "were more likely to be animalized in a Darwinist-Freudian sense."[39]

In this context, Sinclair's description of Jurgis as a "dumb beast of burden" is uncritical and also partly demeaning. By portraying Jurgis in this manner, Sinclair was rehearsing the prejudiced views of the middle class (of which he was a part) and regurgitating simplified cultural narratives of animality taken from Freud and Darwin. *The Jungle* conforms to a reductive view of working class immigrants, Lundblad argues, by seeing them "as more animalized than members of other economic classes."[40] Jurgis, too, is "animalized" from "the very beginning" of the novel – represented as a "working-class animal who cannot control his sexual instincts," for instance, or as someone who is especially prone to violence.[41] But if *The Jungle* animalizes Jurgis and his fellow workers on the model of a crude reading of Darwinist-Freudian ideas, it also partially resists and repels those narratives. Indeed, one of Lundblad's key arguments is that, as widespread as Darwin and Freud had become, their ideas never completely monopolized popular culture but co-existed, sometimes uneasily, with other ways of interpreting culture and society. Or, as Lundblad writes, "texts from the turn of the century that are often thought to epitomize" a Darwinist-Freudian understanding also "include varied forms of resistance to the Darwinist-Freudian jungle."[42] Popular understandings of animality, that is to say, were incompletely and inconsistently assimilated into American culture – and there were often "alternative formulations" to the dominant cultural perspectives.[43] *The Jungle*, according to Lundblad, is one such text: although the novel reproduces, in a number of unreflective ways, the views of popular culture, it also embodies and expresses "alternative epistemologies" that "resist the biological determinism" associated with Darwinist-Freudian explanations of human behaviour.[44] Specifically,

39 Lundblad: *Birth of a Jungle*, pp. 4, 92.

40 Ibid., p. 92.

41 "Progressive-era labor reform," Lundblad continues, "becomes a way for middle-class reformers to distance themselves from the 'animals' for whom they want to advocate." (Ibid., p. 93.)

42 Ibid., p. 5.

43 Ibid.

44 Ibid., p. 109.

Lundblad argues that there is an implicit "Christian framework" in *The Jungle*, as when the narrator passes judgement on the "crimes" committed in the stockyard "dungeon" in stark moral (and Christian) terms. In this way, Lundblad writes, the stockyard could be "judged as a monstrous corporation that leaves death and destruction in its wake, not because of an amoral, social Darwinist drive to survive but rather out of a malice that is almost incomprehensible."[45] Sinclair's language of animality, in other words, has a complex range of registers – sometimes crudely 'Darwinist,' at other times implicitly Christian, and more often an indeterminate mix of both.

By approaching 'animality' in this open-ended manner, Lundblad's analysis opens up different ways of reading Sinclair's text: he offers, in particular, a way of seeing Sinclair's metaphors as the site of messy, multiple and sometimes contradictory cultural discourses on class, labor and modernity. But one might add another element to Lundblad's reading of animality in *The Jungle*, something perhaps so obvious that it is easily missed. In addition to its complex Darwinist-Freudian-Christian framework, animality in *The Jungle* is also shaped by Sinclair's practical experience of the stockyards. *The Jungle,* that is to say, is not only a description of the slaughterhouse but also a product of it, in the sense that the novel is shaped by the images, practices and conditions of the Chicago system. The pacing of Sinclair's language, the particularity of his metaphors, and his "endless deadpan flow of concrete detail,"[46] all bear testament to the speed, energy and materiality of the stockyards.

The language of slaughter, of course, is nothing new in literature. Scenes of slaughter are vividly described in the Bible, the Talmud, and the Quran, and in poems and stories from a variety of traditions, from the *Odyssey* to *Gilgamesh* to *Beowulf.* But my claim here is that there is a special intensity to Sinclair's language which is only possible with the development of the *industrial* slaughterhouse – with the emergence of a system, that is, which dispatches hundreds of animals per day, which relies on cheap human labor, and in which men and women are thought of as nearly as expendable as the animals they kill. It is in this sense that *The Jungle* is configured *by* the stockyard as much as it is 'about' the

45 Ibid., pp. 110–111.

46 Dickstein: Introduction, p. 57.

stockyard: the novel's language is impressed by the weight of the industrial experiences it describes, including the increasing division of labor, the corralling of unprecedented numbers of animals into a single space, and emerging technologies of animal slaughter.

The following animal images from Sinclair's novel, which pertain to Jurgis' incarceration in prison, his reflections on the experience of Chicago, and his time in the surrounding countryside as a tramp, reveal the impression the stockyard left on Sinclair's language.

> [Jurgis] was of no consequence – he was flung aside, like a bit of trash, the carcass of some animal. (154)

> When night fell [Jurgis] was pacing up and down his cell like a wild beast that breaks its teeth upon the bars of its cage. Now and then in his frenzy he would fling himself against the walls of the place, beating his hands upon them. (153)

> They had put [Jurgis] behind bars, as if he had been a wild beast, a thing without sense or reason, without rights, without affections, without feelings. (155)

> Jurgis could see all the truth now [...] He and his family, helpless women and children, struggling to live [...] – and the enemies that had been lurking for them, crouching upon their trail and thirsting for their blood! (171)

> Poor Jurgis was now an outcast and a tramp once more. He was crippled – he was literally crippled as any wild animal which has lost its claws. (267)

These images are inspired by the experience of modern urban spaces and, crucially, by the rise and development of factory farms. The intensity of American industrial life, its vast impersonality, and the way it made human lives seem expedient, was contemporaneous with the development of technologies for transporting, confining and slaughtering animals – and all these experiences are subconsciously at work in Sinclair's language. The novel's language of animality, then, cannot simply be attributed to a crude popularization of Freud and Darwin, or to a bourgeois animalization of the proletariat class, but has something to do with the development and experience of the industrial stockyard itself. Thus, when Jurgis is described as a "bit of trash" as he is thrown in jail, and then swiftly likened to the "carcass of some animal," Sinclair is not simply revealing his own stereotyped views of the working class (although this is perhaps also at work) but drawing on experiences taken from the industrial slaughterhouse. Similarly, when stockyard workers are taunted by a foreman for holding a strike – "You went out of here like cattle, and like cattle you'll come back!" (259) – Sinclair is revealing, perhaps more than he himself knows, the extent to which human workers were 'animalized' by the mechanized indifference of the killing floors. The experience of animals under capitalism – vulnerable, frightened and exploited – provided Sinclair with immediate, if subliminal, images for the powerlessness of his human characters.

Sinclair is not alone in using the language of the stockyard to describe the experience of industrial modernity. Tillie Olson's novel, *Yonnondio*, for instance, which partly describes stockyard conditions in Omaha, Nebraska, is equally charged by images and experiences from the stockyard. "Abandon self, all ye who enter here," the narrator remarks at one point. "Become component part, geared, meshed, timed, controlled."[47] The narrator's description of the Omaha factory bears powerful resemblances to Jurgis' experience of Chicago:

> Hogs dangling, dancing along the convey, 300, 350, an hour; Mary running along the rickety platform to keep up, stamping, stamping the hides. To the shuddering drum of the skull crush machine, in the spectral vapour clouds, everyone the same motion all the hours through [...].
> Geared, meshed: the kill room: knockers, shacklers, pritchers-uppers, stickers, headers, rippers, leg breakers, breast and aitch sawyers, caul pullers, fell cutters, rumpers, splitters, vat dippers, skinners, gutters, pluckers.[48]

The stockyard infiltrates the very language of Olson's novel: her descriptions capture the repetitiveness of labor ("stamping, stamping"), the violence of the work ("the shuddering drum of the skull crush machine"), and the sense in which the factory workers are "timed" and "controlled" by the speed of production. Obliquely, too, the passage registers the workers' fatigue, who, after a day of work, can no longer distinguish between "300" or "350" hogs – a significant difference but one which cannot be appreciated under these fast and furious conditions. Like Jurgis and Elzbieta, the characters in *Yonnondio* have become extensions of the stockyard, "geared" and "meshed" by the speed of the production line. But what is crucial about stockyard metaphors in *The Jungle*, what becomes decisive, is how the lives and suffering of nonhuman others are marginalized even as they provide new images of capitalism's biopolitical force and authority. Images of animal oppression come to stand in for human oppression, but in a way that tends to obscure the original

47 Tillie Olson: *Yonnondio. From the Thirties*. Lincoln: Bison 2004, p. 165. Olson's novel was written in the 1930s and published in 1974.
48 Ibid., pp. 165–166.

referent. Hence, Jurgis feels himself treated like a "carcass," but gives no thought to the basis of the "carcass" metaphor. Likewise, Elzbieta's "gift of insensibility" ends up limiting her ability to draw connections between her own creaturely suffering and that of nonhuman others, even as she works in the midst of them in the cannery.

In *The Greening of Literary Scholarship*, Steven Rosendale argues that "there are compelling reasons for reexamining novels like *The Jungle* for their ecocritical perspective."[49] This is because, although *The Jungle* is set almost entirely in urban spaces, the existence of the stockyard involved and implicated a whole network of relations between country and city. In a brief but acute reading, Rosendale goes on to show how issues of pollution and environmental degradation are in fact central to the novel, even though Sinclair does not dwell on these topics at any length. Surprisingly, Rosendale says little about the treatment of animals in *The Jungle*. However, his method of reading 'eco-critically' – his desire to connect city and country, for instance, or his awareness of what is often suppressed or excluded from any text, points the way to an animal reading of the novel, one which attends to Sinclair's animals not merely as metaphors but which acknowledges their reality as autonomous, living creatures. This reading also has an ethical dimension. By reading animal pain back into *The Jungle*, alternative interpretations can restore the text's original referent, making nonhuman lives – and their 'moral claims' – present. Thinking in this way, however, does not simply mean literalizing Sinclair's metaphors, such that the "hog squeal of the universe" refers *only* to animal pain. A more integrated approach – what might be termed a *creaturely* reading – involves showing how *both* human and nonhuman suffering are at stake in Sinclair's language of animality.[50] (This also involves showing how, hidden in the

49 Steven Rosendale: In Search of Left Ecology's Usable Past. *The Jungle*, Social Change, and the Class Character of Environmental Impairment. In: Steven Rosendale (ed.): *The Greening of Literary Scholarship. Literature, Theory and the Environment*. Iowa City: University of Iowa Press 2002, pp. 59–76, here p. 63.

50 For 'creatureliness' as a shared condition of both humans and animals as embodied, vulnerable beings, see Anat Pick: *Creaturely Poetics. Animality and Vulnerability in Literature and Film*. New York: Columbia UP 2011. As Cora Diamond notes, however, acknowledging the vulnerability we share with others can be a difficult and even "wounding" experience: "The awareness we each have of being a living body, being 'alive to the world', carries with it exposure to the bodily sense of vulnerability to death, sheer animal vulnerability, the vulnerability we share with them. This vulnerability is capable of panicking us. To be able to acknowledge it at all, let alone as shared, is wounding; but acknowledging it as shared with other animals, in the presence of what

novel's purportedly anthropocentric foundations, there are fragments of a half-articulated interspecies ethics at work.) When the foreman compares the striking workers to "cattle," for instance, his insult summarizes the degrading labor conditions of the Chicago system, one which mercilessly objectifies human life. But, more than this, the comparison encodes the lives of other animals: the creaturely suffering of hogs, cows, sheep and horses. These experiences, which animate the very life of the novel, are also suppressed by it.

Changes in Ways of Seeing

It is no exaggeration to say that the system perfected in Chicago led to profound changes in the ways animals were treated and understood in North America. As the methods of the stockyard became generally accepted, the novelty of killing a single animal with hundreds of men – what initially struck Jurgis as "wonderful" and "uncanny" – lost its strangeness. Mass slaughter, occurring at a rate unthinkable in previous decades, and at speeds which placed enormous pressure on workers, was naturalized as the dominant form of meat production. The logic of capital dominated creaturely life in entirely new ways, and the ethical configurations that emerged from these patterns of relating were as profound as they were lasting. "Abstract, standardized and fungible," Cronon writes, animals were now "governed as much by the nature of capital as by the nature that gave them life."[51]

It is worth rehearsing the major developments that led to this new configuration, not least because they continue to undergird contemporary relations between humans and animals in industrial settings. First, in the era of factory slaughter, animal bodies were commoditized into ever more discrete parts. Or, as one character puts it in *The Jungle*, in a phrase apparently often-invoked in the Chicago stockyards, "They use everything about the hog except the squeal" (131). Second, the volume of animals being processed in 'disassembly' lines created new relationships between worker, animal and consumer, in that the sheer numbers of animals being slaughtered eradicated the possibility for certain forms

we do to them, is capable not only of panicking one but also of isolating one." (Cora Diamond: The Difficulty of Reality and the Difficulty of Philosophy. In: Stanley Cavell / Cora Diamond / John McDowell / Ian Hacking / Cary Wolfe: *Philosophy and Animal Life*. New York: Columbia UP 2008, pp. 43–89, here p. 74.

51 Cronon: *Nature's Metropolis*, p. 259.

of recognition – the recognition, for instance, of particular animals as *individual* animals and therefore, to use Tom Regan's term, as "subjects-of-a-life."[52] The slaughterhouse anonymized animals by virtue of its scale. Third, the rise of Chicago as the centre for meat-packing in the Midwest changed the spaces in which animals were reared and the environments through which they travelled. Specifically, there was a development away from animals grazing on open prairies to their sequestration on fenced pastures. This spatial change was accompanied by a development in diet, as animals moved from eating wild-grasses to grains such as corn, a change which could adversely affect an animal's health.[53] But just as animals were being increasingly sequestered on ranches, they also began to traverse once unthinkable distances on their way to the market, a phenomenon made possible by the growth of American railroads, developing technologies of refrigeration, and Chicago's increasing monopoly over the national market. With the development of the stockyard, nothing less than a redefinition of human-nonhuman relations was at stake.

The influence of the Chicago system in all of this cannot be overemphasized. The changes happening in Chicago led to a more general re-patterning of the American relationship to the landscape and animal life, changes at once very broad and extremely specific. At the most general level, for instance, animals were increasingly being seen in market terms, as saleable items whose bodies were configured by market forces. Flesh *as* money became the new and dominant equation. But this change, which occurred at the level of economics, was also dialectically related to other, more concrete changes in human-nonhuman relations. Farmers, for instance, began worrying over the weight their animals lost on the way to Chicago (since animals were valued by the pound, lighter animals meant smaller profits). As such, new techniques were developed to make the process of handling animals more efficient. In one particularly dramatic example, Cronon notes that some farmers began stitching "shut the eyelids of particularly obstreperous [hogs]" whose "bad humour" would slow the journey from pasture to slaughterhouse, resulting in the loss of time and money. "Once blinded in this

52 Tom Regan: *The Case for Animal Rights*. Berkeley: University of California Press 2004.

53 For a discussion of the effects of corn-rich diets on cows, see Michael Pollan: *The Omnivore's Dilemma*. London: Bloomsbury 2006, pp. 77–78.

way," Cronon writes, "they could still keep to the road by following their companions, but were less inclined to make havoc."[54]

Then there were the injuries animals sustained during freight travel, the numbers of which, it bears stressing, were historically unique – a result of the collaboration between the developing technologies of rail-travel and Chicago's growing monopoly over American meat production. What would have been counter-intuitive for the small-scale farmer (a system in which animals were placed in dangerous and potentially fatal proximity to each other) was seen, on the industrial scale, as a form of acceptable collateral damage, not least because the body parts of the animals could still be used. As the narrator of *The Jungle* observes, "the packing-house had a special elevator upon which [injured animals] were raised to the killing-beds" (63). Even hogs with cholera, the narrator remarks, contracted "in the course of a two or three days' trip, in hot weather and without water" could be turned into "lard" (256). The stockyard's emphasis on efficiency – together with its disregard for sanitary laws – normalized processes that would otherwise have been disingenuous and even off-limits to earlier farmers.

Over time, the dominance of the industrial model precipitated a gradual shift from the low-scale form of husbandry, one which was based on the notion of stewardship (a problematic and often violent relationship in itself[55]), towards a market-intensive method of farming, a method that led to wholly different modes of relating to nonhuman others. In an earlier era, for example, one "was not likely to forget that pigs had died so that people might eat," Cronon writes, "for one saw them grazing in familiar pastures, and regularly visited the barnyards and butcher shops where they gave up their lives in the service of one's daily meal."[56] Industrial farming, however, changed these relationships in some of the most fundamental ways possible. The Chicago system led to a trend in which most animals were unknown to their consumers, sent from hundreds of miles away, and slaughtered by people one would never meet. With the development of refrigeration in the late 1870s, moreover, the slaughter of animals – traditionally reserved for the winter seasons, when cool temperatures preserved meat from rotting – became a

54 Cronon: *Nature's Metropolis*, p. 226.

55 See, for instance, David A. Nibert: *Animal Oppression and Human Violence. Domesecration, Capitalism and Global Conflict*. New York: Columbia UP 2013.

56 Cronon: *Nature's Metropolis*, p. 256.

year-long activity, and gradually ushered in a different sense of relationship between humans, animals, time and the seasons.[57]

In all of these cases, too, what emerges most strongly is how the new ethical configurations emerging between humans and nonhumans were being systematically effaced by the same structures which made them possible. When Sinclair's narrator observes that slaughter is "buried out of sight and memory" (36), he is making the same fundamental observation as Paula Young Lee, who writes that "the slaughterhouse exists in order to provide a covert space where physical and symbolic disarticulations can take place."

> From a historical perspective, the introduction of the slaughterhouse system inaugurated a radical shift in human-animal relations, as it institutionalized the industrial compartmentalization of a particular segment of the animal kingdom. Today, livestock animals are subsumed into a linear system that conceives them mostly as meat [...] Inside the modern industrial system, [...] livestock is born to die, following constricted corridors leading directly from pasture to slaughter.[58]

In these industrial spaces, Cronon argues, the animal "died a second death."

> Severed from the form in which it had lived, severed from the act that had killed it, it vanished from human memory as one of nature's creatures. Its ties to the earth receded, and in forgetting the animal's life one also forgot the grasses and the prairie skies [...] that seemed more and more remote in space and time.[59]

It is in this sense that *The Jungle* offers an early critique of industrial stockyard conditions – unconsciously, and simply by observing what animal others experienced. Sinclair's intentions may have been explicitly socialist, but the act of describing the stockyards forced a broadening of attention, one which showed how the forces exploiting human workers were also exploiting nonhumans. "There were some with broken legs

57 As Cronon writes: "Time itself gained new meaning under these circumstances, for in the most literal sense it had become money. During an animal's foreshortened lifespan, the old seasonal alternation of fat summers and lean winters gave way to a system of continuous growth, in which food supply – whether in the form of hay or shocked corn – was grown and stored so that there need be no interruption to the steady accumulation of future cash in well-muscled flesh. Farmers and ranchers thus truncated the cyclical time of natural reproduction to make agricultural production as rapid and linear as possible." (Ibid., p. 224.)

58 Lee: Housing Slaughter, p. 2.

59 Cronon: *Nature's Metropolis*, pp. 256–257.

and some with gored sides," Sinclair's narrator remarks of animals newly arrived on trains. There were also some "that had died, from what cause no one could say; and they were all to be disposed of, here in darkness and silence" (63). Or, as the narrator remarks later in the book, in a sharply observed and nearly unbearable passage,

> A time of peril on the killing beds was when a steer broke loose. Sometimes, in the haste of speeding-up, they would dump one of the animals out on the floor before it was fully stunned, and it would get upon its feet and run amuck. Then there would be a yell of warning—the men would drop everything and dash for the nearest pillar, slipping here and there on the floor, and tumbling over each other. This was bad enough in the summer, when a man could see; in wintertime it was enough to make your hair stand up, for the room would be so full of steam that you could not make anything out five feet in front of you. To be sure, the steer was generally blind and frantic, and not especially bent on hurting any one; but think of the chances of running upon a knife, while nearly every man had one in his hand! And then, to cap the climax, the floor boss would come rushing up with a rifle and begin blazing away! (111–112)

This distressing image of the steer is echoed in a later scene of the novel, when Jurgis compares himself to a "wounded animal in the forest", "forced to compete with his enemies upon unequal terms" (216). The two passages are deeply linked. The bewildered steer, running for life, offers an analogue for the exploited worker. The exploited worker, in turn, speaks to the fate of industrialized animals. When Jurgis calls himself one of the "packer's hogs" (299) towards the end of the novel, he is therefore drawing on a powerful but suppressed association, one inextricably bound up with the rise of industrial farming: the legacy of the stockyard is the efficiency with which it exploited vulnerable bodies, human and nonhuman alike.

II

Animality and Its Intersections
The Politics of Human-Animal Relations

Black Dogs, Bloodhounds, and Best Friends

African Americans and Dogs in Nineteenth-Century Abolitionist Literature

Brigitte Fielder

> H is the Hound his master trained,
> And called to scent the track
> Of the unhappy fugitive,
> And bring him trembling back.[1]

Harriet Beecher Stowe's 1852 abolitionist novel, *Uncle Tom's Cabin*, alludes to the injustice done to enslaved African American people by comparing their treatment with that of animals. Discussing his status as chattel (despite having a white father), George Harris complains, "I had a father—one of your Kentucky gentlemen—who didn't think enough of me from being sold with his dogs and horses, to satisfy the estate, when he died."[2] George later compares this treatment to the love of his black, enslaved mother: "To him I was no more than a fine dog or horse: to my poor heartbroken mother I was a *child*." (393) The

1 Hannah Townsend / Mary Townsend: The Antislavery Alphabet (1847). In: Deborah DeRosa (ed.): *Into the Mouths of Babes. An Anthology of Children's Abolitionist Literature*. Westport: Praeger 2005, pp. 72–76, here p. 74.

2 Harriet Beecher Stowe: *Uncle Tom's Cabin*, ed. by Elizabeth Ammons. New York: Norton 2010, p. 101. Henceforth page numbers will be cited in-text.

abolitionist implication is, of course, that George is not a dog or a horse, and that there is an important difference between how people and animals ought to be treated. As the original subtitle of Stowe's novel, "The Man Who Was a Thing,"[3] suggests, chattel slavery's fundamental problem was not individual slaveholders' treatment of enslaved people, but the very system that made these people saleable, like 'things' – or nonhuman animals.

Proslavery arguments, of course, would blur the legal, social, and ideological boundaries between human and nonhuman by insisting upon black people's allegedly inferior humanity. These dehumanizing arguments simultaneously sought to deny black people's intellectual abilities, their capacity for social and political equality, and their right to personal freedom. Rendering George as a saleable animal in his slaveholder-father's estimation therefore strips him of the consideration one ought to give to another human being. It positions him in the role of an animal who has no rights to personhood himself, but who is the legal property of his 'master,' able to be bought and sold – and even beaten and killed – by his 'owner.' Stowe's abolitionist argument, in contrast, depends upon her readers' belief in the inherent humanity of enslaved people. Stipulating that humans ought to be treated differently than (domesticated) animals, who are legal property, made to work for the benefit of an owner, Stowe expects us to recognize an injustice in enslaved people's dehumanization and to advocate for their being treated differently.

Nineteenth-century comparisons of enslaved people and animals took various forms and evoked various human-animal associations. Although George likens his status as saleable to that of a dog or a horse, the former association holds particular resonance in the abolitionist context. Comparing a person to a dog is a common insult and likening enslaved people's treatment to that of dogs a common antislavery accusation. As one of Stowe's characters puts it, "Treat 'em like dogs, and you'll have dogs' works and dogs' actions. Treat 'em like men, and you'll have men's works" (96). The antislavery argument that a person was unfairly treated and disadvantaged when treated like a dog was one of the most prominent connections made between enslaved black people and dogs in the long nineteenth century. While nonwhite people were compared to other kinds of animals – such as nonhuman primates

3 This designation is deliberately gendered in Stowe's subtitle, given the differences between women's and men's political and social rights.

in eighteenth- and nineteenth-century works of natural history and scientific racism – comparisons to pets resonated differently. To compare an enslaved person to a dog is to make a different kind of human-animal correlation than making racist comparisons between black people and nonhuman primates. It is also different from comparing them to laboring farm animals, like horses or cattle. While an inherent racism underlies each of these human-animal comparisons, examining the specificity of the comparison to dogs reveals not only the rhetorical and material dehumanization of slaveholding but also the similarly problematic resonances of abolitionist literature. Stowe's abolitionist argument counters a common (and specific) proslavery one that likened black people to subordinate but well-loved pets. But other references to dogs are not merely metaphorical; these illustrate enslaved peoples' material relationships with nonhuman animals. Besides seeing enslaved people compared to dogs in *Uncle Tom's Cabin*, we also see them both in adversarial and violent relationships with dogs used to hunt fugitives and also with dogs as beloved pets of their own.

This essay will explore the different appearances of dogs in Stowe's novel in order to map out and analyze the contradictions inherent in the comparisons of enslaved African Americans to dogs and their various relationships to and with them. Reading Stowe's *Uncle Tom's Cabin* for both its importance as an abolitionist literary phenomenon as well as for the ways it is representative of the most common ways we see dogs depicted in abolitionist literature, I focus on this text as an exemplar of the way dogs operated in simultaneous and even contradictory ways as antislavery writers depicted their relations to enslaved black people. Abolitionist arguments that decried black people treated 'like dogs,' depictions of bloodhounds employed in slave-hunting, and black people's relationships with familiar dogs as pets point to the competing yet complexly-related resonances of dogs in abolitionist literature. When the complexity, variety, and contradictions of dogs' relationships to enslaved people in abolitionist literature are taken into account, we see a fuller human-animal landscape than is visible when we focus solely on African American people's dehumanization. While the dehumanization of African American people is, undoubtedly, an important factor in the history of racial oppression, the multifaceted comparisons and relations of black people to animals presents a richer picture of how both oppression and resistance occurred in a landscape of not just human, but also human-animal relations.

"Black Dogs"

George Harris' complaint of being valued only as chattel speaks to the animalization of enslaved black people that abolitionist literature meant to counter. Antislavery advocates often stressed the humanity of enslaved people in response to arguments that dehumanized black people as a justification for their enslavement. That George complains about being treated like a dog is significant. The specificity of this association speaks simultaneously to the injustice of his legal status as chattel, the dehumanization of enslaved people, the specific use of 'dog' as an insult, and both proslavery and antislavery arguments that might employ the relationship between people and pets as an analogy for interracial relations. In the narrative of Jermain Loguen, an abolitionist who had escaped slavery by way of the Underground Railroad, we see the slaveholder Manasseth verbally assault the enslaved Jarm: "Don't stand there staring at me, you black dog! Off with your shirt, or I'll whip it off—hide and all!" and then, "Cross your hands, or I'll take your life, you d—d black dog!"[4] Accompanied by threats of violence, the meaning of the epithet to suggest a position of submission is obvious. In a hotel scene of Kentucky slaveholders, Stowe gives us an image of "rifles stacked away in the corner, shot-pouches, game-bags, hunting-dogs, and little negroes, all rolled together in the corners" (93). This list equates these items' status as property. Dogs, "little negroes" and various objects are lumped together as parallel, all of these the mere accoutrements of a hunting party. In this instance, we only get a glimpse of what or who is listed here; none of these enter into this scene as characters. But the lens of abolitionism tells readers that there is something wrong with the equalizing effects of this list: Stowe's combined antislavery and animal welfare writings argue that, as living creatures, neither "little negroes" nor hunting dogs ought to be reduced to the status of inanimate objects.

Beyond this association of legally owned 'things,' we see not only a categorical or associative link between enslaved people and dogs as property in both Loguen's narrative and *Uncle Tom's Cabin*, but also a direct use of this link as a method of dehumanization. Simon Legree, speaking of breaking Tom's will to resist him, claims "He'll beg like a dog this morning" (345). And "Down, you dog!" Legree shouts, as he strikes Tom with a riding whip (346). Using the word "dog" as an epithet,

4 Jermain Wesley Loguen: *The Rev. J. W. Loguen, as a Slave and as a Freeman. A Narrative of Real Life.* Syracuse: J. G. K. Truair 1859, pp. 239–240.

Legree incorporates this association into his physical and psychological abuse of slaves. As a metaphor that suggests Tom's subservient position, Legree's first statement relates notions of power and dependence: the structural and physical violence that was supposed to hold enslaved people in check subjected them to a force from which they might also beg mercy. The accompanying proslavery argument reversed the causality of this relation, holding that enslaved black people were subject to white power *because* of their inherent inferiority and, therefore, dependence. Like Loguen's representation, "you d—d black dog," Legree's interpellation of Tom as "you dog" is part of the system's literal brutalization, as slaveholders seek to dehumanize the enslaved.

The specificity of this interpellation is important here, calling up not simply human-animal relations but those between people and pets. Proslavery notions of plantation life imagined enslaved people as incorporated into the familial structure of white slaveholding households. Often characterized as either children or pets, enslaved black people were subjected to a position of dependence in domestic structures of power.[5] When Augustine St. Clare calls his enslaved manservant, Adolph, a "poor dog" (160) he suggests this paternalism with a sympathy that implies some degree of caring and affection while also maintaining strict racial hierarchies in its dehumanization. If enslaved people were imagined to belong to some kind of plantation 'family,' positioning them as pets only reinforced notions of racial hierarchy through the use of human-animal ones. Even when considered as family members, the place and role of dogs in the domestic realm still suggested their subjugation. While dogs might be represented positively, their positive traits were mostly testaments to their subservience, marked not as relationships of equality but of obedience, faithfulness, and unquestioning loyalty.[6]

The rhetorical antislavery questions, "Am I not a man and a brother?" and "Am I not a woman and a sister?" also played on notions of family, suggesting not only inclusion in the sphere of humanity but also framing humanity itself as a structure of kinship. This suggestion of family was

5 For a comparison of late nineteenth-century attitudes towards children and pets, see Susan J. Pearson: *The Rights of the Defenseless. Protecting Animals and Children in the Gilded Age*. Chicago: University of Chicago Press 2011, pp. 21–57.

6 For a discussion of positive and negative characteristics ascribed to dogs and cats in the later part of the nineteenth century, see Keridiana Chez's contribution to this volume.

important because it resonated with the ideal of a universal Christian family, but also because its framing of sibling relations countered proslavery depictions of familial hierarchies that depicted enslaved people only as children within plantation paternalism. Acknowledging humanity and kinship, these questions challenged racist arguments that separated black and white people on the basis that racial difference was akin to difference in species. They also suggested an equality of familial roles. By referring to brotherhood and sisterhood (with God himself as the family's implied parent), these antislavery mottoes refused characterizations of black people as perpetual children with white people functioning in the role of parents.

Proslavery advocates did not have a monopoly on the rhetoric of white stewardship over black people, however. Critics of white abolitionism have long shown how abolitionist texts contributed to racist discourse by employing models of white supremacist stewardship and paternalism rather than racial equality. Katherine Grier notes Stowe's racialized depictions of dogs in her series of children's stories published in *Our Young Folks*, comparing them to her depictions of African American people in *Uncle Tom's Cabin*.[7] Similarly, Lesley Ginsberg shows how Stowe's depiction of her characters' racialized relationships to animals contributes to a "sentimentalized version of slavery."[8] Elsewhere, I have argued that such comparisons produced antislavery and animal welfare literature that resembled one another in ways that nineteenth-century readers readily recognized, showing us that abolitionist literature did not simply work to distance enslaved people from comparisons to animals.[9] As Grier notes, Mrs. Shelby's characterization of enslaved people as "these poor, simple, dependent creatures" and her lamenting the sale of "such a faithful, excellent, confiding creature as poor Tom" is "suspicious."[10] Stowe does not employ comparisons of her black characters and dogs only in the explicit critique of slavery's mistreatment.

7 Katherine C. Grier: *Pets in America. A History*. Chapel Hill: University of North Carolina Press 2006, pp. 214–215.

8 Lesley Ginsberg: "I am slave for love". Race, Sentimentality, and Harriet Beecher Stowe's Fiction for Children. In: Monika Elbert (ed.): *Enterprising Youth. Social Values and Acculturation in Nineteenth-Century American Children's Literature*. New York: Routledge 2008, pp. 97–115, here p. 112.

9 See Brigitte Fielder: Animal Humanism. Race, Species, and Affective Kinship in Nineteenth-Century Abolition. In: *American Quarterly* 65,3 (2013), pp. 487–513, here p. 498.

10 Grier: *Pets in America*, pp. 214, 455, fn. 111.

Stowe's imagery produces problematic associations in her depiction of Tom, in particular. During a scene in which Tom learns of Haley's intentions to have sold Eliza and her son separately, we read, "Tom, whose great heavy mouth had stood ajar during this communication, now suddenly snapped it together, as a big dog closes on a piece of meat, and seemed to be digesting the idea at his leisure" (61). A dehumanizing illustration however we understand Stowe's intent, this and similar animalistic depictions of black characters point to abolitionism's inability to fully embrace antiracism by disentangling itself from the discursive nexus of racialization-as-animalization. Widespread contemporary associations of dogs and loyalty make comparisons of Tom to dogs even more worrisome. During Eva St. Clare's illness, "Tom, at last would not sleep in his room, but lay all night in the outer verandah, ready to rouse at every call." Miss Ophelia, Augustine St. Clare's abolitionist cousin from the North, asks him, "Uncle Tom, what alive have you taken to sleeping anywhere and everywhere, like a dog, for?" (268) Jennifer Mason has argued that Stowe's language of animality allowed her to use human-animal comparisons that were not simply disparaging, and elsewhere I discuss the possibility of nonracist human-animal comparisons.[11] Still, it is difficult to read the kinds of human-animal connections she makes as racially neutral. Ophelia's characterization of Tom as "like a dog" may be one part of Stowe's indictment of a racist vein of abolitionism. It may also serve to illustrate the 'dog-like' qualities – loyalty, submissiveness – with which she imbues her protagonist.

Because pet animals – like dogs – were common in white, northern households, they may have been more familiar than nonwhite people as companions to Stowe's northern readers. Abolitionist children's literature not only often resembled animal welfare literature, but writers sometimes used the familiarity of household animals as mediators to garner sympathy for enslaved characters, as black people would be less familiar to their child audience.[12] St. Clare presents such an argument to Ophelia, which compares interracial affection with interspecies affection for household animals. St. Clare, though a slaveholder, derides his cousin's repugnance at a show of physical intimacy between Uncle Tom and Eva, holding "You would think no harm in a child's caressing a large dog, even if

11 See Jennifer Mason: *Civilized Creatures. Urban Animals, Sentimental Culture, and American Literature, 1850–1900.* Baltimore: Johns Hopkins UP 2005, pp. 95–118; Fielder: Animal Humanism, pp. 489–490.

12 See Fielder: Animal Humanism, pp. 498–501.

he was black; but a creature that can think, and reason, and feel, and is immortal, you shudder at; confess it, cousin" (196). Predominantly white populations and racial segregation made African Americans less familiar to many northern white people than animals like household pets might have been, while the ubiquity of enslaved servants rendered black people familiar in slaveholding households. Ironically, this familiarity led to more intimacy between white and black people in slaveholding households than in many northern, antislavery ones. As the above scene illustrates, the abolitionist humanization of black people did not simply mean that white people would view them as equals. Humanization itself involved various hierarchies of age, gender, class, and race. Neither did the racist dehumanization of black people position them in the generalized realm of 'animals' in this hierarchy. Individual animals' specificity in discourses about slavery created complexities of human-animal relations that worked in tandem with human hierarchies.

George Harris complicates the human-animal hierarchy as he tells us that, as an enslaved man, he had "not a living soul that cared for me more than a dog" (101). This sentiment goes beyond the mere dehumanization of black people but suggests a hierarchy in which the enslaved might figure as even lower than animals in white racist estimations. George continues, "Why, sir, I've been so hungry that I have been glad to take the bones they threw to their dogs" (101). The extent to which George is poorly treated and poorly fed suggests that he is not simply treated *like* a dog but, in fact, worse than one. Indeed, as Michael Lundblad argues with regard to his distinction between 'animal' and 'savage,' American racism complicates simple human-animal hierarchies that are based on evolutionary logic. Lundblad shows how nonhuman animals are sometimes elevated above nonwhite people in white, racist literature.[13] The case of George's claim that he is not cared for more than a dog – either affectively or in white people's material treatment – shows how notions of human-animal relations are not simple species hierarchies but also racialized ones. Moreover, enslaved people were not simply equated with animals in their dehumanization, but put into different kinds of relationships to various nonhuman animals than free, white people.

13 Michael Lundblad: *The Birth of a Jungle. Animality in Progressive-Era U.S. Literature and Culture.* New York: Oxford UP 2013, pp. 139–140.

Bloodhounds

Most often, abolitionist literature has depicted African American people's relationship to dogs as an adversarial one.[14] This is for good reason. The use of dogs to hunt self-emancipated people has a long history in the Americas. Sarah E. Johnson traces the practice to the eighteenth-century Caribbean, calling this use of dogs by white supremacist enslavers "canine warfare."[15] Meant not only as a pragmatic tool for tracking people, dogs were also employed as weapons of terror. The violence dogs could inflict when hunting people as prey inspired fear, but did not entirely deter people from risking their lives to escape. Stories of the violence done to escapees haunt abolitionist texts, making yet another case against slavery by showing it to be an inhumane system of violence. Beside the danger of being tracked, caught, and re-enslaved, the violence dogs could do to their prey presented an additional danger for attempts at self-emancipation.

In the antebellum United States, the use of dogs to hunt fugitives was notorious. Popular abolitionist texts, such as Abel Thomas' 1864 anti-slavery children's text, *The Gospel of Slavery: A Primer of Freedom*, illustrated dogs' danger to enslaved people. (Fig. 1) Images and accounts of 'bloodhounds' or other dogs used to hunt enslaved people also appeared in slave narratives by writers such as Henry Bibb, William Wells Brown, and Solomon Northup. In her 1862 narrative, Harriet Jacobs writes of an incident in which her son was attacked and injured by a dog and recounts the slaveholder Mrs. Flint's gleeful reaction to hearing the child had been bitten: "'I'm glad of it,' replied she. 'I wish he had killed him. It would be good news to send to his mother. *Her* day will come. The dogs will grab *her* yet.'"[16] For Mrs. Flint, the dogs' potential to harm enslaved people, as well as to track escapees, is a source of sadistic pleasure.

Uncle Tom's Cabin contributed to dogs' notoriety, mentioning slave-hunting dogs throughout. Discussing a slave-catching party of "some

14 For a discussion of how bloodhounds appear in abolitionist critiques of slavery's violence, see John Campbell: The Seminoles, the "Bloodhound War", and Abolitionism, 1796–1865. In: *The Journal of Southern History* 72,2 (2006), pp. 259–302.

15 See Sara E. Johnson: You Should Give Them Blacks to Eat. Waging Inter-American Wars of Torture and Terror. In: *American Quarterly* 61,1 (2009), pp. 65–92, here p. 67.

16 Harriet Jacobs: *Incidents in the Life of a Slave Girl, Written by Herself.* New York: Penguin 2000, p. 138.

Fig. 1: "B Stands for Bloodhound". From Abel Thomas: *The Gospel of Slavery: A Primer of Freedom*. New York: T.W. Strong 1864.

six or seven, with guns and dogs," St. Clare mentions, that "People, you know, can get up just as much enthusiasm in hunting a man as a deer, if it is only customary" (214). The scene St. Clare goes on to describe continues this language of dehumanization that equates self-emancipated people with hunted animals. This language distinguishes them from dogs and shows their relationship to them when dogs are employed as hunting tools:

> Well, the dogs bayed and howled, and we rode and scampered, and finally we started him. He ran and bounded like a buck, and kept us well in the rear for some time; but at last he got caught in an impenetrable thicket of cane; then he turned to bay, and I tell you he fought the dogs right gallantly. He dashed them to the right and left, and actually killed three of them with only his naked fists, when a shot from a gun brought him down, and he fell, wounded and bleeding, almost at my feet. The poor fellow looked up at me with manhood and despair both in his eye. I kept back the dogs and the party, as they came pressing up, and claimed him as my prisoner. (214)

Acknowledging this situational likeness to hunted animals as well as the escapee's humanity, St. Clare also illustrates the adversarial relationship between dogs and self-emancipated people.

The threat of dogs is a feature of other scenes. We see Cassy, a woman Legree holds enslaved, note the danger of slave-hunting dogs, telling

Tom "Down in the darkest swamps, their dogs will hunt us out, and find us. Everybody and everything is against us; even the very beasts side against us,—and where shall we go?" (363) Cassy is correct to anticipate this use of dogs; she and Emmeline are pursued by dogs when they are found missing and they escape only by hiding in the garret on Legree's own plantation – the one place he is not looking for them.

Uncle Tom's Cabin is an odd case in the depiction of slave-hunting dogs, as its most prominent scene of dogs hunting black people does not appear in the novel at all. No dogs are available to hunt Eliza, a woman enslaved by the Shelbys in Kentucky, as she famously carries her child across the frozen ice of the Ohio River and into a 'free' state. In fact, characters even discuss the unavailability of dogs to do so. As the slave trader Haley laments of the Shelby plantation, "your master don't keep no dogs (I pretty much know he don't) for trackin' out niggers" (52). Haley's failure to catch Eliza is, in part, due to the unavailability of this weapon. Considering using dogs later, he worries that the harm dogs might do to a person would devalue his property. When one man tells him "Our dogs tore a feller half to pieces, once, down in Mobile, fore we could get 'em off," Haley responds, "Well, ye see, for this sort that's to be sold for their looks, that ar won't answer, ye see" (64). Because Eliza's and her son's value lies in the idealization of mixed race 'beauty,' the danger of damaging "their looks" in order to catch them does not make good business sense.

The novel's absence of dogs in Haley's chase of Eliza was revised in many stage productions of *Uncle Tom's Cabin*, however. An indication of the centrality of dogs in stories about fugitivity, many stagings inserted dogs into Eliza's scenes and even made this a central feature of the production.[17] John W. Frick writes, "Of these interpolations into stage Uncle Toms, undoubtedly the most prominent and popular was the addition of dogs to chase Eliza across the ice and perhaps pursue Cassy and Emmeline as they attempted to flee Legree's plantation."[18] This addition of dogs to the Eliza plot served to exacerbate the danger of Eliza and her child's escape. As "Uncle Tom" shows became more

17 I owe thanks to Alex W. Black for bringing this feature of several stage productions of *Uncle Tom's Cabin* to my attention.

18 John W. Frick: *Uncle Tom's Cabin on the American Stage and Screen*. New York: Palgrave Macmillan 2012, p. 123. Frick is wrong, however, in his claim that "There had been no dogs in the novel" (ibid., p. 124).

prevalent even than Stowe's novel itself, scenes like this also worked to associate dogs almost exclusively with their role as human-tracking bloodhounds in abolitionist fiction. As Frick argues, once it was customary to see dogs in this role in stagings of *Uncle Tom's Cabin*, "to produce the play without dogs was show business suicide."[19] The popularity of including dogs in this scene is evident, as Jo-Ann Morgan writes that "the notion of slavering, bloodthirsty hounds lapping at the heels of runaways was fraught with heart-stopping thrills."[20] Such productions also made enslaved people's adversarial relationship to dogs in scenes of hunting and fugitivity one of the most iconic racialized human-animal relationships in the United States.[21]

Dogs used to hunt slaves might be better understood as working animals rather than pets in their importance to and relationship with slaveholders. Johnson discusses how dogs were also abused by this practice, deliberately starved and beaten in order to 'train' them to behave even more viciously toward their prey.[22] Both William Wells Brown's abolitionist novel *Clotel* and Stowe's *A Key to Uncle Tom's Cabin* reproduced an advertisement for "Negro Dogs" for hire "to catch runaway negroes" for a fee.[23] Kept as much for this purpose (or perhaps more so) as for their companionship as pets, dogs' role in the slaveholding system likely produced racialized readings of human-dog relationships. In her discussion of the image *Hunter with Dogs*, Anna Mae Duane acknowledges the different meanings such an image might hold for free white children and formerly enslaved black children. She writes, "For a student… [whose family had run away from slavery], the picture of a white man with dogs on a hunt was more likely to elicit nightmarish

19 Frick: *Uncle Tom's Cabin*, p. 125.

20 Jo-Ann Morgan: *Uncle Tom's Cabin as Visual Culture*. Columbia: University of Missouri Press 2007, p. 50.

21 As Johnson has traced the use of dogs in canine warfare from the eighteenth-century Caribbean colonies to their employment as military dogs at places like Guantánamo and Abu Ghraib, one might make a similar argument about the continuation of these adversarial, racialized human-animal relations in the use of police dogs against civil rights protesters in the twentieth- and twenty-first century United States.

22 Johnson: You Should Give Them Blacks to Eat, p. 85.

23 See Harriet Beecher Stowe: *A Key to Uncle Tom's Cabin. Presenting the Original Facts and Documents Upon Which the Story Is Founded. Together with Corroborative Statements Verifying the Truth of the Work*. Boston: Bosworth 1853, p. 109; William Wells Brown: *Clotel; or the President's Daughter*. London: Partridge & Oakley 1853, p. 73.

Fig. 2: Chapter 35 Headpiece illustration: Cassy, Legree, dog. From Harriet Beecher Stowe: *Uncle Tom's Cabin; or, Life Among the Lowly*. Illustrated Edition. Designs by Hammat Billings. Engraved by Baker, Smith, and Andrew. Boston: John P. Jewett 1853.

associations with the slave-catcher than the idyllic image of pastoral leisure that whites would likely feel the piece conveyed."[24] The difference between being the hunter and the hunted is key here, and this racialized relationship positions dogs as a point of reference for this particular form of white supremacist power and dehumanization.

The alignment of slaveholders with slave-hunting dogs even goes so far as to make another human-animal comparison. Stowe compares both Haley and Legree – the most notoriously brutal slaveholders of the text – to dogs in the novel. (Fig. 2) Regarding Haley, she writes "Indeed, could our readers fancy a bull-dog come unto man's escape, and walking about in a hat and coat, they would have no unapt idea of the general style and effect of his physique," (57) with Tom later referring to Haley's "clean, sheer, dog meanness" (61). Stowe's representation of human slave-hunters as doglike is evident, as Alex Black notes, in the seamlessness of the "shift from 'human bloodhounds' to

24 Anna Mae Duane: *Suffering Childhood in Early America. Violence, Race, and the Making of the Child Victim*. Athens: University of Georgia Press 2010, pp. 172–173.

bloodhounds" when the novel is translated to the stage.[25] Cassy later warns Tom that, having crossed Legree, he will find his ill will "hanging like a dog on your throat,—sucking your blood, bleeding away your life, drop by drop" (347). This animalization works differently than the racist dehumanization of black people that abolitionism seeks to counter. Attributed to their behavior, the viciousness of slave-hunting dogs in the text provides a backdrop for these comparisons to human viciousness. Carrying out the same 'inhumane' tasks toward enslaved black people, white slaveholders and hunting dogs are unable (or refuse) to comprehend their commonality with the people they track and hold captive. These comparisons turn the tables on proslavery arguments about enslaved people by instead arguing that slaveholders are the ones who are 'less than human.'

In the *Antislavery Alphabet* of this chapter's epigraph, "H is the Hound," bloodhounds figure as a staple of antislavery discourse in the United States. Indicating the ubiquity of depictions of slave-hunting dogs, we also read here what is perhaps an unwitting comparison of the hound and the fugitive. When we read "H is the Hound his master trained / And called to scent the track / Of the unhappy fugitive" it is unclear whether the "his" refers to the Hound or the unhappy fugitive, both of whom are implicated by the possessive and both of whom are legally owned by a "master." While this confusion hints at the dehumanization of enslaved people discussed earlier, the coupling of the dog and the slave in terms of their similar legal position and material conditions might also make possible the event of their solidarity with – rather than their adversity to – one another.

Best Friends?

Before he attempts to escape slavery, Stowe's George worries about the possibility of his death and its effect on his family: "I shall be kicked out and buried like a dog, and nobody'll think on it a day after,—*only my poor wife*!" (104) Again evoking the similar treatment of dogs and enslaved people, George worries that he might be so dehumanized that his death would not be mourned. He then modifies his statement, however. As he tells us, enslaved black families love and care for one another,

25 See Alex W. Black: *Print and Performance in American Abolitionism, 1829–1863*. Unpublished Dissertation, Cornell University, Ithaca, NY, 2013, p. 23.

even when the conditions of enslavement make the basic logistics of maintaining familial relationships extremely difficult. George would not die unmourned, because his wife, Eliza, would mourn him. To be "like a dog" is not necessarily to be uncared for.

Moreover, George himself cares for dogs. When he is first introduced, we learn that his wife had given him a pet dog, Carlo, who he frames almost as a member of this family. He tells Eliza, "the creature has been about all the comfort that I've had. He has slept with me nights, and followed me around days, and kind o' looked at me as if he understood how I felt" (15). The shared understanding George supposes is a result of the dehumanizing effects of slavery. He seems to view his situation as one only the fellow-enslaved and owned animals might fully recognize.

As Stowe continues George's conversation with Eliza, we read a heartbreaking scene that shows how both George and Carlo are subject to the will of white slaveholders.

> "[...] Well, the other day I was just feeding him with a few old scraps I picked up by the kitchen door, and Mas'r came along, and said I was feeding him up at his expense, and that he couldn't afford to have every nigger keeping his dog, and ordered me to tie a stone to his neck and throw him in the pond."
>
> "O, George, you didn't do it!"
>
> "Do it? not I!—but he did. Mas'r and Tom pelted the poor drowning creature with stones. Poor thing! he looked at me so mournful, as if he wondered why I didn't save him. I had to take a flogging because I wouldn't do it myself [...]" (15, fig. 3)

Both George and Carlo are not only property, but property who can be physically abused and even killed. Both are similarly subject to white violence and, like the Hound and the "unhappy fugitive," to the will of the same owner. Just like George and Eliza cannot (legally) protect their child from being sold away from them, George cannot protect his pet dog from being stoned and drowned. For abolitionists, this scene evokes a kind of double pathos, as readers are expected to feel sympathy both for "poor little Carlo" and for George, who is unable to save him. Here we add to the list of slavery's atrocities the prevention of enslaved people from maintaining relationships of stewardship and care over their nonhuman companions (15).

Dogs do appear as pets to black people in antislavery literature and in the African American press, however. While most scholars have prioritized discussions of dog-keeping in the nineteenth-century United States as a phenomenon of white, middle-class domesticity, pet dogs

Fig. 3: "Carlo's Death". From Harriet Beecher Stowe: *Uncle Tom's Cabin; or, Life Among the Lowly: A Tale of Slave Life in America*. Illustrated by George Thomas, Esq., and T.R. Macquoid, Esq., and Engraved by William Thomas, Esq. London: Nathaniel Cooke 1853.

were known to be held not only by the black middle classes, but by enslaved black people, as well. Further, such dogs were often a matter of contention for slaveholders. Grier discusses dogs kept by enslaved people on George Washington's plantation, noting contention over such dogs mating with slaveholders' purebred dogs and the problem of preventing them from poaching livestock. While they might have been a nuisance to the slaveholding class, such dogs were often a boon to the enslaved, especially if used, as Grier suggests, "to help their owners augment their diet by hunting wild animals."[26] For George, Carlo is – perhaps because the dog is associated with his wife – mostly a source of comfort. And, as the above passage shows, George's feelings for the dog are also a source of vulnerability. Just as slaveholders used enslaved people's kinship relationships as another avenue through which to inflict emotional harm or terror, the killing of Carlo serves as a violent performance and reinforcement of white domination.

26 Grier: *Pets in America*, p. 35. On enslaved people's use of dogs for hunting and fishing, see Scott Giltner: Slave Hunting and Fishing in the Antebellum South. In: Diane D. Glave / Mark Stoll (eds.): *"To Love the Wind and the Rain." African Americans and Environmental History*. Pittsburgh: University of Pittsburgh Press 2006, pp. 21–36.

Fig. 4: "Eliza comes to tell Uncle Tom that he is sold, and that she is running away to save her child". From Harriet Beecher Stowe: *Uncle Tom's Cabin; or, Life Among the Lowly*. [First Edition.] Illustrated by Hammatt Billings. Boston: John P. Jewett 1852.

Dogs kept by enslaved people were not only a point of vulnerability, however. While Cassy laments that "even the very beasts side against us," this is not entirely true for Stowe's enslaved people. As Eliza is fleeing the Shelby plantation with her child, we read about her encounter with "Old Bruno, a great Newfoundland": "She gently spoke his name, and the animal, an old pet and playmate of hers, instantly, wagging his tail, prepared to follow her, though apparently revolving much, in his simple dog's head, what such an indiscreet midnight promenade might mean" (33–34). Even the irregularity of Eliza's movement doesn't make Bruno a threat to her. He follows her to Uncle Tom's cabin, where she eventually asks Tom's family to shut the door on him so that he does not follow her as she escapes. (Fig. 4)

Bruno – and his relationship to Eliza – comes up again when Haley is lamenting Shelby's lack of slave-hunting dogs. As Sam, another man enslaved on the Shelby plantation, banters with Haley, delaying his pursuit of Eliza, he mentions Bruno at the same moment in which he indicates the non-adversarial relationship between enslaved people and dogs on the plantation. When Haley inquires about dogs, Sam assures him, "thar's Bruno—he's a roarer! and, besides that, 'bout every nigger of us keeps a pup of some natur or uther" (52). This description of exactly the wrong kind of dogs for Haley's purposes is practically a taunt, as Stowe mentions that "Sam knew exactly what he meant, but he kept on a look of earnest and desperate simplicity" (52). Articulating this friendly relationship to dogs, Sam shows how enslaved people might challenge the system by which human-animal relations only meet white supremacist ends. The presence of black-owned dogs thus also presents a means of re-thinking what kinds of animals were pets – and to whom – in the plantation system. This reorientation of human-animal relations beyond the predominant power structures that aligned dogs with white enslavers makes their presence important for thinking about how enslaved people resisted this power structure and how such resistance could sometimes be interpreted in terms of interspecies cooperation.

If the relationships between George and Carlo and Eliza and Bruno are affectionate ones, this is decidedly different than the relationships we see between enslaved people and the dogs used to hunt them. William Link notes that Virginia slaveholders sought specifically to regulate African American dog ownership, implying a connection between this restriction and other restrictions on black freedom and mobility.[27] Beside the threat dogs may pose to their livestock, another worry slaveholders might have had is that this particular human-animal alignment would upset their own framing of dogs as adversaries to black people. In the instance of Carlo, Stowe shows the human-animal relationship of pet and keeper as one that was denied to enslaved people because their status as property prevented them from functioning as either owners of or stewards over the animals in their care. But this relationship also indicates an inability to absolutely control animals and forge them into tools of white supremacy. Grier writes that "it seems that campaigns to prevent slaves from keeping dogs were never successful."[28] In light of slaveholders' cultivation of adversarial relationships between dogs and enslaved people, forging friendly relationships with canine companions might be viewed as a subversive act.

While the dogs that are friendly pets to enslaved people in Stowe's novel are distinct from the dogs meant to hunt and capture them, the

27 William A. Link: *Roots of Secession. Slavery and Politics in Antebellum Virginia*. Chapel Hill: University of North Carolina Press 2003, pp. 150–151.

28 Grier: *Pets in America*, p. 35.

possibility of overlap here is an even greater danger to white slave-holding power. In his 1853 narrative, *Twelve Years a Slave*, Solomon Northup admits to deliberately abusing his enslaver Epps' dogs so that they will fear him:

> I concluded, in that case, to be prepared for Epps' dogs, should, they pursue me. He possessed several, one of which was a notorious slave-hunter, and the most fierce and savage of his breed. While out hunting the coon or the opossum, I never allowed an opportunity to escape, when alone, of whipping them severely. In this manner I succeeded at length in subduing them completely. They feared me, obeying my voice at once when others had no control over them whatever. Had they followed and overtaken me, I doubt not they would have shrank from attacking me.[29]

Countering the violence of slave-hunting dogs with preemptive violence of his own, Northup uses slaveholders' own tactic of abuse to subvert the power relations inherent in this type of human-animal relationship.

Northup also describes a similar strategy, neutralizing the threat of slaveholders' dogs by turning them into allies (or at least neutral parties) who are unwilling to do slaveholders' bidding. Also enslaved with Northup on Carey's plantation is a nineteen- or twenty-year-old mixed-race 'girl,' named Celeste. She appears at Northup's door one night, and tells him "Carey's dogs won't follow me. They have tried to set them on. There's a secret between them and Celeste, and they won't mind the devilish orders of the overseer."[30] Northup goes on to explain that Celeste "had no fear of Carey's dogs, any more than I had of Epps'. It is a fact, which I have never been able to explain, that there are those whose tracks the hounds will absolutely refuse to follow. Celeste was one of them" (162). Subtler, perhaps, than Northup's own violent tactics, Celeste aligns herself with these dogs in a way the slaveholder cannot detect.

Martin Delany describes powers similar to Celeste's in his response to *Uncle Tom's Cabin*, *Blake; or, The Huts of America*, serialized in *The Anglo-African Magazine* in 1859 and reprinted in *The Weekly Anglo-African* from 1861 to 1862. An enslaved woman, Aunt Rachel, explains to *Blake*'s protagonist, Henry, that the night-patrollers and their dogs are not a threat to the enslaved on their plantation because the dogs

29 Solomon Northup: *Twelve Years a Slave*. New York: Penguin 2012, p. 159.

30 Ibid., p. 162.

have been 'charmed': "God bless yeh, honey, da blacks do'n mine dem noh der 'nigga-dogs' nutha. Patrolas feahd uh de black folks, an' da black folks charm de dogs, so da cahn het 'em."[31] Dogs that cannot hurt them are not a threat to enslaved people and slaveholders are cowed without this powerful tool of oppression at their disposal.

Blake's Oba/Grande family are also dog charmers, and this has granted them special privileges and security on their plantation: "Grande was foreman on the plantation of Jenkin, probably because of his superior intelligence; but most probably because of the fact that from the day of his advent on the place, the bloodhounds were known to fondle with his family, and never could be made to attack or even bay after one of them."[32] Coupling this diffusion of the slaveholder-dog alignment with the prospect of armed slave rebellion in Delany's novel, the practice of "dog charming" is a powerful skill enslaved people impart to one another.

> Secrets were exchanged concerning dog charming between Henry and his new friend Grande, and much information was obtained concerning the character of Cuban planters, as well as the designs of the slaves. They were ripe for a general rising, said the old man, but God only knew where they would find a leader. These things and many more were made known to him during three days' secretion in the family.[33]

Delany makes the cultivation of this human-animal relationship a part of Henry's preparation for organizing emancipation and revolutionary efforts.

Conclusion

The various resonances of dogs described here show how abolitionist literature's associations between enslaved African American people and dogs were multifaceted and contradictory. Reading dogs in *Uncle Tom's Cabin* and other abolitionist literature – including literature by African American writers – we see dogs and black people paired in scenes ranging from racist dehumanization to radical human-animal associations. This discussion of race and species shows that we must attend to the specificity of human-animal relationships to fully understand how

31 Martin R. Delany: *Blake; or, The Huts of America*. Boston: Beacon 1970, p. 90.

32 Ibid., pp. 172–173.

33 Ibid., p. 173.

these resonances fit into the broader context of race, racialization, and racism in the American nineteenth century. Paying attention to these complexities allows us to more fully comprehend the resonances of race and species in these literary representations.

The nineteenth century saw discourses of race and species that were closely intertwined. Transatlantic discussions of science and pseudo-science produced literature on human and nonhuman taxonomies and natural histories that often conflated race and species categories in their arguments and overwhelmingly sought to justify global white supremacist endeavors of imperialism, enslavement, and oppression. As I have shown in this chapter, the long history of how race and species have overlapped includes the racialization of human-animal relationships, a phenomenon that requires scholars of animal studies to acknowledge the complexities of how race and racism have come to bear on the diversity of human-animal relationships, which speak not only to the heterogeneity of animals, but that of humans as well. Scholars of animal studies cannot afford to ignore the ways race and racism inflect upon animal studies scholarship or to relegate discussions of the intersections of race and species to simplistic, ahistorical comparisons, rather than careful analysis.

Further, animal studies scholarship must engage closely with – rather than merely appropriate – scholarship on race and racism in order to avoid performing yet another form of appropriative violence upon people of color. I argue that this work necessitates an historicist treatment of animals that takes into account the racialization of human-animal relationships as well as other intersectional human identities that come to bear upon interspecies relations, an engagement with writing by nonwhite people that also recognizes the fields of scholarship most appropriate for their study, and the incorporation of a more diverse spectrum of voices within the realm of animal studies scholarship. This chapter is an attempt to add my own scholarly voice and methodologies in nineteenth-century American literary studies, the critical study of race and racism, and early African American literary studies to this interdisciplinary field.

Man's Best and Worst Friends

The Politics of Pet Preference at the Turn of the Twentieth Century

Keridiana Chez

In the nineteenth-century's flood of animal-focused writing, dozens of accounts of inconsolable dogs standing vigil by their ailing or dead human companions fostered the belief that the dog's primary reason for living was its human. Building on centuries of existing lore about the faithful dog, these testimonies supposed that when a dog's master or mistress died, it would pine without reprieve, haunting graves and refusing all food so as to expedite its own death. In contrast, cats were reputedly unfazed by the death of their masters or mistresses. Selfish, cruel, and incapable of disinterested fidelity, cats eschewed meaningful attachments to humans.

Yet towards the last third of the nineteenth century, representations shifted. The below sketch of "A Cat's Attachment" (1885) figures a cat in a posture thereto exclusively associated with dogs: the posture of the faithful, inconsolable pet by the graveside. Another such account from 1877 describes how "at the death of her mistress, [the cat] wandered about her chamber, mewing most piteously; and after the body was consigned to the grave, it was found stretched upon the tomb, lifeless, having expired

Fig. 1: "A Cat's Attachment". From Elizabeth Surr: *Pets and Playfellows; or Stories about Cats and Dogs*. London: Nelson & Sons 1885, after p. 118.

from excess grief."[1] Evocative of Edwin Landseer's celebrated paintings of faithful dogs by human corpses – *Attachment* (1829) and *The Old Shepherd's Chief Mourner* (1837) – the devoted cats are depicted as heartbroken over their master's or mistress' grave, refusing to abandon them even in death. After over a century of prejudice that insisted that cats were incapable of becoming attached to their humans, these cats surprised because they behaved like dogs.

Grappling with the intricacies and implications of this shift in attitudes, the first section of this chapter surveys the cultural history of

1 Henry Hupfeld: Cats. In: *Encyclopaedia of Wit and Wisdom*. Philadelphia: McKay 1877, pp. 37–38, here p. 37.

the dog/cat dichotomy and how claims made about each also shaped human gender dynamics (and vice versa), particularly at the height of the humane movement's successful redefinition of cruelty towards animals in the latter half of the nineteenth century. Multiple representations, fictional and non-fictional, described dogs as masculine (referred to as 'he') and cats as feminine (assumed to be 'she'), polar opposites assigned admirable and reprehensible traits respectively. Humanity's sense of affront at failing to secure feline favor or submission – for cats did not appear to love and obey humans as dogs so visibly did – propelled the production of a complex discursive-imaginary apparatus linking felinity with femininity to the detriment of both. The next section explores how, according to these narratives, intimacy with each species was supposed to affect humans in prescribed ways: while the dog saved souls, the cat disabled its human companions. When they provided men with the company of dogs and assigned to women the exclusive propensity to gather cats, nineteenth-century Americans[2] were engaging in interspecies, homosocial practices of gender production. The chapter then closes with a snapshot of how *fin-de-siècle* gender shifts – overcivilized effetes, mannish New Women – also intersected with representations of and practices towards cats and dogs. Though to some extent writers successfully revised the cat to take on the dog-like capacity for fidelity, at the nineteenth century's turn, feline independence was increasingly appropriated by (male) dogs (and men). Knots in the threads of ever-evolving gender discourses, these intersections not only reveal the complex dynamics of the cross-species production of gender but also the ways in which animal bodies and expressions of animals' corporeal agency are actively involved in knowledge production, in this case, gendered discourses of felinity and caninity.

Dog vs. Cat

The graveside trope required one simple but dramatic element: the mourning animal's grief would be so great as to suppress its primal instincts (to eat, to live). As proof, many accounts would include details such as humans failing to entice the starving animal with delicious foods and/or resorting to brute force to remove the animal. The ability

2 By 'American,' I refer not only to recognized citizens, but rather to all people living in the United States and shaping the fluctuating definition of Americanness.

to supplant another animal's primal needs with human social and cultural expectations – in this case, proofs of love and rituals of mourning – testified to the human power to attract the absolute devotion of a member of another species. In that sense, dogs were the success story of a domestication recast as an interspecies love story; cats, in contrast, were reminders of human failure.

The eighteenth-century French naturalist Georges-Louis Leclerc, Comte de Buffon, author of the widely circulated *Histoire Naturelle*, drew stark lines between cat and dog. For the dog, Buffon offered hyperbolic encomiums: "without having, like man, the light of intellect, [the dog] has all the warmth of emotion [...] no ambition, no interest, no desire for vengeance: no fear except of displeasing; he is all zeal, all ardor and all obedience."[3] A "faithful animal whose every feeling attaches itself to his owner's person," the dog was praised as humanity's most trustworthy friend and devoted servant.[4] Buffon's views dominated discourse on the dog, gaining particular traction during the nineteenth century's pet-keeping mania when, alongside the birth and spread of the humane movement, the dog was reclassified from beast of burden to beloved family member.[5]

The most celebrated canine virtue was the selflessness that allowed the dog to 'attach' all its 'feelings' to its master's 'person,' thus adopting human needs and wants as his own. The ultimate proof was, of course, throwing itself in harm's way to save a human life. One of the first animal viewpoint novels published in the U.S., Margaret Marshall Saunders' *Beautiful Joe* (1894) features a dog that repays his mistress' kindness by risking his life to save her from burglary and arson.[6] In turn, dogs were also thought uniquely capable of unconditional and undying love. No matter how poor or how cruel (or, in the case of graveside narratives,

3 Georges-Louis Leclerc de Buffon: *Morceaux Choisis de Buffon*, ed. by Hemar Clinquer. Paris: Delagrave 1867, p. 129.

4 Ibid., p. 135.

5 For more on the American humane movement and pet-keeping, see Diane L. Beers: *For the Prevention of Cruelty. The History and Legacy of Animal Rights Activism in the United States*. Athens: Swallow Press / Ohio UP 2006; James Turner: *Reckoning with the Beast. Animals, Pain, and Humanity in the Victorian Mind*. Baltimore: Johns Hopkins UP 1980; Katherine C. Grier: *Pets in America. A History*. Chapel Hill: University of North Carolina Press 2006.

6 Margaret Marshall Saunders: *Beautiful Joe*, ed. by Keridiana Chez. Peterborough: Broadview 2015.

how dead), human masters could expect their dogs to never abandon them. Thus in Saunders' *"Boy," the Wandering Dog: Adventures of a Fox-Terrier* (1916), a prized Boston Terrier is carelessly rejected by his mistress, simply because he has fallen out of fashion, but he continues to pine for her even as he passes into the hands of a loving new owner.[7] Most poignantly, Mark Twain's *A Dog's Tale* (1903) critiques the practice of vivisection by portraying a loyal dog that remains naively trusting of a master who uses her puppy for pointless experimentation.[8] Contrasting the dog's pathetic credulity against the human's wanton cruelty, the story emphasizes how very ungrateful and undeserving humanity must be to perform such acts on such loving animals. These superlative representations of dogs as heroes and devotees, however complimentary, ultimately delimited canine existence and agency to performances of unconditional fidelity to humankind.

To predict Buffon's opinion of cats, negate everything he said about the dog. Possibly the most-cited expert on feline faults, Buffon argued that one must look beyond the cat's apparently docile exterior to its irredeemable core: "although these animals, especially when young, might have gentleness, they have at the same time an inner malice, a false character, a perverse nature, that increases with age, and that training (*l'education*) does no more than disguise (*masquer*)."[9] Indeed, in a particularly invective-laden paragraph, he emphasizes the inconsistency between the cat's corrupt nature and its 'seductive' appearance.[10] Thus, feline abilities such as stalking and hunting prey were read not as admirable or useful skills, but rather as evidence of cunning and evil: "they know to muffle their step, dissimulate their designs, spy the occasions, wait, choose, seize in an instant the opportunity to strike their blow."[11] All observable behavior was explained to the detriment of the cat: if the cat behaved affectionately, it was a ruse; if the cat scratched, its true

7 Beanie's new owner is a 'colored' woman who keeps the houses of women like his first owner, a wealthy white woman. Beanie insists that it is not his new owner's modest household that he rejects; simply, his first human will forever be his only love. He is an example of the typical canine ideal for most of the nineteenth century: unconditionally loyal to the point of non-reason. Margaret Marshall Saunders: *"Boy," the Wandering Dog. Adventures of a Fox-Terrier.* New York: Grosset & Dunlap 1916, p. 101.

8 Mark Twain: *A Dog's Tale.* New York: Harper & Brothers 1904.

9 Buffon: *Morceaux Choisis*, p. 136.

10 Ibid.

11 Ibid.

self was revealed. Any challenge posed by feline corporeal agency to human-centered discourses seemed easily surmounted by the premise of feline deceit, the Other to canine candidness.[12]

Buffon's views on the dog remained popular well into the twentieth century – what of his hostility towards cats? Katharine M. Rogers has argued that by the nineteenth century, the curmudgeon naturalist's views "would have been extravagantly idiosyncratic,"[13] but aspersions against cats were profuse across the period: "They're selfish things; they think of nothing but their own comfort; they haven't a bit of sympathy";[14] they are "ungrateful"[15] and "cunning"[16] and exhibit "greediness" along with "cruel scratching";[17] they are "bold, unblushing, presumptuous"[18]; they "pretend attachment" but this is "mere hypocrisy".[19] Arguably, the need to libel the cat was even greater in the nineteenth century, when, as Rogers herself notes, cats were catching up to dogs in popularity. This brought them "into direct competition with dogs [...] thereby infuriating some dog lovers."[20] The opening image to this chapter, featuring a cat by its master's grave, was not exemplary of the predominant discourse that persisted in defaming all things feline.

Experts had long insisted that the cat's primary attachment was to itself, and then secondarily, to its locus: its loyalty was allegedly conditioned on the ampleness of the cupboard and the coziness of the hearthrug. Other living creatures were as furniture to the cat, which, in its uncompromising felinocentrism, seemed to think that "the world and everything in it were made and exist for cats."[21] Ironically, when a detractor

12 This is not to suggest that nonhuman agency did not affect these anthropocentric discourses. Although these discourses and texts were and are apparently human products, they are arguably always already co-shaped through intercorporeal and intersubjective relations between species.

13 Katharine M. Rogers: *Cat*. London: Reaktion 2006, p. 88.

14 Mary E. Clemens: *Getting and Giving*. London: Nelson & Sons 1884, p. 11.

15 Pets and What They Cost. In: *Eclectic Magazine of Foreign Literature, Science, and Art*, May–August 1856, pp. 410–415, here p. 411.

16 MacLeod: Talks about Familiar Animals. In: *The Teachers World* 5,1 (1893), pp. 10–11, here p. 11.

17 The Cat. In: *Young Israel* 1,10 (1871), pp. 455–459, here p. 455.

18 A Pleasant Bit of Humor. In: *Arthur's Home Magazine* 11 (1858), p. 258.

19 The Awkward Man. In: *Brighton Magazine* 5 (1822), pp. 623–635, here p. 630.

20 Rogers: *Cat,* p. 86.

21 W. H. Larrabee: Cats and Their Friendships. In: *Popular Science Monthly* 37 (1890), pp. 91–102, here p. 96.

said, "[m]y cat loves the dog and horse [it sleeps with] exactly with the tender sentiment we have for foot-warmers and railway rugs,"[22] he suggested that the cat exploited its fellow beings in precisely the same way humans used nearly every animal they did not eat. For the dog, on the other hand, emphasis was placed on its attachment to the family members, making the locus irrelevant. A common theme was that dogs fell in interspecies love, usually imagined as a strictly asexual form of innocent affection and admiration. In Saunders' *Beautiful Joe*, on first sight of his mistress the dog's thoughts are "I had never seen such a beautiful girl, and I think so still,"[23] and in Ethelbert Talbot's *Tim: The Autobiography of a Dog* (1914), the dog that meets his "young mistress" for the first time finds her voice "so gentle and sympathetic that I soon fell in love with her."[24] In *Beautiful Joe*, the dog follows his mistress as she changes abodes, quickly adapting to his new 'homes' so long as she is nearby. The family cat, on the other hand, refuses to remain with one of the brothers for the duration of his summer visit to an aunt's house. "[T]hough he had kept her with him the whole time, she had acted as if she wanted to get away,"[25] and eventually the cat runs off and finds her way home by traversing nearly fifty miles. While *Beautiful Joe* sought to emphasize feline intelligence with this story, in the broader context of contemporary cat discourse, the cat's homecoming was also read as further proof of its inability to attach itself to humans: she prefers the house to the brother.

In the patriarchal tradition, of course the admirable traits of the dog were ascribed to men; of course the derogatory traits of cats were ascribed to women. Dogs were "little boy-children" (faithful, brave, honest) as cats were "little girl-children" (deceitful, materialistic, egotistical).[26] In the case of dogs, boys would be encouraged to aspire to be like their canine friends; in the case of cats, girls would be admonished against becoming what they were already prone to become. Certainly, as

22 Philip Gilbert Hamerton: *Chapters on Animals*. Boston: Roberts Brothers 1893, p. 48.

23 Saunders: *Beautiful Joe*, p. 63.

24 Ethelbert Talbot: *Tim. The Autobiography of a Dog*. New York: Harper & Brothers 1914, p. 7.

25 Saunders: *Beautiful Joe*, p. 114.

26 Anne Herendeen: The Case of Mouser vs. Bowser. In: *Everybody's Magazine* 41,1 (1919), p. 41.

Rogers documents, male authors found representations of cats convenient to "berat[e] slatterns" and "insubordinate wives."[27] As Kathleen Kete and Rogers have explored in their richly historicized work, the cat was also a highly sexualized creature, particularly because of its nocturnal habits and the unabashed noise of feline mating.[28] Female cats were judged aggressively sexual in a transgressive way: this "pet of children, the admired habitué of the drawing-room or the salon by day, may become at night a wild animal, [...] frequently making night hideous with its cries."[29] The 'natural' reality of a cat's barbed penis, combined with the noises of presumed pain during feline copulation, seemed like evidence of the female cat's perverse, sexual masochism. If women were like cats when they were apparently docile, then they would also be like cats when they defied the norms of middle-class women, for whom sex was not usually supposed to be anything more than reproductive.

Yet in spite of all these texts expounding on felinity – the natural histories, periodicals, and fiction – the feline remained veiled under a suspicious cloud of ineffability. According to centuries of lore, the cat harkened from the devil, associated with witchcraft and the supernatural.[30] Even as they made specific claims about cats, commentators added vague warnings such as: "of the cat it must be said that of all animals it is the most mysterious"[31] and "[t]here must be something mysterious and almost supernatural"[32] about the cat. Writers capitalized on its enigmatic reputation by deploying the cat as a symbol of the occult, as in Edgar Allan Poe's *Black Cat* (1843), where a murdered cat's revenant haunts her murderer.[33] Although the protagonist is so unsympathetic that the reader must want to root for the abused cat, her sheer creepiness

27 Rogers: *Cat*, p. 138.

28 Kathleen Kete: *Beast in the Boudoir. Petkeeping in Nineteenth-Century Paris*. Berkeley: University of California Press 1994, pp. 120–121; Rogers: *Cat*, pp. 114–140.

29 Edward Howe Forbush: *The Domestic Cat. Bird Killer, Mouser, and Destroyer of Wildlife*. Boston: Wright & Potter 1916, p. 7.

30 Rogers: *Cat*, pp. 49–68.

31 Samuel Rockwell Reed: *Offthoughts about Women and Other Things*. Chicago: Belford, Clarke & Co. 1888, p. 47.

32 Pussy. In: *Harper's New Monthly Magazine* 40,238 (1870), pp. 481–489, here p. 487.

33 Edgar Allan Poe: Black Cat. In: *The Works of Edgar Allan Poe*, ed. by Edmund Clarence Stedman / George Edward Woodberry. New York: Scribner's Sons 1914, pp. 42–54.

forestalls readerly attachment. Saunders' sequel to her first dog novel, *Beautiful Joe's Paradise; or, The Island of Brotherly Love* (1902), features a cat necromancer who possesses invaluable powers yet is shunned by her fellow islanders, who are almost all males (dogs, monkeys, bears, lambs, and elephants in "brotherly love"). On Beautiful Joe's paradise, animals that die before their masters wait patiently to be reunited. One of the few female islanders, Pussy is a special case "sent there to be educated" so that "she will get some love into her heart,"[34] as if contrary to predominant assumption males were the more loving sex. Beautiful Joe remarks that being a "very honest dog[,]" he "hated queer or mysterious things."[35] Shrouded in mystery, the cat remains an outcast even as her powers are indispensable to the operation of the plot.

Saunders' attitude towards the feline and its assumed interconnections with the feminine echoed a more widespread cultural concern. Even as they were included in the family, the cat/femininity was tagged as a potential threat. As an 1897 description by the "home angel" portrays the "charmed spot [of the] family circle":

> There sits grandfather in his deep chair, gazing at the embers, dreaming of his childhood; there grandmother opposite with her inseparable knitting, thinking of how she can make the little ones happy; there father and mother talk of by-gone days, when they were courting, and there the children play their merry games, the baby rolls on the floor and Tabby nods in the warm corner, while faithful old dog Tray watches her with sleepy, yet alert eyes, from the hearth-rug. It is a happy group.[36]

In this portrait of domestic bliss, the title of "home angel" refers not only to the mother, who would be expected to receive such honors, but also to the dog. In fact, the mother is textually deemphasized so that Tray can punctuate the family roll call. The dog takes the active role of "watching over" the family of which the mother is just another part. "[S]leepy," yet "alert," Tray seems on guard against the threat ensconced within the family: Tabby, the cat who does not appear to pose any danger. What appears to be an idyllic picture belies a domestic space fraught with intersecting anxieties about felinity and femininity. Just as the necromancer Pussy in *Paradise* and Tabby the nodding cat are

34 Margaret Marshall Saunders: *Beautiful Joe's Paradise; or, The Island of Brotherly Love*. Boston: Page 1902, p. 97.

35 Ibid., p. 95.

36 Family Circle. In: *American Home Magazine* 1,1 (1897), p. 16.

included yet mistrusted, marked as "queer" and "mysterious," so is the wife and mother by extension, given the linkage of women and cats. According to this description, the cat/feminine requires constant vigilance on the part of the dog/masculine, and given the apparent distraction of the human mother, the dog has taken over as the new "home angel." Arguably, the dog/cat dynamic thus also represents concealed gender hostilities in the supposedly safe haven of the household – ruptures in the separate spheres ideology that bound middle-class women to the domestic role. The scene paradoxically suggests that the wife and mother whose duty it was to produce domestic harmony was in fact the family's greatest liability; like the cat, she may unpredictably erupt in disruptive, antidomestic ways.

By depositing human gender in animal bodies, gender was inscribed and reinforced as an essential reality, strengthening the assumption that masculinity and femininity were 'natural' and that the former was superior to the latter. Canine faithfulness and feline detachment were thus constructions of Otherness that shadowed and shaped human discourses of masculinity and femininity.

Canine Enablers, Feline Disablers

"Boys, as a rule, prefer dogs to cats to make pets and companions of[,]" said one commentator, "but the latter animals are the favourites of the girls."[37] Under this same-sex, same-gender arrangement, boys and men would be improved by the company of faithful dogs. With their disinterestedness, dogs were held up as models for boys, who "must learn to obey like a dog."[38] At the same time, in mastering their dogs properly, males would develop the ability to restrain their own 'animal' impulses.

Yet a dog's company promised still more, particularly for boys. Richard Felton Outcault's *Buster Brown's Autobiography* (1907), along with his popular comic strip, is an iconic example of the "a boy and his dog" relation. The mischievous Buster Brown and his dog Tige are represented as inseparable partners in a world where adults and their doings are mere props in the child's drama. "Dear old Tige,—all that summer when we

37 Vernon S. Morwood: *Facts and Phases of Animal Life*. New York: Appleton 1883, p. 171.

38 Lucretia P. Hale: *Stories for Children*. Boston: Leach, Shewell & Sanborn 1892, p. 129.

first became acquainted he stuck to me like a brother,"[39] Buster Brown narrates. Dogs are great friends, according to Buster, because "he is your friend because he loves you, and not for what there is in it"[40] – an adult concern foisted upon a child. "If I was happy, he sprang up and barked with joy. If I was sad he hung his head and tail and was as downcast as I was," says Buster Brown, and if he were pondering over a bird, "Tige would look as meditative as a human being and do just as I did."[41] The dog's exact copying (one is tempted to call it aping) creates the illusion of absolute resonance, of two beings distinct but so well-matched as to never disagree. The way in which the dog's companionship enriched the boy's life was both practical, in that they wreaked mischief together, and emotional: "He knows how to sympathise [*sic*] with a friend. He can cure a bump or a bruise for me by just licking it."[42] The ability to create flawless resonance was deemed essential to the relation that so strengthened the boy and dog. In Saunders' *Paradise*, the human boy appears to his faithful dog as "a prince, a king in gorgeous clothing," as "the whole world with Paradise thrown in,"[43] and in turn the boy describes his dog as "my friend—more brother than dog,"[44] begging the question: why does the boy's "brother" have to be a dog?[45]

Child psychologists argued that a companion like the dog was essential to the development of boys because another human being would fail to provide the kind of companionship required: a shadow, a prop, a resonator. Experts such as Mabel Marsh pointed out that a pet animal was ideal because it had "sufficient individuality [...] without either the weakness that another child usually shows for wanting the same things at the same time, and appealing to the ordeal of combat if he is not given them."[46] Indeed, from a pet "neither rivalry nor exaction is to be

39 Richard Felton Outcault: *Buster Brown's Autobiography*. New York: Stokes 1907, p. 3.

40 Ibid.

41 Ibid., pp. 3–4.

42 Ibid., p. 4.

43 Saunders: *Beautiful Joe's Paradise*, p. 348.

44 Ibid.

45 If we take Saunders' *Beautiful Joe* as a contrasting example, the portrayal of a dog and his mistress would emphasize how the mistress nurtured the dog, and how the dog repaid the kindness by guarding and/or rescuing her from danger.

46 Mabel A. Marsh: Children and Animals. In: *Studies in Education* 2 (1902), pp. 83–99, here p. 83.

feared," thus allowing the child to "most fully ope[n] his heart" and "lavis[h on the pet] the treasures of his affections."[47] The logic is familiar enough – the idea that pets are easier to love than people still has currency – but it is significant that dogs were prescribed to children to serve, essentially, as emotional training wheels. While girls would be encouraged to take up pets as pretend babies to nurse, boys were presumed to require an easier love object: a worshipful double. The nineteenth century's dog-keeping mania was more a concerted effort on the part of people with growing authority and cultural clout than a mistake, as Monica Flegel has noted,[48] and while domination was certainly part of the relation, as Yi-Fu Tuan has argued,[49] the pet has always been about more than domination: boys in particular were taught that alongside domination comes affection. In the boy-and-his-dog trope, the boy does not have – perhaps cannot maintain – any close human friends, because no human companion could or would provide ready approbation and unconditional attachment. The canine enabler fulfilled a role that only a nonhuman animal was thought capable of, molding and shaping young boys' emotional capacities by their own candid selflessness – work that was presumed impossible with an ontological equal.

Unlike the dog, the companionship of cats generally signaled the accompanying human's bad character. "[V]ery young ladies" would be excused for liking cats, while spinsters over age thirty were lambasted.[50] The unfortunate old maid was portrayed as "the cat's only friend,"[51] suggesting that no one else in their right mind and with an adequate life would bother with that animal. A refrain from a popular song named *Poor Old Maids* went "nursing cats is all we do,"[52] emphasizing that an unmarried childless woman with cat companions engaged in an illegitimate and all-consuming occupation. Some commentators begged the public to pity their loneliness, citing unmarried women's attentions towards cats

47 Marsh: Children and Animals, p. 83.

48 Monica Flegel: *Pets and Domesticity in Victorian Literature and Culture. Animality, Queer Relations, and the Victorian Family*. New York: Routledge 2015, p. 4.

49 Yi-Fu Tuan: *Dominance and Affection. The Making of Pets*. New Haven: Yale UP 1984.

50 Pets and What They Cost, p. 410.

51 Stories About Cats. In: *Humane Advocate* 3,3 (1908), pp. 202–203, here p. 202.

52 Poor Old Maids. In: *The United States Songster*. Cincinnati: James 1836, pp. 174–175, here p. 174.

as proof of their affectionate natures,[53] while others spurned spinsters for wasting affection "which might be much better bestowed on their fellow-creatures."[54]

Yet cats were more than a signal that their keepers were somehow deficient: while canine companionship was empowering, intimacy with cats was believed to be detrimental to moral, emotional, and spiritual character. In other words, cats *produced* old maids through their power to attract the excessive devotion of women. A short scene in a children's book illustrates the detrimental dynamic imagined between a human and her feline disabler. "[S]he cares no more about what's happening in the house than the stuffed squirrel does," a boy tells his sister: "I believe if you were to break your leg to-morrow, that thing wouldn't stop purring for half a minute, nor so much as get up off the hearth-rug to see what was the matter."[55] In this children's book, a boy confounds his sister's feelings for her cat by trying to point out the irrationality of her feelings: she cares for some "thing" that does not reciprocate, which is foolish if not dangerous. And shortly we see why. The girl finds herself silently agreeing with her brother, but continues to caress the unresponsive cat: "as she felt it was all too true, she could only gently rub up the fur about Tabby's ears."[56] *Because* she agrees that the cat does not reciprocate her affections, she feels compelled to continue to render rubs. Reduced to an object, the cat is likened to something like a vacuum or a black hole absorbing precious and finite human affection. As per a contemporary, "[t]o fall beneath the fascination of a cat [...] is to be under a spell," a relation distinct from the fortifying "[f]riendship" of a dog.[57] Alluding to the cat's seductive powers and supernatural associations, this author suggests that nothing sincere exists in a human-cat relationship. Even those who acceded to the cat's ability to sincerely care for a human would add that it required a degrading degree of investment on the human's part: "abject slavery to a cat's every whim sometimes seems to win its real regard and affection, or at least its appreciation[,]"

53 Flegel: *Pets and Domesticity*, p. 64.

54 Defence of Old Maids. In *Hogg's Weekly Instructor* 88 (1846), p. 159.

55 Clemens: *Getting and Giving*, p. 11.

56 Ibid., p. 12.

57 Ella Fuller Maitland / Frederick Pollock: The Etchingham Letters. In: *Saturday Review of Politics, Literature, Science, and Art* 97,2533 (1904), pp. 496–497, here p. 497.

and "[r]arely is such service offered except by women[,]" who seem to invest even more "when the object of their attentions manifests only indifference."[58]

Lacking, one supposes, the wisdom, restraint, or self-respect of her brother, the girl seemingly cannot stop herself from rubbing the cat's ears: as expressed by *Godey's*, quoted above, she "must have something to love,"[59] and if that be cats, then she is in danger of pouring out all her love onto an animal that will give nothing in return. Without outside intervention, nursing cats will become all that she will do. To add insult to injury, the cat merely "pur[rs] with a deeper satisfaction than ever, utterly undisturbed by the brother's reproaches."[60] The cat is certainly neither 'sister' nor 'friend': instead, the girl becomes the cat's servant or slave.

Even less generous detractors accused both mistress and cat of gross solipsism, describing the human's engagement as onanistic.[61] Any appearance of intercorporeality was considered masturbatory, as a cat's "caressing ways bear reference simply to themselves."[62] Thus detractors conjectured that perhaps the real motivation for this female impulse to love where no love was to be had was that women used cats for self-pleasure. For example, one writer opined that gazing at a contented cat would "pu[t] a feeling of rest and contentment into the mind of the person who looks at it"[63] and in that sense – in that passive, non-interactive, unengaged sense – a cat provided some small benefit. Another said that the presence of a cat would allow someone to not feel "absolutely alone"; so, he asked rhetorically, "why inquire too closely into the sincerity of her gratitude?"[64] With this question, he suggested that women chose to be fooled into believing that cats reciprocated their affections, drawing pathetic comfort from willful self-delusion. Both cat and mistress were thus depicted as two solipsistic beings, each using the other yet unattached. While reciprocity likely existed in fact, each party in the relation was paradoxically presumed to be wholly disinterested in

58 Forbush: *The Domestic Cat*, p. 17.

59 Children's Pets. In: *Godey's Lady's Book and Magazine* 62 (1861), p. 94.

60 Clemens: *Getting and Giving*, p. 12.

61 Flegel: *Pets and Domesticity*, p. 21.

62 Philip Gilbert Hamerton: *Chapters on Animals*. Boston: Roberts Brothers 1893, p. 48.

63 Miller: *Stories of the Dog*, p. 31.

64 Hamerton: *Chapters on Animals*, p. 48.

reciprocating. Thus, these representations denied the possibility of sincere or mutually beneficial interspecies love stories between cats and their mistresses. Instead, the interspecies pair formed an unhealthy affective economy that drained human participants of positive affect.

The cat's reputation for being 'less affectionate' did not fully account for the vehemence the cat faced, however: there was also a sense of affront borne out of a human sense of entitlement to be loved, an entitlement so taken for granted that it was not articulated except in the form of anger when such entitlement was denied. Humans fancied that they owned dogs both in mind and body, as proven by dogs' willingness to follow human commands (sit, heel, stay, love) and abdicate bodily autonomy. According to Tuan, a good pet was defined by its submission to affectionate caresses.[65] The cat, however, defied both: not only did she refuse human demands, she also rebuffed human attempts at limiting her corporeal agency by denying them unrestricted access to her body. If the measure of an animal's amiability was the extent to which one could access its body at any time and without restrictions, then the cat was repulsive for rejecting human caresses.

The reiterated focus on the cat's tendency to scratch without warning evidences the human presumption of a license to touch and handle the nonhuman. In a 1918 children's poem entitled *O My! She Scratches Me*, the narrating little girl says: "O see this darling little cat, / She's nice as she can be; / She is the dearest little cat, / And yet she scratches me."[66] At her nicest and "dearest," the cat remains an unpredictable love-object, returning caresses with violence in the short space of an "[a]nd yet."[67] When a misreading of or disregard for nonhuman cues elicits the outstretched claws, one ought to perhaps accept the sharper communiqué without rancor. But the way these interactions were read was in the tone of a tragedy: the reiterated drama of the spurned human lover. In return for what a human blithely offered as a loving caress, the cat might duck, refuse to purr, or scratch – the human's loving overture was thus cruelly rejected. The sense of tragedy was amplified by the emphasis on the apparent unpredictability of such scratches, harkening back to Buffon's admonitions that the cat was not as she appeared. "Who would have guessed such dreadful claws / Were hid beneath those velvet paws, / To

65 Tuan: *Dominance and Affection*, p. 171.

66 Carrie Jacobs-Bond: *Tales of Little Cats*. New York: Volland 1918, n. p.

67 Ibid.

scratch us if she chose?"[68], pondered another poet, positing the cat as a tease: surely something covered in velvet exists to be touched. Resentful anger was precisely the response that could be expected from a human who presumed himself to be entitled, by virtue of being human, to bestow caresses upon an animal that would not be allowed to say 'no' or even 'not now.'[69]

Appropriating Independence

In the course of the century the dog generally profited from his elevation into petdom, a rise propelled by the narrative of canine fidelity. While many forms of cruelty persisted, and arguably new cruelties arose alongside intensified breeding and dog shows,[70] the use of dogs as motive power was by and large phased out and the idea of animal abuse was, at least publicly, no longer socially sanctioned. The cat, on the other hand, remained the subject of intense contest, its capacity for fidelity a question of greater import than ever.

These negative associations of the cat persisted in spite of the humane movement that was so successful in refashioning the dog from beast of burden to pet. Perhaps in response, authors of fiction produced revisionist representations of feline character to contest this continuing anti-cat prejudice. These new fictional cats were not dogs in cat suits, but they did perform certain traits hitherto ascribed to dogs and denied of cats – namely, the capacity to sincerely love and show affection to humankind. S. Louise Patteson's *Pussy Meow: The Autobiography of a Cat* (1901), was explicitly written as the 'cat version' of Saunders' *Beautiful Joe* (which in turn was marketed as the 'dog version' of the English bestselling equine autobiography, Anne Sewell's *Black Beauty*, 1877). Meow, for example, claims that reading *Beautiful Joe* had "filled [her] with a desire to be as good and useful a cat as Joe was a dog."[71] She performs displays of recognition, attachment, and affection for her mistresses, including a reunion scene in which she "climbed up to her [mistress'] face and

68 Tommy's Clever Trick. In: *Frank Leslie's Popular Monthly* 3,1 (1877), p. 447.

69 Rogers has noted that cat-bashing was also a way "to censure women who seduce [men] but do not requite their love"; these aspersions also betray the logic that to this day is invoked to justify sexual assault ('she asked for it'). Rogers: *Cat*, p. 127.

70 Harriet Ritvo: *The Animal Estate. The English and Other Creatures in the Victorian Age*. Cambridge: Harvard UP 1987, pp. 82–121; Tuan: *Dominance and Affection*.

71 S. Louise Patteson: *Pussy Meow. The Autobiography of a Cat*. Philadelphia: Jacobs 1901, p. 28.

covered her cheeks with kisses."[72] She even becomes "best of friends" with a dog.[73] Although she is the subject of some abuse at the hands of cruel boys, she defies anti-cat stereotypes by never scratching the hands that feed her.

Miranda Eliot Swan's *Daisy: The Autobiography of a Cat* (1900) chronicles the life of an affectionate, introspective cat, very devoted to his mistress. In this case, humaneness is taught through a series of cautionary tales where horrible abusers meet their just desserts. All the worst offenders are boys and men.[74] "If we are cruel," Daisy says, "we learn it of human beings."[75] Repeatedly the novel argues that the infamously negative traits of cats were the product of nurture, not nature: "[I]f they defend themselves, refusing to have their eyes poked out with sticks, tin pails tied to their tails, and lighted matches held to their noses, and bite or scratch, then they are denounced as vile, and are given bad characters that will follow them through life."[76] Daisy thus identifies the vicious logic of cat abuse: these defensive responses became rationales for their abusers' actions. At the same time, Daisy also considers the problem from the anthropocentric perspective. Identifying herself as a Christian cat, Daisy worries herself "sick, trying to solve the problem, [of] how I could reform my race" so that they could be better treated by humans.[77] In attempting to elevate the cat's position in human society, Swan's *Daisy* claimed that "when Adam and Eve left the garden, a dog walked by his master's side, and a cat by the side of the mistress"[78] – presenting both as equally faithful animals for each respective gender.

Saunders followed in 1913 with *Pussy Black-Face; or, The Story of a Kitten and Her Friends*, about a self-described "naughty young kitten."[79]

72 Ibid., p. 38.

73 Ibid., p. 25.

74 At one point, Swan suggests that the cat is no worse than, or perhaps even superior to, non-white humans. "Think of the heathen cannibals, eating human flesh. To them the fat little baby is just like a chicken. Then the Indians—did a cat ever worry a rat worse than they tortured the white men? When you think of this, can you conscientiously say we are worse, or even as bad as human beings?" (Miranda Eliot Swan: *Daisy. The Autobiography of a Cat*. Boston: Noves Brothers 1900, p. 164.)

75 Ibid., p. 15.

76 Ibid., p. 48.

77 Ibid., p. 34–35.

78 Ibid., p. 131.

79 Margaret Marshall Saunders: *Pussy Black-Face; or, The Story of a Kitten and Her Friends*. Boston: Page 1913, p. 1.

As with Patteson's Meow, when she wanders off she falls victim to the cruelty of boys. Contesting the belief that cats did not attach to humans, Black-Face is loyal to her family, generally kind, and unusually civic-minded. While Saunders' first autobiographical animal, Beautiful Joe, would simply relate his philanthropist mistress' words, Black-Face has her own independent impulse towards charity and kindness. Comparing her situation to that of a homeless cat's, she asks, "Why am I wrapped in a fur cloak, and why is she out in the cold? Am I a better cat than she is? Probably not."[80] She then seeks out this homeless cat and convinces her to follow her home, where she would be well taken care of. Rather than simply reward this do-goodery, the novel surprises: the homeless cat is not very nice after all. Slyboots – a name that denotes her crooked nature – does not simply serve as a pitiful object of rescue. Much to Black-Face's consternation, Slyboots takes advantage of her good-will, taking over her bed and monopolizing their mistress's attention.

Rather than whitewashing cats into 'good' characters to curry human favor, the story includes and normalizes a range of feline behavior. Slyboots, the homeless cat who turns out to be cunning and selfish, is no less beloved by her mistress; she is not cast out for being a 'bad' cat, nor is she left home alone when the family travels to the country for diversion. In spite of her solitary inclinations, she learns to belong, and given the choice to remain in the country she firmly refuses: "I'm the Denvilles' cat and I've got to stick it out with them."[81] Another cat named Blizzard proves a scheming, ill-minded strategist, but is never simply dismissed as a hopeless case. These 'bad' cats are fully accepted in their respective human families. In contrast, many dog stories seem to negate the possibility of a 'bad' dog, and at best include one or two undesirable animal characters only to serve as the narrator's Other. In Saunders' *Beautiful Joe*, the "snapping and snarling and biting" Bruno is preemptively shot in the head and the vagabond dog who rejects human mastery, Dandy, dies a mangy death.[82] In Saunders' *"Boy"*, this role is fulfilled by the Boston Terrier, an inactive lapdog that lacks self-respect.[83]

80 Marshall Saunders: *Pussy Black-Face*, pp. 34–35.

81 Ibid., p. 302.

82 Saunders: *Beautiful Joe*, p. 149.

83 The dog that was man's best friend had to be masculinized; thus, feminized dogs like toy breeds or lapdogs were explicitly excluded from general discussions of dogs. On the representation of lapdogs and women, see Jody L. Wyett: The Lap of Luxury.

To some extent, these cat stories successfully countered the continuing discrimination against cats, offering plausible alternative interpretations of observable cat behavior and endowing feline character with dimensionality. The cat's widely-acknowledged tendencies towards unsavory behavior liberated cat characters from the simple dichotomy of good vs. evil. In turn, to the extent that cats were thought as reflections of women, perhaps these female authors also expanded their own representational opportunities.

Kete has argued that in France, at the *fin de siècle*, the cat's thorough "rehabilitat[ion]" marked the end of the use of organic nature to represent "the past" as distinct from "modernity."[84] But in the U.S., these markers were contested throughout the century and especially during the Progressive Era, when hegemonic gender relations were threatened by phenomena such as the rise of the New Woman and the women's suffrage movement.[85] A piece from 1899 suggests that the cat persisted as a metaphor for modernity's problematic disruption of the traditional social order: as "the embodiment of the modern ideals of self-advancement—of egoism, in a word[,] [...] the cat has become the accepted ideal of our *fin-de-siècle* standards," while the dog stood for "the things that have gone out."[86] And yet, in the first two decades of the twentieth century, the cat's independence – hitherto, the cat's fundamental flaw – became a powerful metaphor for a more vigorous and undomesticated masculinity that was able to resist and negate the degenerative effects of civilization.

The historian Gail Bederman has argued that at this time the Victorian virtue of 'manliness,' characterized by restraint and civility, was supplanted by a 'masculinity' that borrowed heavily from race- and class-based ideas and anxieties regarding the superiority of white civilization.

Lapdogs, Literature, and Social Meaning in the "Long" Eighteenth Century. In: *Literature Interpretation Theory* 10,4 (2000), pp. 275–301.

84 Kete: *Beast in the Boudoir*, p. 117.

85 For the New Woman in the American context, see, for example, Carroll Smith-Rosenberg: *Disorderly Conduct. Visions of Gender in Victorian America*. New York: Oxford UP 1986, pp. 245–296; Jean V. Matthews: *The Rise of the New Woman. The Women's Movement in America, 1875–1930*. Chicago: Dee 2003; Charlotte J. Rich: *Transcending the New Woman. Multiethnic Narratives in the Progressive Era*. Columbia: University of Missouri Press 2009.

86 Anna Bowman Dodd: Dog Love and Cat Worship. In: *Souvenir Book of the Women's Auxiliary to the Building Committee of the Medical Society of the County of Kings*. New York: Eagle 1899, p. 136.

In spite of its vaunted achievements, throughout the second half of the century, the white man's civilization was increasingly held responsible for widespread emasculation. Too much brainwork led to weak bodies and neurasthenia, a popular diagnosis for white middle-class men supposedly always on the brink of 'overcivilization.' To reenervate the race, the bourgeoisie turned to dark-skinned and/or working-class men, groups that were regarded as less civilized, more primitive. Not only were they thought of as repositories of a savagery now highly coveted, but they were – under evolutionist ideas – thought closer to animality.[87] Though Bederman limits her discussion to human players, this contest for a more animal masculinity logically spilled over onto other species that had long been co-producing gender discourses.

Scholars have discussed the ways in which the idea of wildness became a key resource for the forging of a 'new' masculinity by a (re)turn to the more primordial/animal qualities of the human.[88] Some, most prominently Theodore Roosevelt, willingly immersed themselves into the 'savage' spaces of the now vanishing Western frontier or hunted dangerous beasts in the African jungle.[89] Much closer to home, however, man's best and worst friends were also entangled in these changing gender discourses. As the cat's 'wildness' became appropriated for masculinity, the dog's faithfulness increasingly signaled emasculation. Suddenly, writers complained that "in general the dog is overestimated and the cat underestimated."[90] Suddenly, dogs possessed "a sycophantic and transparent nature, fawning for notice, and abject under whipping."[91] Suddenly, the fact that the cat "uses us" as if "we exist for his delectation," like "a hearth rug to be jumped on and sat on, a curry comb to titillate him," was proof that "the cat is vastly superior to the dog, which is

87 Gail Bederman: *Manliness and Civilization. A Cultural History of Gender and Race in the United States, 1880–1917.* Chicago: University of Chicago Press 1995; John Pettegrew: *Brutes in Suits. Male Sensibility in America, 1890–1920*. Baltimore: Johns Hopkins UP 2007.

88 E. Anthony Rotundo: *American Manhood. Transformations in Masculinity from the Revolution to the Modern Era*. New York: Basic 1993, pp 227–232; Kelly Enright: *Maximum Wilderness. The Jungle in the American Imagination*. Charlottesville: University of Virginia Press 2012; Michael Lundblad: *The Birth of a Jungle. Animality in Progressive-Era U. S. Literature and Culture*. New York: Oxford UP 2013.

89 For a contemporary account, see Axel Lundeberg / Frederick Seymour: *The Great Roosevelt African Hunt and the Wild Animals of Africa*. New York: McCurdy 1910.

90 Psychic Development of Cats and Dogs. In: *Appleton's Popular Science Monthly* 52 (January 1898), p. 427.

91 Reed: *Offthoughts*, p. 46.

faithful to those who maltreat him."[92] The cat was now praised for not "giv[ing] up her wild ways as completely as the dog."[93] And so the cat was repositioned as a new symbol of the past – not of the chivalry or "[t]he graces developed by servitude; the discipline of one's lower nature"[94] attributed to the dog, but rather of a revisionary past that posited the existence and recuperability of an ancestral man more vigorous and primitive, as yet untamed by civilization. "How wonderful it is," said Charles Livingston Bull, well-known wildlife illustrator, "that down through the uncountable ages the cat, of all domestic animals, has been changed so little by its environments."[95] Recast as a living fossil, the cat went from being reprehensibly cruel (and feminine) to an embodiment of a new masculinity defined by its physicality and its readiness to resort to violence as an expression of power. The cat's supposed ontological liminality between primordial wildness and civilized domestication was now reinterpreted in more positive terms as a remarkable tenacity to retain an original, more ferocious nature evocative of the species' evolutionary past. In this light, the cat not only commanded human respect but could even serve as a corrective model for those about to lose their way in the debilitating complexities of modernity.

Authors belabored to reframe the "sycophantic" and "abject" dog to resemble the cat who would not so easily give up her "wild ways." As Jennifer Mason notes, turn-of-the-century conceptions of companion animals became even more muddled as the dog was rewritten with the cat's trademark independence.[96] Representations of man-dog relationships were reframed to insert increasing measures of apparent canine agency, performances of dogs making independent, self-interested choices and being surprisingly discriminate about intimate attachments with humans. That dog that, as per most representations hitherto, would have unconditionally loved a human simply for being human, became an animal capable of rejecting human companionship. Jack London's two dog novels, *The Call of the Wild* (1903) and *White Fang* (1906), feature dogs crossed with wolves for remasculinization. They distance

92 Here and There. In: *Fur Trade Review* (1904), p. 520.

93 Kent: *Puppy Dogs' Tales*, p. 125.

94 Dodd: Dog Love, p. 136.

95 Charles Livingston Bull: What Do You Know About Cats? In: *Boy's Life Magazine* 2,11 (January 1913), p. 14.

96 Jennifer Mason: *Civilized Creatures. Urban Animals, Sentimental Culture, and American Literature, 1850–1900*. Baltimore: Johns Hopkins UP 2005, p. 161.

themselves from mankind; they kill with abandon. Even stories that did not resort to 'wolfing' the dog found ways to reinvent it. For example, the protagonist of Saunders' *"Boy"* is a revamped version of her first dog novel's vagabond character, Dandy, and in this second iteration the masterless dog becomes an admirable figure. While in *Beautiful Joe*, the dog that refuses to be mastered meets with a lonely death, by 1916 the vagabond dog breezily declares, "I had had many homes, many masters and mistresses."[97] He is not "a perfect dog"; he humbly presents himself as "just a good plain, American every-day sort of dog,"[98] empowered to be discriminate about who he serves – an assertion of animal/canine agency within an overarching framework of human dominion and animal servitude. "I can't love persons unless I respect them," he asserts, limiting his performance of canine fidelity towards the one master he has elected to love: "He just suited me [...]. I felt that I could die for him."[99] What would have been considered any human master's due, a dog rushing headlong into the arms of death for the sake of his master, had become merely hypothetical. Here, a dog named "Boy," elevated to humanness, "could" die for his master, but could also choose not to do so; his unconditional devotion was now conditional. This new latitude for agency and disobedience did not unmake the dog, but rather raised him in man's esteem.

If the cat's independence was now an attractive trait, did the cat's reputation (and treatment) improve? As the earlier discussion of unpredictable claws suggests, cats remained for the most part suspicious even as some authors endeavored to portray them as affectionate creatures. Rudyard Kipling's *The Cat That Walked By Himself*, a popular read in the U.S. as part of his 1902 *Just So Stories*, exemplifies the paradoxical relationship between man and cat at this point. From the outset, the Wild Cat (pointedly male) and Wild Man are linked by their shared resistance to domestication and domesticity. "[T]he wildest of all the wild animals was the Cat," but "[o]f course the Man was wild too. He was dreadfully wild."[100] The Wild Man's wildness is at risk from the moment that

97 Saunders: *"Boy"*, p. 63.

98 Ibid., p. 192.

99 Ibid., p. 63.

100 Rudyard Kipling: The Cat That Walked By Himself. In: Id.: *Just So Stories for Little Children*. New York: Doubleday, Page 1902, pp. 197–223, here pp. 197–198.

Woman chooses a "nice dry Cave" in which to "keep house."[101] "Wipe your feet, dear," she says, marking Wild Man's unwilding.[102] Rosalind Meyer's early reading seems to hold true, at least for the story's opening: the Cat seems to represent the undomesticated part of Man. Wild Dog, Wild Horse, and Wild Cow readily make their contracts with Woman in the face of her domestic temptations: the Wild Dog provides hunting and guarding services for roast bones, the Wild Horse provides transportation for sweet grass, and the Wild Cow becomes the "Giver of Good Food" for grass.[103] In contrast, the Wild Cat seeks to trade as a peer, to exchange goods and services without friendship or servitude. He is at first rejected, but then brokers a deal: if he secures three words of praise from her, he will earn entry, then proximity to the hearth, and finally milk. In spite of herself, Woman finds herself praising the cat when it thrice proves useful. Victoriously nestling by the fire, the cat chants his trademark refrain: "[I]t is I [...]. But *still* I am the Cat who walks by himself, and all places are alike to me."[104] He insists that Woman remains his "Enemy" (as well as the "Wife of my Enemy and Mother of my Enemy"), refusing to acknowledge friendship or a fixed role in the domestic circle.[105] For the Cat, everything is transactional: no emotional services will be rendered. So far, the Cat is the *fin-de-siècle* man's new hero – fiercely independent even as he appears to have acquiesced to the comforts of domesticity.

Yet Kipling's Man eventually breaks with the Cat, still aligning himself exclusively with the valuable, enabling companionship of his "First Friend," the dog.[106] While Woman's commitments to the Dog, Horse, and Cow sufficed to forge family-wide deals, Man and Dog excuse themselves from her deal with the Cat, insisting instead on structurally different contracts that unilaterally exact services on the pain of punishment: the Cat must catch mice or get five things thrown at him (boots, a stone axe, a piece of wood, and a hatchet). The Cat promises to catch mice as

101 Ibid., p. 198.

102 Ibid.

103 Wild Cow is the only animal that does not talk, signaling the edibility of her body and its products. Note that the cat's milk, and perhaps also the dog's roast bones, likely come from cow. Ibid., p. 210.

104 Ibid., p. 218, original emphasis.

105 Ibid.

106 Ibid., p. 210.

demanded, but then adds his refrain, "*still* I am the Cat who walks by himself, and all places are alike to me."[107] Disingenuously, Man says that had the Cat not said that last part, he "would have put all these things away for always and always and always," but given the Cat's declaration of independence, "now I am going to throw my two boots and my little stone axe (that makes three) at you whenever I meet you. And so shall all proper Men do after me!"[108] The Dog then demands his own separate, punitive terms (that Cat must amuse the Baby or be chased by the Dog), and reacts poorly when the Cat agrees but insists that he remains "the Cat that walks by himself."[109] And so, because the Cat refuses to submit to these self-serving contracts, he earns abuse by man and dog for all perpetuity, suggesting that the only nonhuman animals that could and should enter into intercorporeal intimacy with humans would be those animals who accede to the self-erasure of unconditional love.

If the Cat is a cat, then the reneged contracts and arbitrary violence suggest that the great hatred against felines by both men (and the dogs they have claimed as their own) is somehow a fair and reasonable consequence of the cat's perverse insistence on remaining independent. The predominant narrative was still preserved: the Cat's insistence on transacting with them *without affective ties* remains a deeply wounding offense. Though Man and Dog behave inconsistently, irrationally, and unfairly, each is justified by their sense of affront – that Cat will not give something for nothing, will not be their friend or servant, will not relinquish its identity and agency.

If Cat represents modern man's precious wildness, then this ending also suggests Man's internal struggle: he hates his own wildness and punishes it for asserting itself – or Man is jealous of the Cat's stubborn retention of a wildness he must renounce. Even if Man initially aligns himself with the Cat's wildness, he orchestrates a dramatic break, which is as much his choice as it is an emotional overreaction. At the *fin de siècle*, feline corporeal agency was redeemed, but strictly as a symbol for men to emulate; the actual animals themselves remained beyond the limits of man's intimacy. Men were now encouraged to be like cats and yet dislike cats – to the point of violence – creating a paradoxical dynamic of self-loathing.

107 Kipling: The Cat That Walked By Himself, p. 219.

108 Ibid.

109 Ibid., p. 220.

Conclusion

In his famous illustration of animal alterity, Jacques Derrida describes an encounter that takes place in his bathroom as he stands "*frontally* naked" before the unflinching gaze of his truly little cat.[110] With her eerie, almost supernatural inaccessibility, the cat's gaze deranges a naked Derrida who describes himself as vulnerable to the castrating bite that threatens but never comes – and from this uncanny encounter, Derrida develops a valuable critique of anthropocentrism. Donna Haraway has argued that Derrida went "right to the edge" of actually engaging with his actual cat before being "sidetracked by his textual canon of Western philosophy and the literature and by his own linked worries about being naked in front of his cat."[111] Derrida's abortive encounter insists that his cat does not serve "as an allegory for all the cats on the earth, the felines that traverse myths and religions, literature and fables," engaging in a wishful theatrics of nudity wherein the philosopher attempts to consider a being or thing as outside of culture and discourse.[112] In effect, the nudity that he embraces (for he also emphasizes his nakedness) is analogous to the imagined nudity of his cat. The feline gaze that has launched a thousand philosophers' metaphysical ships hinges on the discourses that have represented the female cat as a detached being that observes humanity from the vantage point of a peer or a superior rather than a submissive dependent. Indeed, as Alyce Miller and Erica Fudge have noted, the point would not have been made if the cat had been a dog.[113]

To look at the companion animal with an emphasis on the discourses shaping the companionship is to focus on the purposes of human-animal intimacy and its alleged effects on those involved. More than

110 Jacques Derrida: *The Animal That Therefore I Am*, trans. from the French by David Wills. New York: Fordham UP 2008, p. 4, original emphasis.

111 Donna Haraway: *When Species Meet*. Minneapolis: University of Minnesota Press 2008, p. 20.

112 Derrida: *The Animal That Therefore I Am*, p. 6.

113 Alyce Miller: What if Derrida's Cat Had Been a Dog? http://www.alycemiller.com/2011/01/what-if-derridas-cat-had-been-dog.html (accessed December 6, 2015); Erica Fudge: The Dog, the Home and the Human, and the Ancestry of Derrida's Cat. In: *Oxford Literary Review* 29 (2007), pp. 37–54. In a timely intervention, Susan Fraiman questions the way Derrida has been enshrined as the patriarch of the field of animal studies. Dubbing this vein of scholarship "pussy panic," she critiques its failure to credit groundbreaking feminist scholarship as well as its renunciation of ties to cultural studies. Susan Fraiman: Pussy Panic versus Liking Animals. Tracking Gender in Animal Studies. In: *Critical Inquiry* 39 (2012), pp. 89–115, here pp. 92–93, 100.

allegorical stand-ins for humans, cats and dogs were bodies employed as repositories for human constructs of gender. For most of their cultural history, dogs were masculinized and represented as unconditionally faithful while cats were feminized and represented as incapable of love, even as they were linked to the femininity that historically has been linked with excess feeling. Experienced by humans as a mortal affront, an insult to the human species, the cat's independence became the seed for all the other charges levied against its species. At the same time as dogs and cats were gendered according to the predominant binary, however, the propagation of a rivalry between dogs and cats contradicted the supposed complementarity of masculinity and femininity. Interspecies homosocial couplings operated with the premise that men would be improved through their intimacy with dogs and that women, in spite of any efforts to dissuade them, would find themselves unduly attracted to the feline companions that would contribute to their emotional and moral impairment. This persisted even as representations of cats reached for canine fidelity and representations of dogs appropriated and incorporated notions of feline independence.

The entangled evolution of these discourses evidences the extent to which they were produced through the gendering of the nonhuman, where other species did not merely reflect but also, by their own agency, influenced human constructions of other animals, displacing narratives inscribed unto them back on human bodies. This account also highlights how gender discourses affected interspecies practices of intimacy and vice versa, as well as how moves that seem to elevate any particular animal's position might remain double-edged. The illustrator Charles Livingston Bull might have held up the cat's apparent preservation of complete agency as a model for boys, but in the same breath he noted the exception that existed in Boy Scout Law that allows for the killing of cats "known to be wild."[114] Even as the cat's 'primitive,' 'wild' independence became the subject of appropriation for *fin-de-siècle* masculinities, the very same ascription still justified its marginalization and destruction.

114 Bull: What Do You Know, p. 14.

"Sheep is Life"

The Navajo, Cultural Genocide, and the Animal as Cultural Property and Historical Witness

Aimee Swenson

> No important step has taken place [in building the United States] without a contribution from the flock, its fleece, or its master. Few indeed were the military expeditions leading to the settlement of this continent that did not have their quota of sheep with advance party or train. The distribution of flocks over the country rarely failed to be identified with the great moves that brought civilization to the wilderness. Sheep accompanied Conquistador and Puritan, miner and soldier, merchant and farmer, into each new region, and provided the raw materials that attracted trails, markets, woolen mills, packing houses, and finally highways and trucks [...] Flockmaster and flocks alike have participated in, or created, the long series of situations that have wielded us into the nation of today.[1]

Part One: Domesticated Livestock and Geographic Ontologies

As human cultures develop, so too does their relationship with the animal environment in which they reside and of which they are a part. Coevolution of species (human and animal) is actual and necessary, particularly in the realm of human interactions with domesticated

1 Edward N. Wentworth: *America's Sheep Trails. Histories and Personalities.* Ames: Iowa State College Press 1948, p. vii–viii.

livestock animals.[2] Humans could not have developed without the inclusion of animals into their emerging or developing societies; animals exemplify representations of many things, including human social and cultural development. Livestock predates countless other animal species as symbols in human cultures, primarily because the keeping of livestock and the forms of human-animal interaction it brought about precede human relations with the species of companion animals we are familiar with today, such as dogs and cats and birds. Livestock species have been fundamental to human existence for over 15,000 years and were thus essentially the forebears of companion animals.[3] Livestock accompanied humans through diverse landscapes, over long periods of isolation, and through various environmental tribulations. Livestock were integral to the settlement of people in various regions, over extensive spans of time.[4] Not only did they give their flesh as a primary food source to ensure human survival, they were also an important part of humans' *social* and *affective* environments. Livestock must be cared for through grooming, training, birthing, milking, shearing. This physical interaction with livestock animals developed into a human care ethic, and while the status of animals within this ethical system could vary widely and individually, the very act of caring for the animal in a physical sense arguably ensured a consideration of livestock as a form of companion animal. As human history advanced, the development and integration of successful livestock breeds continued, and the first of these successes were sheep.[5] Essentially, these relationships and

2 Stephen Budiansky: *The Covenant of the Wild. Why Animals Chose Domestication.* New Haven: Yale UP 1992, p. xi.

3 I specifically refer to the process of livestock domestication. Dogs predate all other animals as companion species, and this is evidenced by the existence of companion dogs in the archeological record dating back 30,000 years. See Mietje Germonpré / Martina Lázničková-Galetová / Mikhail V. Sablin: Palaeolithic Dog Skulls at the Gravettian Předmostí Site, the Czech Republic. In: *Journal of Archaeological Science* 39,1 (2012), pp. 184–202.

4 Richard Yarwood / Nick Evans: Taking Stock of Farm Animals and Rurality. In: Chris Philo / Chris Wilbert (eds): *Animal Spaces, Beastly Places. New Geographies of Human-Animal Relations.* London: Routledge 2000, pp. 99–115, here p. 100.

5 Roger A. Caras: *A Perfect Harmony. The Intertwining Lives of Humans and Animals Throughout History.* New York: Simon & Schuster 1996, p. 15. While this text provides an overview, many other historical sources support this statement. Some sources claim that the goat was the first domesticated animal, but neither animal has unanimous support. The bone structures studied as evidence have been viewed as potentially belonging to either species. There exists more evidence that sheep were first, as wool fibers were quickly employed for functional use after domestication, and

developments are the fundamentals of both cultural and animal geographies. Considerations of animals are increasingly finding resonance within the discipline of geography in ways that ensure a deeper understanding of humans and animal worlds as multi-spatial, multi-temporal, and by no means mutually exclusive.[6]

Resulting from these historical relationships, which are at once cultural, sentimental, and geographic, human and ovine lives blended together into a complex emotional geography. Beyond care ethics, consumption, and companionship, an ingrained sense of the animal's presence – both spiritually and physically – was able to manifest. As is the case with other species, sheep often evoke an affectionate human reaction, which is reflected by the wealth of historical accounts of sheep as models of purity and innocence, symbols of youth and abundance, and archetypes of longevity. They have been sacrificed and blessed by an equal plethora of spiritual entities, and there is little doubt as to why. They are the beautiful, serene, quixotic animal who has given exorbitantly to human existence.

As previously noted, sheep emerged at the forefront of livestock domestication.[7] They were a species successful in quickly adapting to human needs, and their relationship with humans was established early on. Indeed, much of 'human' history finds its expression in small woolen beasts weaving through the terrain. The act of shepherding is performed from a physical position behind the animal, in response to which the animal moves forward. Shepherding is characterized by co-performance and reciprocal movement: the human is driving the animal forward, but in turn the animal is driving the *human* through the landscape. Sheep do not willingly follow anything but other sheep, and therefore sheep do not follow humans, they *accompany* them. Sheep have molded the ways in which humans traversed the globe, into new spaces and beyond boundaries, guiding human civilizations for almost 15,000 years.[8] Humans have chosen these trajectories over earth based

some archeological findings support that spun wool was found prior to the evidence of domesticated goats.

6 Henry Buller: Animal Geographies I. In: *Progress in Human Geography* 38,2 (2014), pp. 308–318, here pp. 309, 310, 312.

7 Juliet Clutton-Brock: *Animals as Domesticates. A World View through History*. East Lansing: Michigan State UP 2012, p. 41.

8 Wentworth: *America's Sheep Trails*. See the entirety of chapter 1 for a comprehensive yet simplified introduction to the trajectory of sheep domestication.

upon the routes most fitting for the sheep; humans dare not go where their sheep may not lead, and sheep may not go beyond the periphery of the watchful gaze of their shepherd. This early development is one of interwoven human-ovine existence, of mutual development, and we might wonder whether (sheep) domestication is characterized by human agency or animal agency or both – a question Henry David Thoreau effectively recapitulates as "I am wont to think that men are not so much the keepers of herds as herds are the keepers of men, the former are so much the freer."[9]

The melodic, rhythmic cadence of grazing and scratching, shuffling quietly about, with a soft clink of bells that emerges from a flock can evoke even in the least sentimental a feeling of spirituality. Occasionally a bleat will erupt in an effort to commune with offspring or flock members, resulting in a new direction of movement from the latter, or a semi-graceful spring to action in an oft all-too-eager response of unfounded fear. Surveying the movement of a flock can be mesmerizing in any landscape. Relaxing the eyes, rhythms of white undulate in calming and harmonizing patterns, weaving and roaming through the terrain. It can be easy to understand why sheep are so entrenched in the divine beliefs of many a culture. And it can be difficult to imagine these peaceful and mesmerizing beasts to be among the principal historic tools of colonizing peoples, the motivation of bloody wars, and even the unwitting architects of indigenous genocides the world over.

Animals, regardless of (the limits of) their own agency, have disproportionately served the human, and therefore we must respond to, and acknowledge, their influence as cultural arbitrators. Further, because animals have both accompanied and been shaped by human historical development, it should be expected that they embody those histories in their respective genetic and anatomical compositions, which are in turn charged with human cultural value.[10] This essay seeks to expand on the idea that animals act as historical witnesses and cultural property by

9 Henry David Thoreau: *Walden*, ed. by J. Lyndon Shanley. Princeton: Princeton UP 1989, p. 56.

10 Carmine Di Martino: Husserl and the Question of Animality. In: *Research in Phenomenology* 44,1 (2014), pp. 50–75, here pp. 51, 58–59. A phenomenological analysis of animal experiences should always (attempt to) go beyond considering these experiences as valuable only in relation to human experience. Di Martino, in her discussion of Husserl, addresses human history and culture as something that cannot be wholly experienced by, and applied to, animals. Nevertheless, the historical ontology of animals can be derived to some extent from human perception and documentation.

examining a specific historical scenario, that of the Navajo people of the Southwestern United States, in which livestock engendered an elaborate shift in human cultural existence, resulting in the animal being utilized as an instrument to destroy the transformed culture.

Claude Lévi-Strauss, well-known for his statement that "animals are good to think with," would perhaps agree that they are not only good to think with but indeed of absolute necessity to think with. Animals provide associative and conceptual representations that translate into projections of multispecies relationships in space and time.[11] As Thomas Nagel has famously argued, we remain unable to think *as* another animal, in the sense of adopting the perspective of a nonhuman being and perceiving and experiencing the world from this perspective.[12] We, as humans, are our own animal, and our ability to think *with* animal others means recognizing the ways in which they coexist in mutual space and time and in co-constitutive relationality with the human animal. The notion of the 'human animal' implies a sense of anthropocentric hierarchy which also tends to find its way into our scholarly deliberations. As I move forward in my discussion, I would thus like to emphasize the reciprocity between, and coevolution of, species – here exemplified by the history of human-ovine relations.[13] This does not mean ignoring the seemingly unavoidable fact that the notion of domesticated livestock always in some way alludes to servitude and is shaped by asymmetrical power relations. Domesticated animals, after all, were 'developed' in order to contribute to human survival, success and productivity.[14] I encourage the further exploration of both the representations of this particular kind of human-animal relationship

11 Johanna Hoorenman: *Writing 'that animal darkness'. Galway Kinnell, Gary Snyder, James Merrill.* Unpublished dissertation, Trinity College Dublin, 2010, p. 20. Also see recent contributions from the field of multispecies ethnography: Eben Kirksey / Stefan Helmreich: The Emergence of Multispecies Ethnography. In: *Cultural Anthropology* 25,4 (2010), pp 545–576; Eben Kirksey: *The Multispecies Salon.* Durham: Duke UP 2014.

12 Thomas Nagel: What Is It Like to Be a Bat? In: *The Philosophical Review* 83,4 (1974), pp. 435–450.

13 Budiansky: *Covenant of the Wild*, p. xi. Budiansky is skeptical about coevolution as a system that implies mutually responsive evolution on the part of both the domesticated and the domesticating, and he argues that this has most likely not been the case. Particularly with regard to human-ovine relations, I would object to his statement, and I would argue that humans have indeed altered ways of living in response to animals.

14 Ibid., p. 24.

and the (co-)performances through which it is defined and potentially transformed. At the very least, additional assessments of the ontologies of livestock animals and their existence in 'human' histories beyond the contemporary world should be fostered.[15]

I want to argue here that in order to adequately understand human historical development and, in fact, the 'human condition' as such, we must first and *only* do so in the company of animals, including domesticated livestock. We must comprehend how such animals have shaped our integration in, and the formation of, the nature-culture landscapes in which we reside. We must recognize how these particular animals have constructed and altered our food systems. We must appreciate how livestock animals have enhanced or enabled the actual physical performance of human life. We must realize that the making and taking of animal life is facilitated by our strongly hierarchical relationships with the livestock animals we have surrounded ourselves with. In deliberating such things, it becomes less difficult to imagine that livestock animals are often key cultural signifiers of human existence, underpinning different cultural practices and traditions and ethnic histories throughout the world. Scholars are moving closer to a more complete understanding of these complex and multi-faceted relationships, but inevitably we must move forward with the understanding that acknowledging the prevalent role of nonhuman animals in the development of human existence is indeed the only adequate manner in which we can conceptualize the progression of human life.

Part Two: Navajo Culture and Human-Ovine Relations

Any understanding of the historical transformation of the Navajo people into a reservation society remains incomplete without taking into account the integral role of sheep in this process. The Navajo, once Plains hunters and gatherers, were the only native people who adjusted their cultural lifeway to that of shepherding.[16] The relationship

15 David Lulka: Stabilizing the Herd. Fixing the Identity of Nonhumans. In: *Environment and Planning D: Society and Space* 22,3 (2004), pp. 439–463, here p. 439.

16 For the history of Navajo food systems and agricultural practices, see, for example, Peter Iverson: *Diné. A History of the Navajos*. Albuquerque: University of New Mexico Press 2002; Marsha L. Weisiger: *Dreaming of Sheep in Navajo Country*. Seattle: University of Washington Press 2009; Richard White: *The Roots of Dependency: Subsistence, Environment, and Social Change Among the Choctaws, Pawnees, and Navajos*. Lincoln: University of Nebraska Press 1988, pp. 212–314.

between human, landscape, and animal is integral to the appreciation of the complexity of Navajo culture and society, their identity as a people, and their history within the North American political landscape. This chapter ends only a few years before the beginning of the stock reduction programs that started in the 1920s and continue to this very day. The initial stock reductions began after extensive ecological assessments had been undertaken throughout the region from the late 1800s to the 1920s. The conclusions drawn from these assessments were that the Navajo in particular had increased both their human and sheep populations beyond a sustainable threshold and had seemingly created a drought-ridden region. This prompted government intervention in the form of mandatory stock reductions to reduce the drain on the environment.[17]

It is important to consider the topic of this chapter in its connection with the current issues of forced relocation and stock reductions and their continuity with the original practices of displacement and eradication that began over 200 years ago. Today, stock reductions are still presented in terms of ecological necessity, even though the problem is no longer an ecological one but has to do with land acquisition for mining operations. The progressive extermination of Navajo culture has not ceased but continues in subtler forms, with the conflict now centered on natural resource extraction. As their physical and cultural landscape continues to degrade, the future of the Navajo people is uncertain. The one constant in this process is a focus on the Navajo sheep as a tool for the manipulation of their culture.[18]

17 For more on this subject, see chapter 6 of Weisiger's *Dreaming of Sheep*, particularly her discussion of the theory of "ungulate irruption" (Weisiger: *Dreaming of Sheep*, pp. 132–135). Chapter 5 of Iverson's *Diné* considers the development of the eighteen land management districts assigned to the reservation to determine landscape carrying capacity as well as the introduction of the "sheep unit," which defined the load per animal on the range and stock allocation management per Navajo household (Iverson: *Diné*, pp. 154–155). These actions were integral to the initiation of governmental stock reduction policies. George Boyce's *When Navajos Had Too Many Sheep. The 1940s*. San Francisco: Indian Historian Press 1974, extends the discussion beyond the initial stock reductions.

18 Richard White claims that as a result of flock increases after the Navajos' release from Bosque Redondo, "changes in the land and changes in people came simultaneously, but this does not mean that one caused the other" (White: *The Roots of Dependency*, p. 215). I would disagree with this statement and, in a sense, this essay challenges his claim. An understanding of the way in which the Navajo utilize the land – its primary purpose being shepherding – shows that to change that form of land use means to change the culture of the people who engage directly within that landscape.

The Navajo-Churro sheep were the first domesticated sheep to be introduced to and shaped by the North American continent. And while many shepherding cultures have flourished for centuries throughout the world, few are as fundamentally tied to the animal as the people who shepherd these particular sheep. Many pastoral cultures are shepherds to sheep as a species of livestock, conforming to market conditions or land availability, with the breed often being less important than the species itself. In many instances, what are now rare breed animals were bred in response to specific cultural or economic demands, rather than the culture manifesting or reshaping itself as a response to the breed. But the Navajo people are a unique culture with a unique breed of sheep, and this specificity needs to be taken into account in understanding the plight of the Navajo and the role of the sheep in their demise.

The history of the sheep as part of Navajo social and cultural existence is not generally well known outside of their society and that of its expansionist-minded antagonists, but it remains integral not only to an understanding of Navajo culture and the contemporary physical and cultural landscape which continues to challenge their way of life, it also provides insight into the formation of the United States as a political entity emerging from primarily Anglo-centric settler colonies. This history has generally been presented with a focus on land acquisition and the colonialist enforcement of Euro-American 'rights' to the natural world, but the exploitation of the land and the disintegration of Navajo existence has occurred through a unique channel: sheep. The sheep have never been simply a food source or part of an economic system; they are so deeply embedded into their lifeway – the way of being Navajo –, that to remove them from the people is to remove an essential aspect of who they are *as* a people.

Most of the small amount of historical literature available on the subject of sheep in North American history is written through a predominantly settler colonialist lens, at a time during the mid-1900s when the memory of territorial expansion was still relatively fresh and when the still-young Navajo reservation lands were increasingly under pressure by natural resource extraction projects.[19] Little if any thought was given to the recognition of the indigenous histories that had shaped the

19 For the introduction of sheep to North America and their resulting relationships with both native peoples and landscapes, see Wentworth: *America's Sheep Trails*, and Charles W. Towne / Edward N. Wentworth: *Shepherd's Empire*. Norman: University of Oklahoma Press 1945.

continent, but the literature still offers some insight into the effects of sheep on both North American ecological and political landscapes. It also provides evidence of the violent measures taken against indigenous populations as bands of European settlers pushed westward, essentially clearing the landscape of humans and animals alike to acquire land for grazing and development. While the literature on sheep introduction and production in North America has for the most part dismissed the existence of indigenous peoples as little more than a nuisance, the sheep and their husbandry needs were integral to colonizing and expansionist efforts. This specific animal had never been present in this new environment, and the settlers introducing them into this new world were doing so mostly based on their experiences with European environments, food systems, and husbandry practices. Accordingly, few were able to fully recognize the role of sheep as a foreign being in a new landscape. The effect the sheep would have on both the people and the land was an experience that no human – regardless of culture – was prepared for.

As a new creature introduced into the landscape, one can only begin to imagine the reaction of the Navajo upon first encountering sheep. They were foreign yet easily adaptable to the needs of the Navajo. The Navajo already knew how to spin and weave with cotton acquired through trade and from the techniques learned from the Pueblo. In time, these textile techniques were adapted to the wool produced by the sheep. Beyond questions of subsistence, the sheep were also a spiritual answer for the Navajo – they symbolized the promise of a new and prosperous lifeway. Since the Navajo were already skillful hunter-gatherers and entirely self-sustaining, it is not likely that there was a dire need to acquire the sheep for reasons of mere survival. Rather, the animals presented themselves to the Navajo and the latter not only seized the opportunity but found that the sheep were already part of what might be termed the subconscious history of their people.

It is said in Navajo history that their people have had sheep in their genetic memory since they became a people. From the moment that sheep entered the cultural life of the Navajo, they, as a people, have customarily presented themselves through their relationship with these animals: as pastoral herders of the North American landscape, as master weavers and spinners, as a spiritual people connected with and through the animal and the land. *Diné bí' íína'* – Sheep is Life – is the

Navajo greeting to the world.[20] The animal established for the Navajo an intimate relationship with the Southwestern environment that is as essential as the roots of the juniper reaching for the deepest water for survival. The sheep perform a tacit yet tangible replication of the harmonic balance of all life on the land. They are symbols of what is good and pure, and they have engendered a rapid shift of the Navajo from a hunter-gatherer to a pastoral-agricultural society. The lore of the sheep had not been verbalized or documented until the actual, physical encounter with the animal, but once this encounter had taken place, these stories emerged as a representation of a pre-existing spiritual history that would henceforward guide the people. In actuality, sheep only came to the Navajos anywhere between 50 to 350 years after the emergence of their people as a cultural entity.

It is believed that sheep were initially introduced to the Navajo by Spanish explorers and colonizers in the sixteenth century. Although many sheep were previously shepherded by expeditionaries thousands of miles throughout what is now Mexico and the Southwestern United States, after many years of unsuccessful exploration all met their demise in the company of gold expeditioners and missionary groups. The first Spanish Merino flocks were brought to the Southwest by Hernán Cortés in 1538, who eventually distributed his sheep among the Spanish missions in Mexico. This established a future offshoot of some flocks of the Hispanic sheep, who were integral to the crossbreeding with the Churro that would occur several decades later. Shortly after Cortés, Francisco de Coronado brought the first Iberian Churra sheep to North America, but all of them were most likely slaughtered or perished in the course of Coronado's unsuccessful gold expeditions – as a result, the land would be devoid of the ovine colonizers for many decades to follow. In 1598, Juan de Oñate descended upon the Rio Grande Valley with another flock of about 3,000 Iberian Churra sheep from which all Navajo-Churro sheep have since originated. These endeavors marked the beginning of the successful colonization of the southwestern parts of the North American continent.[21]

20 'Sheep is Life' is the phrase that has long been utilized by the Navajo to define The Navajo Lifeway. It is also the name of the annual celebration of the Navajo-Churro sheep and the Navajo weavings made from their wool.

21 Wentworth: *America's Sheep Trails*, ch. 2. Also see Lyle McNeal: The Navajo Sheep Project. Churro History. http://navajosheepproject.com/churrohistory.html (accessed March 10, 2016).

The Navajo-Churro sheep, perceived as inferior, scrubby, and unworthy creatures by European settlers, were prized by the Navajo for their ruggedness. They were small and tough, with wool unlike the large European fine-wool breeds, holding little lanolin and thus requiring little to no water to clean after shearing. The sheep produced copious amounts of the tough wool, which meant that they could be sheared twice a year. Also, the particular structure of the fiber enabled it to absorb and hold natural dyes extremely well and it was easy to weave with very little preparation. The fiber was coarse and strong and quickly became the staple of Navajo weaving production, allowing textile products to serve as an economic source.[22]

The modes of coexistence with sheep differed between European settlers and the indigenous cultures of North America, and these differences are crucial to understanding how one culture could see the animal as simply a representation of an economic way of life rather than an embodiment of a culture. European mentalities were based on a perception of the animal as a food source and an economic resource. Sheep had existed in European cultures for thousands of years prior to accompanying the colonizers across the ocean to North America. However, this cultural history was one in which sheep figured as a consumable entity and not as a crucial expression of cultural identity. Had agriculture shifted in much of Europe at that time to concentrate on another species, such as cattle or hogs, the cultural characteristics of the people would most likely have stayed generally intact, with some adjustments to land use and food systems.[23] The focus of most European livestock-centric cultures has been less on species and more on patterns of land use and agricultural economics,[24] whereas for North American

22 Noël Bennett / Tiana Bighorse: *Navajo Weaving Way. The Path from Fleece to Rug.* Loveland: Interweave Press 1997, p. 11; Charles Avery Amsden: *Navaho Weaving. Its Technic and History.* Santa Ana: The Fine Arts Press 1934, pp. 111–150; Susan M. Strawn / Mary A. Littrell: Returning Navajo-Churro Sheep to Navajo Weaving. In: *Textile* 5,3 (2007), pp. 300–319.

23 Multispecies agriculture was indeed prominent in much of Eurasia. However, shepherding and the husbandry of sheep was a primary facet of animal-based agriculture for several centuries. Agricultural shifts, including the use of domesticated animals, do occur regularly throughout human history. For a comprehensive foray into animal domestication and the shifts in human-animal interactions in the context of agriculture, see Clutton-Brock: *Animals as Domesticates.*

24 There are clearly exceptions to this, as are the Pyrenees shepherds and other sheep-centric transhumant societies. However, people from these communities did not often migrate to the New World to reestablish these traditions there. Most of the European settlers in North America were sedentary agriculturalists.

indigenous societies animals also held a spiritual significance, without the dichotomous conception of human and animal life so influential in European history. European settlers labeled and categorized their animals and perceived them through a predominantly utilitarian lens. For indigenous peoples like the Navajo, however, animals were spiritually embodied beings who provided a mutual existence possibly transcending the physical.[25] Europeans were shepherding for a purpose; sheep were a (mobile) food source and land acquisition strategy that was easily manageable. In contrast, the sheep found its way into Navajo society not out of necessity but because the animal was seen as a gift to their people and an answer to a memory that had been unrealized for centuries. Unlike the neighboring indigenous societies which also obtained sheep from colonizers, such as the Apache and the Pueblo, the Navajo cared for their flocks in an effort to permanently incorporate the animal into their society.[26]

As more and more English and Spanish settlers invaded Navajo lands in the eighteenth century, at which point the landscape had become flourishing livestock grazing territory, they brought with them their own histories of shepherding customs and in particular their histories of woolen textile use and production. The settlers were increasingly met with resistance by the Navajo, who had by then developed into accomplished weavers and shepherds and had grown their flocks to tens of thousands. While the sheep had only been a part of Navajo society for less than 200 years, their important role for the identity of the Navajo as a people had already become solidified. The prized weavings still sought after today had been established as a valued commodity within the Navajo community and even more so with traders and collectors in the European settlement populations. Weavings began to be contracted to trading posts and became a primary economic source for the people. Historic grazing lands had now been passed through generations and

25 Paul Shepard: *Thinking with Animals. Animals and the Development of Human Intelligence*. New York: Viking 1978, p. 259.

26 This also occurred in the Hispanic communities to the south. The sheep reared by the Hispanics were preserved genetically, which helped reestablish flocks after Navajo internment, but it is believed that all sheep owned by the Hispanics who were identical to the Navajo-Churro lines were eventually crossbred with Merino sheep for wool improvement in order to meet the needs of the European settlers. This crossbreeding ensured that the only pure Navajo-Churro lines would inevitably be in the care of the Navajo. See Wentworth: *America's Sheep Trails*, pp. 123–126.

were devotedly shepherded by almost every Navajo family. Flocks had grown to a point that they were able to sustain the people as a whole, and a firm transition from hunter-gatherer society to pastoral society had quickly and successfully taken place.[27]

The settlers, however, began to instigate conflict through increased land encroachment and hostile trading behaviors in an effort to crossbreed the Churros with sheep of their own fine Merino and Longwool breeds.[28] The purpose of this was not only to increase flock production and expansion but also to breed out the unappealing features of the Churro and to re-assimilate the sheep into the settlers' European flocks. In the process, the characteristic ruggedness of the Churro breed had to give way to demands for a higher carcass yield and a refined textile production to serve the new American settlers. In response to the often forced acquisition of the animals by the new settlers, the Navajo became increasingly aggravated and protective and began to remove their sheep farther to the Southwest in order to safeguard them. It is at this point that the separation of the Merino and Churro breeds can be identified and that the evolution of the landrace of the Navajo-Churro sheep becomes solidified.[29] Henceforth, Euro-American settlers began a steady drive to rid the landscape of its rather inconvenient native residents.

Beginning in the 1860s, territory and grazing lands were increasingly fought over until the federal government warned the Navajo that they must conform or be subdued. After a long history of intermittent conflict with the settlers, the Spanish, and the Mexicans, the Navajo increasingly engaged in direct conflicts and violent raids against many other Native American peoples of the region, specifically the Ute, Hopi, Pueblo, and Apache. This was in part due to livestock thefts and slave raids, but it was also the result of alliances between other indigenous communities and the federal government. A series of battles began to threaten the governance of Navajo society, as many of their important leaders were killed. Congress in part utilized the resistance of the Navajo as an impetus to increasingly extend the control over their land as well as their use of the land. As the federal government, supported by New Mexican volunteers and other Native American peoples who

27 Strawn / Littrell: Returning Navajo-Churro Sheep, p. 302.

28 McNeal: Navajo Sheep Project.

29 Ibid.

had issues of their own to resolve with the Navajo, was increasingly successful with its forced acquisitions of Navajo territory and developed a stronger resolve to secure the region for American purposes, Congress began to enact legislation that would guide the new 'vision' for the Navajos. The latter included developing outposts for future internments, establishing plans for boarding schools for Navajo children, and abolishing the Navajos' pastoral lifeway in favor of a controlled farming society confined to a limited territory. These plans (deliberately) ignored the important role of livestock in Navajo society, which would have conflicted with the encroaching American settlers and their demands for land to use for their own livestock. Instead, the goal was to eliminate Navajo grazing rights altogether.[30] In July 1863, Army colonel Kit Carson was commissioned to subdue the Navajo as a response to their desperate resistance to encroachment, colonization, and livestock management strategies.

Beginning in January 1864, Army soldiers descended into the Southwest and terrorized the Navajos by destroying their crops, burning their hogans,[31] and slaughtering thousands of their sheep on site by gunfire or by driving them by the hundreds over cliffs. The fall of 1864 saw the beginning of the deportation marches – the 'Long Walk' – of approximately 9,000 Navajos to the Fort Sumner camp at Bosque Redondo, New Mexico, in which several thousand Navajo and Apache prisoners were contained within an area of forty miles over the course of four years. In a final act of violent defiance, a group of Navajo resisted these aggressions in the Canyon del Muerto, but they were defeated through starvation and eventually surrendered and were also sent to Bosque Redondo. The 350-mile march took approximately eighteen days, with a trail of Navajo people said to be ten miles long. The federal government engaged in every possible recourse to forcibly transform the Navajo into a sedentary farming society, with Westernized education imposed upon their children in an effort to eliminate their culture. Inevitably this effort failed for many reasons, and the Navajo were released in 1868 to return to a new life in an ever-shrinking landscape which now included reservation boundaries and boarding schools. All sheep who

30 White: *The Roots of Dependency*, pp. 212–215.

31 Hogans, small houses constructed with the help of wooden poles and mud, are the traditional dwelling of the Navajo people.

remained alive at the time of the marches had been confiscated by the Army or slaughtered. However, some of the Churro lines that had been preserved by the Hispanics to the south lived on. It is descendants of these sheep and those of the governmentally confiscated lines who were used by the Navajo to rebuild the flocks upon their release from internment and the establishment of the reservation.

Part Three: The Animal as Historical Witness and Custodian of Cultural Value

The cultural representation of an animal is an outward expression of the animal as a representative of a specific culture, and often only a specific aspect of this culture. We can think, for example, of the emblematic function of the kangaroo in Australian culture. This function of the animal is evident in various forms of marketing and imagery, but the animal itself is not an embodied representative of the people of Australia. The people of Australia, in contrast to the Navajos' relationship with their sheep, do not enact their daily life through physical interaction with the kangaroo. Animal representation can be a cliché or a form of kitsch in the commercial expression of a culture over time rather than a reflective understanding of the incarnation of a cultural lifeway by the animal.[32] In some instances, as with the Navajo, one must move beyond an understanding of the animal as merely a cultural representation and recognize the animal as a genetic manifestation[33] and historical embodiment of a specific material-environmental existence in time and space, a perspective that is crucial to the understanding of the animal *and* the culture and the uniqueness of both. The Navajo people cannot be wholly understood *as* a culture without understanding their relationship with their sheep. Conversely, one cannot understand the biological existence of the Navajo-Churro sheep without understanding Navajo cultural history. The Navajo-Churro sheep only exist because of, and through, the Navajo people as an aspect of their

32 Adrian Franklin: *Animal Nation. The True Story of Animals and Australia.* Sydney: University of New South Wales Press 2006, p. 123.

33 I argue that genetic manifestation is a result of animal reproduction in response to human interaction and environmental influence. The structure of the animal in physiological and behavioral characteristics – both evidenced in genetic representations of breed characteristics – adjusts generationally through reproduction as a response to interaction and influence.

culture and lived experience, and as part of reciprocal, interdependent histories, which are a fundamental component in the broader consideration of cultural sustainability.[34]

There has been increasing effort to understand the role of livestock and its importance in cultural history, but much of this work has encompassed animal geographies only insofar as they directly relate to food systems or breed conservation.[35] Almost no scholarship addresses a methodology for assigning a 'measurable' cultural value to livestock in order to understand its contribution to cultural life and, more specifically, its importance for cultural sustainability. However, the literature that *does* exist provides a solid foundation for considering these methodologies in scenarios that require an exploration of the importance of the role of the animal in historical ontologies and cultural production. Acknowledging, or allowing for, the presence of the animal in these considerations enables a broader understanding of reciprocal human-animal relationships and their essential interdependence for continuity in place and time.[36]

Gustavo Gandini and Emanuele Villa have proposed a comprehensive methodology for determining the cultural value of livestock in European conservation efforts. This is currently the only methodology that can be found in the existing literature, but its parameters are malleable and applicable to other contexts beyond the authors' research focus and findings. Gandini and Villa's initial framework considers the following: first, every human action is considered a documentation of human culture, and thus actions which encompass the use of livestock should also be included in this cultural documentation – not simply as mere actions within space and time but rather as actions both representative and formative of culture. Second, every examination of the cultural value of human actions must be done through the analysis of their *historical* value, that is, the capability of these actions "to document the world in which they occurred."[37] Understanding these premises and revisiting the case of the Navajos discussed in this chapter, we

34 Virginia DeJohn Anderson: *Creatures of Empire. How Domestic Animals Transformed America*. Oxford: Oxford UP 2004, p. 17.

35 Lulka: Stabilizing the Herd, p. 439.

36 Gustavo C. Gandini / Emanuele Villa: Analysis of the Cultural Value of Local Livestock Breeds. A Methodology. In: *Journal of Animal Breeding and Genetics* 120,1 (2003), pp. 1–11.

37 Ibid., p. 2.

can conclude that the role of sheep in Navajo history means that we have to fully include them in our documentation of Navajo culture and recognize their ability to offer a documentation of the Navajos' historical lifeways and lifeworld.

The Navajo-Churro sheep are essential to the cultural survival of the Navajo, and by removing the sheep, the ties to the landscape and the culture are broken. This is a connection that is quite different from the cases that have been documented in Europe, where the animal functions more as a cultural token but not as the focal aspect (or custodian) of the respective culture.[38] The comprehensive historical documentation of the sheep as a product and representative of Navajo culture effectively positions the relationship between the sheep and the Navajo as quite unique in the way in which it gives rise to a manifestation of Navajo culture in and through the animal. Four parameters presented by Gandini and Villa applied to the Navajo-Churro sheep encompass the vital cultural position of the animal and underline that the breed does in fact have a comprehensive cultural value and functions as a historical witness.[39] First, the Navajo-Churro sheep have maintained a crucial role in the agricultural practices and the broader social life of the Navajo people for a long period of time. Second, animal products derived from the Navajo-Churro are specific to the breed and have been incorporated into Navajo culture, including Navajo foodways and spiritual life, and are recognized for their unique cultural value. Third, the Navajo-Churro sheep have been a key element in the transformation of the Southwestern landscape. Sheep and shepherding practices have shaped Southwestern local ecologies through the actual physical impact of the animals' hooves on the soil and through their consumptive behaviors.[40] Lastly, the Navajo-Churro sheep, beyond the products derived from the animal as mentioned above, are considered an iconic reference to the ancient local traditions of the Navajo, often visually referenced in food

38 For instance, when one thinks of Ireland, one might think of a history of sheep and shepherds in rolling, green landscapes, which allows one to understand that shepherding has been an important aspect of Irish culture. However, the Irish are attached to a multi-faceted history that does not wholly encompass shepherding, which means that sheep are not intrinsically attached to the survival of Irish culture as such.

39 Gandini / Villa: Analysis, pp. 4, 6–8.

40 For a comprehensive overview of the ecological impact of the Navajos' sheep in the Southwest and resulting governmental policies throughout the last 200 years, see Weisiger: *Dreaming of Sheep*; Boyce: *When Navajos Had Too Many Sheep.*

practices, craft, and folklore, and are recognized through various forms of symbolism for their important role in the protection of the Navajos' cultural heritage.[41]

To gain a conceptual understanding of the animal as historical witness, we might think about this by drawing on the French concept of *terroir*, usually employed to describe the 'character' of a wine as it is determined by the specific environmental factors of the region where it is grown. Although we are talking about sheep rather than grapes, we can still use the term *terroir* to refer to the ensemble of properties reflecting a unique biophysical existence. Wool as a biophysical historical indicator represents the lived experience of the animal. Much like a fingerprint, or even a tree ring, the wool fiber of the sheep is unique not only to the breed but to each individual animal. Further, this unique indicator varies through every yearly cycle of life. Generally, sheep produce wool that must be sheared each year; due to the long, dual-coated properties of the Navajo-Churro fleece, these sheep must be sheared every six months to ensure quality fiber production without felting, which would create health concerns for the animal in the harsh high desert landscape. Every fiber contained within the fleece is affected by a multitude of variables the animal experiences within this cycle, such as weather, health, lambing, water access, sun exposure, human treatment, stress, grazing vegetation variation, etc. With each passing year the animal will never move through precisely the same landscape as before, nor will it experience the same weather patterns or ingest the exact same vegetation. The animals may experience an overly cold winter or a long trail to a new pasture. They might ruminate under pine trees rather than juniper. Or they might experience harsh treatment by a new shepherd or a stressful lambing. They may have been stolen or shot at, transported by trucks or trains, or herded into valleys or canyons. Each experience, each day, and each year is thus strongly shaped by human behavior towards the animal and by the animal's response (and sometimes the other way around), by a partnership in which human and animal continuously affect and co-shape each other.

41 Gandini and Villa further their analysis by identifying seven specific ways in which the cultural value of the animal is related to its status as a historical witness, which might then play an important role in the decision whether or not to conserve the breed in question. Although I do find value in further considering these parameters as they might apply to an in-depth study of the contemporary status of the Navajo-Churro sheep population, this is beyond the scope of this chapter.

Each of these experiential variables also influences the physiology of the animal, including the production of proteins, which in turn affects the structure of the wool fibers. The wool fibers thus become markers of the animal's lived experience, and once the animal has been shorn, they enter the sphere of human experience and relations in a more direct way. The Navajo people employ the wool to weave textiles to sleep on, furnish their homes, or clothe their bodies. The wool fibers travel through the hands of shearers, spinners, and weavers, and as such, the *terroir* of the animal becomes interwoven with human experience and culture. These textile animal products, in other words, become repositories of time and lived interspecies relations. Two woven blankets might look identical, but they came from different sheep, which had different shepherds, which fed on different scrub, and ruminated in different sunlight. Such are the biological identifiers of human and animal coexistence in a more-than-human historical space, and in this sense the sheep is an active participant in a cultural history of, but also beyond, the human, in which the animal functions as historical witness.

A Final Consideration

> Our life is connected to the life of the sheep. We are alive and strong because of them, and being close to them, being with them everyday, keeps us strong [...] If we are too far from our sheep, we can become frail.[42]

The term *Diné Bikéyah* defines the area of land that has historically and spiritually encompassed the Navajo people for several hundred years. The land gave birth to the Navajo people beginning in the twelfth century, and it has been encroached upon since the sixteenth. Currently, this encroachment manifests itself particularly in the form of mineral extraction. Peabody Coal has been actively running coal slurry (a liquid coal waste by-product from extraction and processing) and increasing its questionable mining operations on and under the Navajo reservation beginning only sixty years after the reservation was created. For these last sixty years, the mining operations have created droughts and toxic water, leaving little to irrigate crops, provide for livestock, or even to

42 Clarence and Mary Lou Blackrock, October 25, 2014. Clarence Blackrock: Sheep Emergency Recovery Fund. https://www.everribbon.com/sheep-emergency-fund (accessed January 30, 2016).

drink or wash.[43] The mining operations have continued to expand and, in turn, Peabody has lobbied for increased access to reservation land. As a result, ever more land is becoming off-limits to both the Navajo and their livestock. Efforts to tax and confiscate the sheep have increased beyond levels sustainable to an indigenous population mostly living well below the poverty line. Because the Navajo primarily rely on their sheep for sustenance, and on wool for income, removing their sheep enables the federal government to argue that the Navajo are not productively utilizing the land and therefore have neither the need nor the justification to *stay* on the land. Relocation is usually 'offered' in some form, and an increasing number of Navajo decide to leave their homeland.

Pictures posted on the Black Mesa Indigenous Support website in October 2014 show Clarence Blackrock, a Navajo elder, sitting in a small chair by a fire outside his hogan on Navajo reservation land in northern Arizona.[44] A blanket on his lap, his cane resting on his leg, he holds on tightly to a rope tied to a sheep standing by his side. As we learn from the description, the old man is kept awake by fear and a spirit of resistance, should the Bureau of Indian Affairs and the Hopi Rangers arrive in the middle of the night to take his flock of sheep away from him. A few days prior to this photo, reminiscent of the repeated confiscations that have occurred over the previous fifty years, other elders had their sheep taken away, some of them at gunpoint during raid-like operations. Clarence has been a shepherd all his life, just as his parents before him, and his ancestors before them. He probably has not-too-distant ancestors who survived the 'Long Walk' to Bosque Redondo in 1864; ancestors that had their sheep killed or taken away from them in an effort to eradicate their culture and history as a people; ancestors who worked to rebuild their flocks after release from internment; ancestors who hid their sheep in the niches and crevasses of the treacherous terrain of the Four Corners region to save them from a second round of

43 Claudia Rowe: Coal Mining on Navajo Nation in Arizona Takes Heavy Toll. In: *Huffington Post*, June 6, 2013. http://www.huffingtonpost.com/2013/06/06/coal-mining-navajo-nation_n_3397118.html (accessed October 23, 2014); Diné Policy Institute: Diné Food Sovereignty. A Report on the Navajo Nation Food System and the Case to Rebuild a Self-Sufficient Food System for the Diné People, April 2014. http://www.dinecollege.edu/institutes/DPI/Docs/dpi-food-sovereignty-report.pdf (accessed January 14, 2016).

44 Liza Minno: Elders Living in Fear and Heartache. http://supportblackmesa.org/2014/10/elders-living-in-fear-and-heartache/ (accessed January 30, 2016).

violent slaughter during livestock reductions and land clearings in the 1920s and 1930s. Clarence's family has worked to preserve the lifeway of the Diné through shepherding, the spinning of wool, and the weaving of textiles – no matter that the younger generations are exponentially being pushed away from the reservation due to poverty and a lack of educational resources. Now, as the forced stock reductions actively continue to this day over 200 years after they began, the dwindling numbers of elders are primarily the shepherds who remain, holding on to a fading culture at the end of a rope.

III

Exploration, Expansion and Manifest Destiny
Contexts and Legacies

Ardent Creatures

William Bartram and the Limits of Compassion

Neill Matheson

William Bartram has long been included in the canon of U.S. nature writers. His extraordinary 1791 narrative of travels through the American Southeast was read and admired by Samuel Taylor Coleridge, William Wordsworth, and Henry David Thoreau, among many others. Bartram has also been characterized by some scholars as an important early environmental writer, who anticipated twentieth-century ecological thinking. Michael Branch describes Bartram's writing as "proto-ecological," containing "a strain of radical nonanthropocentrism which clearly distinguishes him from his contemporaries."[1] Kerry S. Walters calls Bartram "a pioneering environmentalist" concerned with a range of environmental issues, and especially "horrified at the human disregard for animal life and well-being exemplified in the wasteful blood-sport" widely practiced in his time.[2] Yet relatively little sustained

1 Michael Branch: Indexing American Possibilities. The Natural History Writing of Bartram, Wilson, and Audubon. In: Cheryll Glotfelty / Harold Fromm (eds): *The Ecocriticism Reader. Landmarks in Literary Ecology*. Athens: University of Georgia Press 1996, pp. 282–302, here p. 286.

2 Kerry S. Walters: The "Peaceable Disposition" of Animals. William Bartram on the Moral Sensibility of Brute Creation. In: *Pennsylvania History* 56,3 (1989), pp. 157–176, here p. 157. Walters differentiates Bartram's views on the moral question of animal cruelty from reformist Quaker arguments in the period.

attention has been given to Bartram as a writer profoundly engaged with the human relation to nonhuman animals, in spite of the recent surge of scholarly interest in animal studies.[3] Bartram describes himself as "an advocate or vindicator of the benevolent and peaceable disposition of animal creation in general,"[4] and he takes issue with prevailing anthropocentric assumptions about animals that justify subordination and exploitation. Bartram's *Travels* (1791) often demonstrates a concern for nonhuman animal life, staging scenes of compassion in response to human violence and cruelty towards other creatures. But what these scenes reveal is sympathy's belatedness and impotence, its inability to intervene effectively to forestall violence. Bartram casts himself as a helpless bystander whose compassion isolates rather than empowers him. I argue that this very helplessness enables identification across species boundaries with animal vulnerability and suffering. From *Travels* to his fragmentary manuscript essay "The Dignity of Human Nature," Bartram increasingly positions himself as a marginal voice speaking out against a dominant cultural tradition that takes for granted the subjection of nonhuman animals, naturalizing anthropogenic violence.

Bartram set off from Philadelphia in 1773, on the brink of the American Revolution, traveling for several years through the Carolinas, Georgia, Florida, and as far west as the Mississippi, acquiring plant specimens for an English collector, and recording his observations of natural phenomena and indigenous peoples. He returned to Philadelphia in January 1777. Yet *Travels* avoids mention of impending war with Great Britain, as if the conflict were too remote to have left any mark on the natural world he aimed to describe.[5] In fact, a year after the 1791 publication of *Travels*, Bartram argued in a letter to a friend that wars between nations might be grounds for preferring the "Moral System" of "many Animals which we hold beneath us," presumably because such warfare is an exclusively human domain: "Can any action, affair or concern, strike our understanding with more decisive, & forceble Ideas of Madness,

3 In addition to Walters's valuable early study, one notable recent exception is Julie McCown: Crocodilian Transmission. Correspondence Networks in William Bartram and Thomas De Quincey. In: *Configurations* 22,3 (2014), pp. 361–384.

4 William Bartram: *Travels of William Bartram*, ed. by Mark Van Doren. New York: Dover 1955, p. 222. Henceforth the page numbers for *Travels* will be cited in-text.

5 For a fuller consideration of *Travels* in the context of the American Revolution, see Douglas Anderson: Bartram's *Travels* and the Politics of Nature. In: *Early American Literature* 25,1 (1990), pp. 3–17.

Brutality, Wretchedness, & depravity of Nature, than National Wars?"[6] Yet the more-than-human world turns out to be full of violence and injustice as well, enabling Bartram to reflect across species boundaries on the moral implications of duplicity, subjection, and killing.

'War' and related words appear fairly frequently in the text, sometimes to refer to conflicts with and among Native Americans, but notably also for the human killing of nonhuman animals (the Creeks "wage eternal war against deer and bear" (184)), or predation among animal species ("numerous bands" of fish, "the watery nations," are caught up in "eternal war, or rather slaughter" (195)). The nature Bartram travels through is populated by creatures described in terms that seem to invoke revolutionary rhetoric: the bald eagle is an "execrable tyrant," who "supports his assumed dignity and grandeur by rapine and violence" (35); an especially large alligator is an "absolute sovereign" who domineers over his "lake or lagoon," driving rivals into more marginal spaces (123); the gar is "a warlike voracious creature," seemingly "in league or confederacy" with alligators to "enslave and devour the numerous defenseless tribes" of fish (178); at the "terrible appearance" of the Seminole hunter, "peaceful, innocent nations" of deer and other prey animals "are thrown into disorder and dismay" (165–166).

Like other writers of his time, Bartram habitually uses terms of human political and social organization – 'tribes,' 'bands,' or 'nations' – to describe nonhuman animal species. On some level, for Bartram, it often seems that animals are people too, if not quite citizens. As with humans, there are good and bad actors. My aim though is not to argue that Bartram displaces the language of revolutionary nationalism onto the natural landscape, so that his depiction of the nonhuman world constitutes a fable or allegory in which animals signify, or are reduced to, human political meanings. Rather, Bartram is notably troubled throughout *Travels* by the actual, material violence he finds in more-than-human nature, especially but not only when it is instigated by humans. His concern is biopolitical, with the killing and making killable of nonhuman (as well as human) beings, even if he sometimes borrows language from human political conflict. This concern is already

6 William Bartram to Benjamin Smith Barton, December 29, 1792. In: Thomas Hallock / Nancy E. Hoffman (eds): *William Bartram, The Search for Nature's Design. Selected Art, Letters, and Unpublished Writings*. Athens: University of Georgia Press 2010, pp. 166–170, here p. 169.

evident in the book's remarkable introduction, which advocates for the value of nonhuman forms of life – plants as well as animals – against prevailing ideologies and traditional philosophical arguments. Bartram acknowledges at the introduction's outset that among the "various works of Nature," "men and manners undoubtedly hold the first rank" (15). One virtue of animals is their "use and convenience to man" (21). However, the introduction's primary movement is to complicate and qualify this hierarchy. The "animal creation also excites our admiration," in part because of impressive physical attributes, size, agility, or beauty: "how wonderful is the mechanism of these finely formed self-moving beings" (21). Animals are not just marvelously intricate, elegant mechanisms, they are "self-moving," agential beings, whose "intellectual system" is still more "beautiful, harmonious, and incomprehensible," evidence of an "essential principle" which "secretly operates within" (21). Bartram asks, "that which animates the inimitable machines, which gives them motion, impowers them to act, speak, and perform, this must be divine and immortal?" (21) He challenges a philosophical tradition, most famously associated with René Descartes, that conceives of nonhuman animals as unthinking, unfeeling machines, guided solely by instinct and mechanical reflex, and lacking intelligent minds or souls. Bartram takes on this tradition directly:

> I am sensible that the general opinion of philosophers has distinguished the moral system of the brute creature from that of mankind, by an epithet which implies a mere mechanical impulse, which leads and impels them to necessary actions, without any premeditated design or contrivance; this we term instinct, which faculty we suppose to be inferior to reason in man. (21)

His "we suppose" seems to imply that the assumption that instinct is inferior to reason may not be entirely justified, an argument that he takes up more explicitly elsewhere, and that is perhaps behind his assertion that animals do not engage in destructive "National Wars," unlike his fellow humans. The more salient argument here though is that instinct is an inadequate, impoverished concept to describe the rich mental life of animals. In Bartram's view, nonhuman animals are not simply "unfeeling brutes" or "stimulus-response mechanisms," as Cary Wolfe characterizes the Cartesian position.[7]

7 Cary Wolfe: *Animal Rites. American Culture, the Discourse of Species, and Posthumanist Theory*. Chicago: University of Chicago Press 2003, p. 5.

Bartram argues that animals possess the same mental faculties and traits commonly attributed exclusively to humans. If we observe their behavior, "we shall find manifest examples of premeditation, perseverance, resolution, and consummate artifice" (22) employed to achieve their aims. As illustration, he relates the account of a predatory spider, which he observed hunting "a large fat bomble bee," advancing "obliquely," "under cover of dense foliage," until close enough to attack (24). Describing a scene that for many observers might seem instinct-driven, Bartram instead finds evidence of rationality: the spider's "subtil approaches" clearly demonstrate premeditation and artifice, not just intelligent planning but the ability to employ stealth and deception strategically. Yet it is also evident that Bartram is disturbed by what he sees as brutal violence. He describes a dramatic contest, which ends when the bee becomes "quite exhausted by his struggles, and the repeated wounds of the butcher," finally dying "in the arms of the devouring spider" (24). He admires the spider's efficient use of reason, but he cannot help noting that the purpose served by reason is killing.

Bartram's profound ambivalence about violence and killing is much more apparent in another episode recounted in the introduction, which is intended to illustrate the rich emotional life of nonhuman animals. If animals are intelligent, they are also capable of intense feeling: "The parental and filial affections seem to be as ardent, their sensibility and attachment as active and faithful, as those observed in human nature" (21). Like us, animals are ardent creatures: they manifest active sensibility, the capacity for a full range of emotions, and affectional bonds with others. Bartram offers an anecdote to illustrate this claim as well. Traveling up a river in Florida, he and his companion, whom he calls "my hunter," see a number of bears on the shore. The hunter announces that he will kill a bear for its "skin and oil," choosing one from a pair feeding together. In Bartram's account, they make "oblique approaches," coming closer to "our prey by this artifice, without their noticing us" (22) – language echoed in the description of the predatory spider a couple of pages later. Here Bartram finds himself on the side of the stealthy killers, and is almost immediately remorseful. The hunter shoots his bear, killing it instantly. The second bear smells and paws the body, seemingly unaware of the shot, and "appearing in agony, fell to weeping and looking upwards, then towards us, and cried out like a child" (22). Bartram's simile, "like a child," signals the anthropomorphism that structures this passage; the second bear, which he realizes is "a young cub," reacts to its mother's death with what Bartram characterizes unmistakably as a humanlike emotional response. Not simply a delusive trope, anthropomorphism may encourage a perception of creaturely affinity, rather than the detached observation of a merely instinctive reaction.[8]

Bartram's anthropomorphism conveys his sympathetic identification, which leads him to attempt to intervene to prevent the hunter from killing the young bear:

> The continual cries of this afflicted child, bereft of its parent, affected me very sensibly; I was moved with compassion, and charging myself as if accessary to what now appeared to be a cruel murder, endeavoured to prevail on the hunter to save its life, but to no effect! for by habit he had become insensible to compassion towards the brute creation. (22)

In spite of Bartram's pleas, the hunter kills "the harmless devoted victim" (22). Simile with its implied comparison disappears here: a child and its mother have been murdered, and Bartram feels complicit. He is emotionally deeply affected, "moved with compassion." In the complex affective politics of this scene, Bartram's awakened sensibility produces an identification with the suffering animal, and distinguishes him sharply from his human companion, who remains "insensible to compassion." Emily Ogden argues in a recent essay about Bartram's Philadelphia contemporary Charles Brockden Brown that in the period's "sensibilist culture," strongly influenced by Lockean theory, insensibility was associated with "inner emptiness"; insensibility "marked gradations away from personhood," even in extreme instances, identities that "lie somewhere south of the fully human."[9] Insensibility

8 Anthropomorphism is central to Bartram's depiction of nonhuman living things, both animals and plants. I draw here on recent critical and theoretical arguments aiming to revalue anthropomorphism as a form of representation for nonhuman animals. Summarizing such arguments, Kari Weil proposes a "'critical anthropomorphism' in the sense that we open ourselves to touch and be touched by others as fellow subjects and may imagine their pain, pleasure, and need in anthropomorphic terms, but stop short of believing that we can know their experience." (Kari Weil: *Thinking Animals. Why Animal Studies Now?* New York: Columbia UP 2012, p. 20.) She later cites Frans de Waal's characterization of resistance to anthropomorphism as "anthropodenial," a "willful blindness to the human-like characteristics of animals, or the animal-like characteristics of ourselves" (ibid., p. 45).

9 Emily Ogden: *Edgar Huntly* and the Regulation of the Senses. In: *American Literature* 85,3 (2013), pp. 419–445, here p. 425.

was closely linked to violence, for example in the context of proslavery arguments, which took for granted that slaves were relatively insensible to pain: as Ogden puts it, "the insensibility (to punishment) of a slave justified insensibility (as cruelty) toward him or her. To be locked in the world of dull feelings, then, was to be locked in a world of violence."[10] Bartram's heightened emotional response is evidence of his humanity, in opposition to the insensibility and therefore inhumanity of his companion, the hunter, whose feelings are dulled by the habit of believing animals themselves to be insensible and therefore killable brutes. The view that animals are insensible to pain and suffering was very much in keeping with the philosophical tradition Bartram is contesting in the introduction, but he is also concerned with something more pervasive in his culture – anthropocentric beliefs reinforced by the everyday habits and practices of human-animal relations. By empathizing with the very human bear, Bartram separates himself from the hunter, who falls short by some degree of being fully human. Sensibility as test or measure reveals the bear to be more human than it initially appears, and the hunter less so. Yet Bartram himself is an "accessary," perhaps even more because killing is what makes possible his demonstration of sensibility and identification across species boundaries.

Though this episode might suggest otherwise, Bartram does not condemn hunting in principle in *Travels*. The person he calls "my hunter" presumably performs an important function, providing game to be eaten (if not in this particular instance). Bartram refers to hunting frequently, and reports shooting at and killing animals himself more than once in the book. Instead, it is as if the boundary that separates him from forms of life that are considered categorically killable has suddenly come into question.[11] In *Before the Law*, Cary Wolfe elaborates the notion of framing as a way of conceptualizing the biopolitical consideration of nonhuman animals, arguing that "the question of framing is not simply a logical or epistemological problem but a social and

10 Ibid., p. 426.

11 I take the notion of the categorically 'killable' from Donna Haraway's discussion of human responsibility in relation to animal suffering. Haraway would substitute "Thou shalt not make killable" for the commandment "Thou shalt not kill," arguing that "it is a misstep to separate the world's beings into those who may be killed and those who may not and a misstep to pretend to live outside killing." (Donna Haraway: *When Species Meet*. Minneapolis: University of Minnesota Press 2008, pp. 79–80.)

material one": "Framing decides what we recognize and what we don't, what counts and what doesn't; and it also determines the consequences of falling outside the frame (in the case at hand, outside the frame as 'animal,' as '*zoe*,' as 'bare life')."[12] Along these lines, one could say that in this passage Bartram's sense of the frame that determines the status of nonhuman animals is displaced or opened up, so that this particular animal appears to be inside rather than outside. The result is not a stable position or lasting conclusion, but rather a momentary unsettling, with uncertain consequences. Bartram knows that hunting and killing are ubiquitous, and recognizes that he himself is in some ways complicit with this violence, but for the moment at least he no longer accepts the notion that nonhuman animals are categorically killable because they fall outside of the frame.

Rather than prompting an argument against hunting, the passage's aim seems to be to register Bartram's profound dismay over an especially troubling instance of killing in the context of his argument for the emotional capacity of animals. His response is strikingly echoed in a passage in *Walden*, which appears in the context of Thoreau's ruminations on hunting, fishing, and eating meat in "Higher Laws": "No humane being, past the thoughtless age of boyhood, will wantonly murder any creature, which holds its life by the same tenure that he does. The hare in its extremity cries like a child. I warn you, mothers, that my sympathies do not always make the usual phil-*anthropic* distinctions."[13] Thoreau rejects a merely philanthropic sympathy, love exclusively for the human, calling instead for compassion across species boundaries, based on the perception of shared vulnerability.[14] He implies that the hare's "extremity," its response to an existential threat, exposes a vulnerable life common to both human and nonhuman animals – a life held "by the same tenure" as ours. Bartram's account of the young bear's "agony" particularizes suffering that remains hypothetical in Thoreau, but it similarly invokes compassion for a life exposed in extremity (bear life reduced to bare life).

12 Cary Wolfe: *Before the Law. Humans and Other Animals in a Biopolitical Frame.* Chicago: University of Chicago Press 2013, p. 6.

13 Henry David Thoreau: *Walden, Civil Disobedience, and Other Writings.* Ed. by William Rossi, 3rd ed. New York: Norton 2008, p. 145, original emphasis.

14 I discuss this passage at somewhat greater length elsewhere, see Neill Matheson: Thoreau's Inner Animal. In: *Arizona Quarterly* 67,4 (2011), pp. 1–26, esp. pp. 3, 12.

Bartram takes the side of compassion here, but what is equally evident is that compassion fails to prevent killing. This scenario is repeated later in *Travels* in several variants. One such episode begins when Bartram and his companions, "old expert hunters," startle some deer, which take shelter in a grove of trees. Entering the grove, the hunters find the deer now absorbed in innocent play, unaware of their danger: "we beheld them thoughtless and secure, flouncing in a sparkling pond, in a green meadow or cove beyond the point; some were lying down on their sides in the cool waters, whilst others were prancing like young kids; the young bucks in playsome sport" (174). The idyllic, innocent scene with its vision of precarious happiness and sociability reawakens Bartram's sympathies. As before, he attempts to intercede to forestall killing: "I endeavoured to plead for their lives; but my old friend, though he was a sensible rational and good sort of man, would not yield to my philosophy" (174). Approaching the deer stealthily, with the combination of guile and predatory intent that typically precedes killing in this text, the "lucky old hunter" kills an especially "princely buck" (174). Bartram's intervention is again ineffectual. His friend embodies a rational, pragmatic common sense ("sensible" in this context), which is incapable of recognizing affinity with a "brute creature" (21). He is resistant to empathetic identification with nonhuman animals. Unlike the earlier episode with the young bear, the hunter here is more positively characterized, but in both scenes Bartram's compassion is crucially set off against the unyielding lack of sympathy of a companion whose beliefs are understood to be culturally normative. Bartram acknowledges that he is a "good sort of man" (174), but his benevolence is clearly limited to the sphere of other humans.

Bartram noticeably shifts to a more neutral, matter-of-fact tone to describe the curious operations that dispose of the deer's body: "he opened the body, took out the entrails, and placed the carcase in the fork of a tree, casting his frock or hunting shirt over it to protect it from the vultures and crows" (175). This turn to unsentimental description characteristic of natural history writing ends the earlier episode with the bears as well ("The next morning, after the slaughter of the bears, whilst my companions were striking our tent, I resolved to make a little botanical excursion alone [...]" [22]). Similarly, in a chapter that recounts various encounters with rattlesnakes, Bartram recalls his father's attempt to intercede on behalf of a rattlesnake, after a younger William is narrowly saved from being bitten: "My father pleaded for his life, but our guide was inexorable, saying he never spared the life of a rattle snake, and killed him; my father took his skin and fangs" (224). The attempt to intercede, after its failure, quickly gives way to the naturalist's curiosity and acquisitiveness.

Bartram also tells the story of his own killing of a rattlesnake, again while traveling with his father on an earlier expedition to Florida. His father points out a rattlesnake coiled to strike directly in William's path, so that "another step forward would have put my life in his power" (224). Bartram's fear and anger quickly lead to violence: "The fright and perturbation of my spirits at once excited resentment; at that time I was entirely insensible to gratitude or mercy. I instantly cut off a little sapling, and soon dispatched him" (224). Bartram describes himself as possessed by violent passions here, impelled to violence almost involuntarily, and "insensible" to more compassionate feelings; he briefly exemplifies the killer's insensibility. The claim that this is an entirely impulsive act of passion is perhaps somewhat compromised by Bartram's actions immediately afterward: fastening a vine around the snake's neck, he drags it through the camp "in triumph" (225). Though he tries this snake's flesh when it is cooked, he is later overcome by regret:

> I, however, was sorry after killing the serpent, when coolly recollecting every circumstance. He certainly had it in his power to kill me almost instantly, and I make no doubt but that he was conscious of it. I promised myself that I would never again be accessary to the death of a rattle snake, which promise I have invariably kept to. (225)

At odds with his own violent actions, which he has been unable to prevent himself from committing, he feels remorse at the killing of a creature that he now believes to have been intelligent, and to have consciously withheld violence itself. He vows not to be on the side of such killing again, though his claim to have "invariably kept to" this promise seems to be belied by the previous chapter, which provides an extended, dramatic account of his killing of a rattlesnake during his later 1870s expedition.[15] The episode ends with an abrupt shift from remorse to

15 Bartram does recount one successful intervention, in which he intercedes to save the life of a rattlesnake near his camp, which similarly has declined to bite him or his companions, even though they have walked past it during the night. Though there is initial resistance, he is able to persuade the others to leave "the generous serpent" "undisturbed" (223).

unsentimental description: he remarks that rattlesnakes can easily be killed with "a stick no thicker than a man's thumb" (225), and then turns to reporting the natural history of other snake species found in the region.

These episodes have in common not only the failure of compassion to prevent killing, but also the sense that the scenes they portray are sharply demarcated from the narrative that surrounds them: Bartram recounts an anecdote featuring violence and excited sensibility, and then moves on to other matters, seemingly without any remaining trace of lingering bad feeling. The scenes seem to function more as tableaus designed to illustrate aroused feeling, rather than as stages of a larger argument that builds towards concrete conclusions.[16] Nevertheless, they do reveal that his eyes are repeatedly drawn to animal cruelty and killing. He is alert to and troubled by the violence that he witnesses in others and sometimes in himself, and feels compelled to record it in his narrative. Late in the book, his party comes upon "a litter of young wolves, to which giving chase, we soon caught one of them, it being entangled in the high grass; one of our people caught it by the hind legs, and another beat out its brains with the but of his gun, – barbarous sport!" He then calmly notes that "this creature was about half the size of a small cur-dog, and quite black" (319). At another point, an alligator wanders into the camp, providing a "rare piece of sport" to the men who gather around it: "Some took fire-brands and cast them at his head, whilst others formed javelins of saplings, pointed and hardened with fire; these they thrust down his throat into his bowels, which caused the monster to roar and bellow hideously" (210). Bartram does not indicate whether he himself attempted to intercede in this scene of torture, but he may well have been among those arguing for a merciful death:

> Some were for putting an end to his life and sufferings with a rifle ball, but the majority thought this would too soon deprive them of the diversion and pleasure of exercising their various inventions of torture: they at length however grew tired, and agreed in one opinion, that he had suffered sufficiently; and put an end to his existence. (210)

16 It is true that this episodic quality is more generally characteristic of Bartram's narrative. Christoph Irmscher points out that the narrative's "logic" is primarily "visual rather than chronological"; animated scenes unfold sequentially in what he aptly calls Bartram's "wonderful theater of vision" (Christoph Irmscher: *The Poetics of Natural History. From John Bartram to William James*. New Brunswick: Rutgers UP 1999, pp. 40–41).

He comments that the event illustrates "the intrepidity and subtilty of those voracious, formidable animals" (210), though clearly the humans are more dangerous in this instance.[17]

Bartram's division of participants in this scene into "some" who want mercy and "the majority" who insist on prolonging cruel pleasure reinforces the sense throughout the narrative that his expressions of opposition to cruelty and killing place him in a distinct minority, or isolate him altogether. The prevailing beliefs of his companions and in his culture more broadly take for granted that the killing of nonhuman animals is a normative and ethical activity, except when engaged in cruelly, wastefully, or purely for pleasure, and for the most part even then. Bartram's reservations about killing place him at odds with this common sense. His repeated story of compassion's failure to prevent killing represents the marginality of his views in terms of powerlessness, helplessness. (He is helpless primarily in the sense of being unable to remedy the situation, but perhaps also in being 'moved' involuntarily by compassion, helpless to resist it.) In his influential *The Animal That Therefore I Am*, Jacques Derrida argues for a shift of focus from abilities to inability in thinking about nonhuman animals. He cites Jeremy Bentham's question, "Can they suffer?," which Bentham substitutes for speculations about animals' capacity for language or reason. Derrida suggests that Bentham's question implies "a certain passivity," "a sufferance, a passion, a not-being-able," which replaces the traditional philosophical concern with abilities: "'Can they suffer?' amounts to asking 'can they *not be able*?'"[18] This inability or "nonpower" is the basis for a recognition of the "finitude that we share with animals," and so for "the experience of compassion," which Derrida associates with shared vulnerability, a vulnerability open to the suffering of others, and itself a kind of suffering ("the anguish of this vulnerability and the vulnerability of this anguish").[19]

Bartram's own helplessness in the face of suffering might be taken to reflect an awareness of shared vulnerability. His helplessness is likewise

17 Bartram writes extensively about the alarming abundance of alligators in some locations he travels through, and about his own repeated narrow escapes from huge, aggressive individuals; these are among the most famous passages in *Travels*. For the fullest discussion of alligators in the text, see McCown: Crocodilian Transmission.

18 Jacques Derrida: *The Animal That Therefore I Am*, trans. from the French by David Wills. New York: Fordham UP 2008, p. 28, original emphasis.

19 Ibid.

a form of suffering, as if he finds himself a vulnerable animal for a moment, whether or not his life is directly threatened in these scenes (as it is at various points in the narrative). One might even say that it is less that compassion fails than that failure and inability allow compassion to be fully realized in these moments. If Bartram represented himself as interceding effectively, compassion would be short-lived, exhausted in the intervention that alleviates suffering, rather than lingering as a kind of suspended question, in spite of the narrative's shift of focus to other matters. It is certainly possible to view Bartram's helplessness as in keeping with the harmless, slightly foolish persona of the naturalist, which masks a less innocent relation to power.[20] I want to suggest instead that Bartram's repeated staging of scenes of helpless compassion takes the place of more overt, sustained argument in *Travels*, signaling not only his growing uneasiness with the casual killing of nonhuman animals, but also his sense of powerlessness in the face of overwhelming contrary popular sentiment, a prevailing common sense that naturalizes killing.

The philosopher Cora Diamond's reflections on vulnerability and 'exposure' in relation to nonhuman animals may help to illuminate these ideas in Bartram. In "The Difficulty of Reality and the Difficulty of Philosophy," she considers J.M. Coetzee's character Elizabeth Costello as transfixed by the knowledge of animal suffering: "She is a woman haunted by the horror of what we do to animals. We see her as wounded by this knowledge, this horror, and by the knowledge of how unhaunted others are. The wound marks her and isolates her."[21] Diamond locates in Costello what she characterizes as "a repudiation of the everyday," "a sense of being shouldered out from our ways of

20 I have in mind here Mary Louise Pratt's well-known characterization of the naturalist as a "benign, often homely figure," in apparent contrast to the conquistador – in effect a friendly face in colonialism's good cop-bad cop routine. Mary Louise Pratt: *Imperial Eyes. Travel Writing and Transculturation*. New York: Routledge 1992, pp. 33–34, also pp. 27–28. Thomas Hallock makes the same connection, arguing that *Travels* fits only to a limited extent with Pratt's notion of "anti-conquest," which is not adequate to Bartram's "slippery position" working the "in-between" spaces of the "early national frontier" (Thomas Hallock: "On the Borders of a New World." Ecology, Frontier Plots, and Imperial Elegy in William Bartram's *Travels*. In: *South Atlantic Review* 66,4 (2001), pp. 109–133, here p. 112). Also see Irmscher: *The Poetics of Natural History*, p. 6.

21 Cora Diamond: The Difficulty of Reality and the Difficulty of Philosophy. In: Ead. / Stanley Cavell / John McDowell / Ian Hacking / Cary Wolfe: *Philosophy and Animal Life*. New York: Columbia UP 2008, pp. 43–89, here p. 46.

thinking and speaking by a torment of reality."[22] Bartram too can be described as being "shouldered out" by the violence he witnesses from habitual ways of thinking, from the common sense that takes killing for granted. Diamond proposes that philosophical argument can be seen as a "deflection" that distances us from bodily vulnerability, from "our own sense of what it is to be a living animal."[23] The absence of "general principles" that would clarify the moral significance of animal suffering results in a kind of exposure: "Our 'exposure' in the case of animals lies in there being nothing but our own responsibility, our own making the best of it"; "we are thrown into finding something we can live with, and it may at best be a kind of bitter-tasting compromise," leaving us "endless room for double-dealing and deceit."[24] In my reading, Bartram is exposed in a somewhat similar way: rejecting philosophical tradition and widely held cultural beliefs, he occupies a position that is inconsistent and compromised, objecting strongly at times to acts of cruelty and killing, but eating game, noting or even collecting parts of dead specimens, and sometimes himself participating in killing. Though he alludes to "my philosophy" and appeals at times to principles, he does not articulate a consistent principled position; he is left on his own to sort out his responsibility, "making the best of it."

Diamond suggests that our exposure to animal suffering may be experienced as profoundly isolating:

> The awareness we each have of being a living body, being "alive to the world," carries with it exposure to the bodily sense of vulnerability to death, sheer animal vulnerability, the vulnerability we share with them. This vulnerability is capable of panicking us. To be able to acknowledge it at all, let alone as shared, is wounding; but acknowledging it as shared with other animals, in the presence of what we do to them, is capable not only of panicking one but also of isolating one.[25]

Though Bartram presents himself as a sociable, friendly figure, on good terms with almost everyone, he understands himself in *Travels* as separated from others by his views on the killing of nonhuman animals. One could argue perhaps that his awareness of cruelty and killing rarely seems

22 Diamond: The Difficulty of Reality and the Difficulty of Philosophy, p. 71.

23 Ibid., p. 53.

24 Ibid., p. 72. As illustration, Diamond points to Costello's comment that her vegetarianism is based less on moral conviction than the desire to save her soul, and that she has leather shoes and a leather purse (ibid., pp. 72–73).

25 Ibid., p. 74.

to be experienced as deeply wounding in the book. However, a later text, unpublished in his lifetime, seems to attest to feeling wounded and isolated by his knowledge of the human treatment of animals, as well as suggesting something like the "bitter-tasting compromise" Diamond alludes to.

Bartram's unfinished manuscript essay on "The Dignity of Human Nature," likely written within a few years of the publication of *Travels*, returns to the topic of nonhuman animals in the context of its meditation on human reason and virtue.[26] In fact, his consideration of "animal nature" takes over the middle of the essay; the energy and seriousness with which he engages with it may suggest that this is where his interest really lies. He introduces this ostensible subtopic as if it were a longstanding personal preoccupation: "I consider it a duty incumbent on me to declare my Sentiments freely, on a subject tho of Little moment to Mankind in general at this time, Yet to me of much importance. Namely of the *Dignity of Animal Nature* with respect to the Station or Degree they hold, in the grand System of Creation in this World."[27] He emphasizes that his deep conviction about the importance of this subject places him at odds with "Mankind," which holds it of "Little moment." His sense that this is a radical, heterodox position, making him a kind of lone voice, underlies the discussion that follows. He goes on to acknowledge, following Linnaeus, as in the introduction to *Travels*, that "Man" has been placed "first in the Animal Kingdome,"[28] but the essay in fact profoundly questions this hierarchy, including the supposed differences that it would be based on. He cites Buffon's claim that animals possess only instinct, not rationality, in order to argue that this "truly Wonderful Instinct, An Intuitive Knowledge, or Understanding,"[29] is in many ways superior to reason, or is itself a better form of reason: in fact, humans "act most Rationally & virtuously when our Actions seem to operate from simple instinct, or approach nearest to the manners of

26 William Bartram: The Dignity of Human Nature. In: Hallock / Hoffman (eds): *William Bartram, The Search for Nature's Design*, pp. 348–358. The editors date this essay as "probably written in the mid-1790s." I follow their practice of using the title "The Dignity of Human Nature" for this fragmentary, incomplete document. See ibid., p. 348.

27 Ibid., p. 351.

28 Ibid., p. 352.

29 Ibid.

the *Animal creation*."[30] Even so, he asserts that every animal species has "a Language," and therefore "Intelligence,"[31] and that we have no certain knowledge that animals lack "Intellectual Powers."[32]
The essay's real animus though is against the complacent assumption that humans belong not only to an entirely different ontological order, but also to a superior *moral* order. As Laurel Ode-Schneider notes in her introduction to the essay, the phrase "the dignity of human nature" becomes increasingly ironic as Bartram reiterates it, as if the consideration of nonhuman animals calls any claims for human dignity into question.[33] He seems to mock the very priority of the human:

> I do not say that Man is not the first order of Beings in this World And accordingly his formulation is such as enables him to subjugate, & even tyrannize over every other Animal, & probably would long ere this have destroyd the whole Animal creation, if his Arms were not withheld, by the Supreme Creator & preserver, but this does not prove that because he is the most powerful that he is the most divine.[34]

He implies that being first in the order of creation only means having the most power to "subjugate" and destroy, rather than any higher moral status. The excesses of human violence contradict the belief that humans are more divine than other living things. Inspired by Quaker theology, Bartram asserts that there is a "Divine Intelligence" that "penetrates & animates the Univers," constituting the "Immortal Soul" of all "Living moving beings," even "Vegetables" and the "Elements." Considering human nature, Bartram avows that his "Soul revolts, is destroyed" by the argument "that Man who is guilty of more mischief & Wickedness than all the other Animal together in this World, should be exclusively endued with the knowledge of the Creator, & capable of expressing his love gratitude & homage."[35] In spite of its nominal theme, the essay is scathing in its criticism of human nature. Humans are compared unfavorably to nonhuman creatures in terms of our propensity for

30 Bartram: The Dignity of Human Nature, p. 353.

31 Ibid., p. 355.

32 Ibid., p. 352.

33 Laurel Ode-Schneider. "The Dignity of Human Nature." William Bartram and the Great Chain of Being. Introduction. In: Hallock / Hoffman (eds): *William Bartram: The Search for Nature's Design*, pp. 340–346, here p. 345.

34 Bartram: The Dignity of Human Nature, pp. 352–353.

35 Ibid., p. 353.

violence and domination (man "Acts the part of an Absolute Tyrant"[36]) and our penchant for deceit: "Man is cruel, Hypocritical, a Disembler, his dissemmulation, exceeds that of any being we are acquainted with for he disembles, disemmulation itself."[37] Throughout the essay, Bartram repeatedly condemns dissimulation, which together with violence is for him at the root of human wickedness: "Nay the Whole of Human or Worldly Wisdom is a continual Series or practise of Deceit, fraud, dissimulation & Hypocrissy, & the more Any Man or Woman approaches to Honesty & simplicity, the more he is accounted a Fool."[38] If the association of the human with duplicity and social pretense is traditional, Bartram amplifies it intensely here, but he also avoids turning it into a binary that would exclude nonhuman animals by definition, denying them the intelligence necessary to practice deception. Animals engage in dissimulation also, but only to protect themselves or their offspring, or to acquire food.[39] (Derrida argues that Western philosophy following Descartes has consistently denied that animals have "the power to *respond* – to *pretend*, to *lie* [...]"[40]) Bartram's essay, ostensibly an exploration of human dignity, offers a caustic critique of human dishonesty, iniquity, and destructiveness, especially in our toxic relation to other forms of life. What is remarkable is the shift in tone from the generally optimistic, benevolent outlook of *Travels*. In the essay, Bartram's view of human nature and its impact on the rest of the living world has become much darker. Given the chance, he suggests, humans would destroy "the whole Animal creation," in effect a mass extinction of other forms of life. Now that there is overwhelming evidence of anthropogenic mass extinction, making it impossible to believe that any "preserver" holds back the "Arms" of human destructiveness, this view has come to seem remarkably prescient.

Perhaps the most arresting pages of Derrida's *The Animal That Therefore I Am* are devoted to a sketch of the transformation in the human treatment of nonhuman animals over the last two centuries. He describes

36 Ibid., p. 355.

37 Ibid.

38 Ibid., pp. 355–356.

39 Ibid., p. 349. As I have noted, even in *Travels*, Bartram sometimes observes cunning animal predators, employing artifice to capture their prey, but the stealthy human hunters are more dangerous, cruel, and wasteful in their killing.

40 Derrida: *The Animal That Therefore I Am*, p. 33, original emphases.

an extraordinary acceleration and intensification in the subjection of the "living animal,"[41] for example through the industrialization of meat production, leading to unprecedented violence and cruelty – to what amounts to "animal genocides."[42] He points out that "no one can deny the *unprecedented* proportions of this subjection," and that "no one can deny seriously, or for very long, that men do all they can in order to dissimulate this cruelty or to hide it from themselves."[43] Bartram is of course situated historically on the brink of the two-century period Derrida describes. He belongs to a time in which "traditional forms of treatment of the animal," such as "hunting, fishing, domestication, training, or traditional exploitation of animal energy," are still largely in place, before being "turned upside down" by new developments in control and intervention.[44] Yet Bartram recognizes the enormously destructive potential of the dominant ideology governing human relations with nonhuman animals in his time, and the way this ideology works by naturalizing its values, turning them into the common sense of the "good sort of men" around him, and thus dissimulating its violence and cruelty. His awareness of a nascent human potential for exterminating violence may account for the darkness and even bitterness of the "Dignity" essay, and for his growing impatience with philosophical arguments that would justify the subordination of animals. This impatience is visible in his comments on "the general opinion of philosophers" in the introduction to *Travels*, and in his mocking of philosophers with "Aristocratic" pretensions about "the *Dignity of Human Nature*" in the later essay, but perhaps especially in a passage in his 1792 letter to his friend Benjamin Smith Barton:

> Is it not my Friend remarkeble, very remarkeble, how cautious, even Great men and Philosophers are of allowing to Animals the power & use of *Reason*, They seeme to put invention to the Rack in endeavouring to establish Terms, to exclude from them the possession of that divine faculty, diffused impartially throughout all Animal Nature. What are they afraid of? that the Sperits of Animals will rise up in judgment against them for killing & eating of them?[45]

41 Derrida: *The Animal That Therefore I Am*, p. 25.

42 Ibid., p. 26.

43 Ibid., pp. 25–26, original emphasis.

44 Ibid., p. 25.

45 William Bartram to Benjamin Smith Barton, December 29, 1792, p. 169.

In this ironic, clear-sighted assessment, an entire tradition of philosophical arguments about nonhuman animals has been motivated not only by the wish to justify subordination, but by the fear of what undoing that justification would entail.

Derrida invokes compassion as a crucial response to the history of violence he describes, asserting that we are in the midst of an "unequal struggle, a war (whose inequality could one day be reversed) being waged between, on the one hand, those who violate not only animal life but even and also this sentiment of compassion, and, on the other hand, those who appeal for an irrefutable testimony to this pity."[46] As I have argued, Bartram repeatedly takes the side of compassion in *Travels*. This text together with his later essay place him among the "minority, weak, marginal voices, little assured of their discourse" whom Derrida describes as speaking out against animal cruelty, "in order to awaken us to our responsibilities and our obligations vis-à-vis the living in general, and precisely to this fundamental compassion [...]."[47]

In spite of the pessimism about human nature that runs through the "Dignity" essay, Bartram offers a final hopeful note. Near the essay's end, he proposes a return to foundations, a regrounding that would aim to address the causes of violence and corruption: "Let us begin at the Source since we cannot expect to have pure & salubrious streams unless, we cleans & purify the Fountain or Source."[48] This vision of returning to the source of clear waters recalls the many remarkably transparent natural springs, basins, and fountains that Bartram discovers throughout the Southeast in *Travels*. Their exceptional clarity sometimes furnishes a view of many varieties of fish in apparently peaceful coexistence. In one especially spectacular spring, he sees "innumerable bands of fish," including such predatory species as the "voracious crocodile" and "devouring garfish," "all in their separate bands and communities, with free and unsuspicious intercourse performing their evolutions: there are no signs of enmity, no attempt to devour each other" (150). The transparency of the "crystalline waters" creates an optical illusion: the "amazing and delightful scene, though real, appears at first but as a piece of excellent painting; there seems no medium; you imagine the picture to

46 Derrida: *The Animal That Therefore I Am*, pp. 28–29.
47 Ibid., pp. 26–27.
48 Bartram: The Dignity of Human Nature, p. 356.

be within a few inches of your eyes," so that it seems possible to reach out and touch the fish, "or put your finger upon the crocodile's eye" (151).[49] The dreamlike quality of this scene, in which the boundary between representation and reality is blurred, extends to its image of idyllic, peaceful coexistence: "although this paradise of fish may seem to exhibit a just representation of the peaceable and happy state of nature which existed before the fall, yet in reality it is a mere representation" (151). The fish are the same creatures to be found in other bodies of water, but here the water "is so perfectly clear and transparent, it places them all on an equality with regard to their ability to injure or escape from one another." Bartram explains that predators "take their prey by surprise; secreting themselves under covert or in ambush," whereas "here is no covert, no ambush; here the trout freely passes by the very nose of the alligator, and laughs in his face" (151). In the absence of the conditions for dissimulation, where motives are entirely apparent, it becomes possible to imagine an end to violence. Later he observes a similar scene in another stream, as if this is a recurrent fantasy. In the "turbid" water near the bank "there is eternal war, or rather slaughter," but in the "swift channel," where the water is transparent, all is calm: "when those different tribes of fish are in the transparent channel, their very nature seems absolutely changed; for here is neither desire to destroy nor persecute, but all seems peace and friendship. Do they agree on a truce, a suspension of hostilities? or by some secret divine influence, is desire taken away?" (195) Bartram dreams of a clear, pure space, free of violence, removed from the murky waters where killing takes place, achievable perhaps only through the elimination of desire itself.

49 Irmscher discusses this passage, focusing especially on its "trompe l'oeil" effect. Irmscher: *The Poetics of Natural History*, p. 41.

The Ends of Man

The Zooanthropological Imaginary and the Animal Geographies of Westward Expansion in Antebellum America

Dominik Ohrem

> Passing across borders or the ends of man I come or surrender to the animal, to the animal in itself, to the animal in me and the animal at unease with itself.[1]

> Animality remains a horizon of the human, that of its loss or escape outside of itself.[2]

In the unusually cold winter of 1818, New Hampshire lawyer Estwick Evans left behind the comforts of his home to embark on an arduous "pedestrious tour" through the Michigan and Illinois Territory to the Great Lakes region and other parts of what was then still referred to as 'the West.' Travelling westward, we learn, Evans sought to "acquire the simplicity, native feelings, and virtues of savage life; to divest myself of the factitious habits, prejudices and imperfections of civilization" and "to find, amidst the solitude and grandeur of the western wilds, more

1 Jacques Derrida: *The Animal That Therefore I Am*, trans. from the French by David Wills. New York: Fordham UP 2008, p. 3.

2 Dominique Lestel: Hybrid Communities. In: *Angelaki* 19,3 (2014), pp. 61–73, here p. 62.

correct views of human nature and of the true interests of man."[3] To anyone who might come up with the valid question why he decided to begin his journey in February in the dead of winter, Evans had an answer as well: "The season of snows," he explains, is preferable for those wishing to "experience the pleasure of suffering, and the novelty of danger."[4] In preparation and as part of the accoutrements for his Western trip, Evans picked an outfit that, despite its obvious practicality, seems rather peculiar: "a close dress consisting of buffalo skins" with "epaulettes made of the long hair of the animal," an "Indian apron [...] covered with fine bear skin" buckled around his waist, a fur cap and fur gloves, and "moccasons" made of deer-skin.[5] (Fig. 1) Somewhat unsurprisingly, Evans dubiously fashionable transformation into a bipedal fur-bearer is met with a not always welcome amount of curiosity that at times made him wish he was "less conspicuous,"[6] with some even warning him that his "mode of dress" might result in him being mistaken for an actual nonhuman fur-bearer and shot by hunters on his way through the forested wilderness parts of the country.[7] But despite the isolation, the discomforts and the many dangers – human, animal or environmental – that might be a threat to 'civilized' Americans travelling through the regions of the early West, Evans remained undeterred, even exhilarated, for it was "in the season of danger" that "the human soul triumphs in the conviction of its own indestructibility."[8]

Evans' Western journey and his comparatively little-known written account are one of the earlier nineteenth-century expressions of white Eastern American imaginings and experiences of Western wilderness environments and concomitant fantasies of (temporarily) escaping the 'artifices' of civilization. At the same time, Evans' narrative also anticipates the way in which Manifest Destiny's collective vision of a

3 Estwick Evans: *A Pedestrious Tour, of Four Thousand Miles through the Western States and Territories, During the Winter and Spring of 1818*. Concord: Joseph C. Spear 1819, p. 6.

4 Ibid.

5 Ibid., p. 7. "I think a garment or two of Buffalo or some other warm skin, to be worn occasionally," Evans remarks on the practical advantages of his mode of clothing given the severity of winter in the region, "would [...] save many a man from rheumatism, and even from being frozen to death" (ibid., pp. 27–28).

6 Ibid., p. 26.

7 Ibid., p. 35.

8 Ibid., pp. 89–90.

nation-building process that would gradually encompass most of the continent drew on, and found its expression in, individual narratives of perilous adventure and rugged perseverance on and beyond the frontiers of American society. After the end of the War of 1812, the United States entered what is sometimes referred to as the Age of Manifest Destiny, a period of unprecedented territorial expansion into the regions west of the Mississippi that had been foreshadowed by the purchase of the enormous Louisiana Territory from France in 1803 and a number of subsequent scientific-military expeditions, most famously those of Meriwether Lewis and William Clark (1804–06), Zebulon Pike (1806–07), and Stephen H. Long (1819–20). Even though earlier proponents of the exploration and settlement of the trans-Mississippi West such as Thomas Jefferson could hardly have imagined the rapidity of territorial expansion – Jefferson believed that it would take more than one hundred generations until American settlement reached all the way to the Pacific –, early on the West became a fertile discursive and imaginary environment, a vast domain of untold and untapped economic, political and cultural potential. And indeed, while often commenting critically on the prospects of westward emigration and the risks it posed to both the physical and the economic health of westering individuals and families, Evans no doubt echoed the expectations of many (white) Americans of the time with his estimation that "the prevailing spirit of emigration, from the maritime to the inland frontier, will have a very beneficial influence" and that "great and permanent advantages will arise from the settlement of our western states and territories."[9]

And yet, antebellum visions of the growth of an American 'empire of liberty' (in Jefferson's famous phrasing) and the rampant triumphalism of Manifest Destiny in the 1830s and 1840s notwithstanding, westward expansion also produced a persistent undercurrent of cultural anxiety that continued to unsettle aspirations towards continental dominance and at times even challenged the very desirability of further territorial expansion. While antebellum skepticism of, or outright opposition to, territorial expansion was a multifaceted phenomenon, one long-standing concern focused on the supposedly decivilizing effects of Western wilderness geographies on both individuals and the character of American society as a whole. Insightful

9 Ibid., p. 23.

Fig. 1
Estwick Evans in his buffalo dress, leaning on his rifle, together with the two dogs who accompanied him on his Western journey, only to be "destroyed by wolves" (p. 7).

Frontispiece of Estwick Evans: *A Pedestrious Tour, of Four Thousand Miles through the Western States and Territories, During the Winter and Spring of 1818.* Concord: Joseph C. Spear 1819.

scholarship has addressed this aspect in terms of contemporary ideas about the environmental malleability of race and the supposed danger of racial or civilizational decline because of the 'lure' of the frontier and the absorption of an increasing number of white Americans into 'savage' Western environments.[10] What figures as the particular point of departure for this chapter, however, is the fact that such concerns about the prospects and risks of westward expansion were frequently articulated in the language of animality and human-animal difference, as many contemporaries wondered how the often unpredictable forms of environmental and animal agency and the relations between (civilized) humans and (wild) animals in the sociospatial arrangements of the antebellum West affected those Americans that worked there for extended periods of time or even lived there permanently. Evans' furry metamorphosis may have been a "constant source of amusement" to his contemporaries in "the settled parts of the country,"[11] his animalistic exterior merely a façade which, half-practically and half-humorously, enveloped a stable, unshakable core of refined humanity and as such only served to underscore his status as a specimen of hegemonic white civilization. But as more and more Americans traveled or emigrated to the West, and as Western life became more prominent in antebellum cultural productions, the bodies, behaviors and lifeways of Western humans were regarded not merely with curiosity but also with anxiety and concern, pointing to the fact that (to paraphrase the Derridean epigram to this chapter) self-identified civilized Americans were indeed animals significantly at unease with themselves.

As I want to argue here, such contemporary anxieties about the extent to which Western environments challenged or subverted the supposed ontological bifurcation between human and animal worlds serve to highlight the broader significance of animality in the context of westward expansion and the ways in which the figure of the animal – both

10 See, for example, Richard Slotkin: *Regeneration Through Violence. The Mythology of the American Frontier, 1600–1860*. Middletown: Wesleyan UP 1973; Daniel P. Barr: "A Monster So Brutal." Simon Girty and the Degenerative Myth of the American Frontier, 1783–1900. In: *Essays in History* 40 (1998). http://www.essaysinhistory.com/articles/2012/114 (accessed August 15, 2016); Conevery Bolton Valencius: *The Health of the Country. How American Settlers Understood Themselves and Their Land*. New York: Basic 2004; Katy L. Chiles: *Transformable Race. Surprising Metamorphoses in the Literature of Early America*. Oxford: Oxford UP 2014.

11 Evans: *A Pedestrious Tour*, p. 26.

as an elusive abstraction and a fleshy, living being – inhabited and traversed the discursive, imaginary and material environments of the antebellum West. In turn, Western environments functioned as spaces of ontological speculation and experimentation that influenced shifting conceptions of animality and humanity in an era in which the 'Darwinian revolution' loomed on the horizon. From antebellum times onward, Western environments, their human and nonhuman inhabitants, and the relations between them thus played an important role in what I will refer to as the 'zooanthropological imaginary' of nineteenth-century American culture, a nexus of different and at times conflicting knowledges and imaginings that was not limited to specialist debates in scientific circles but also, and more importantly, extended into the broader cultural sphere through the writings of (amateur) historians, novelists, journalists, businessmen, explorers, travelers and others in a social environment that featured a burgeoning print culture. I use the term 'zooanthropological' in this chapter to indicate the way in which the irresistible figure of the animal inhabits every conception of anthropological difference and human uniqueness. Historically speaking, what Jacques Derrida has famously brought to our attention as the 'question of the animal' has always been inextricably bound up with the 'question of the human' – so much so, in fact, that articulating the one always already, in a mode of inevitable co-articulation, also evokes the other.

The Zooanthropological Imaginary and the Antebellum (Human) Animal

> What an heterogeneous animal is man! — sometimes exalted to an approach towards divinity, sometimes debased to lower than brutality: — A perpetual struggle between the essence and the dregs.[12]

Many contemporaries would likely have agreed with Evans' assertion that the animal world and "the subject of Zoology" offered not only "an inexhaustible source of instruction and entertainment" from which "man may derive important lessons in relation to industry, economy and perseverance" but that it also embodied and displayed "all the passions

12 Fortescue Cuming: *Cuming's Tour to the Western Country* [1810], ed. by Reuben Gold Thwaites. Cleveland: A. H. Clark 1904, p. 223.

and affections incident to human nature" and thus had an "intimate connexion" with the "moral nature" supposedly unique to the complex interiority of human beings.[13] In the decades leading up to Charles Darwin's *On the Origin of Species* (1859) and its unsettling implications for traditional notions of the human-animal boundary, in a debate that spanned across the discursive domains of natural history, (natural) philosophy, theology, politics, literature and other fields, contemporary zooanthropological thought grappled with contested issues such as the boundary between human and animal life, the fixity or malleability of human nature, the importance and fragility of human sociality, and the supposed uniqueness of human moral and reasoning capacities. Due to the increasing popularity of natural history and natural philosophy, articles that addressed issues discussed in these fields were frequently included in general interest magazines like the *North American Review* or *Harper's Magazine*. The growing number of (sometimes short-lived) periodicals published especially from the 1820s onward functioned less as passive receptacles of specialist knowledges or unidirectional avenues for the cultural reception of contemporary scientific, theological and other debates but in fact actively shaped the debates themselves.[14] An 1845 article published in the *Knickerbocker*, for example, pseudonymously authored by "One of the People," defines the study of human nature as an inquiry into "all that essentially belongs to man, physically, intellectually and morally, and whether to him exclusively, or in common with other beings."[15] We learn that the human being is an "omniverous" migratory mammal who, "though for the most part terrestrial, is, under some circumstances, aquatic" and whose "physical nature seems to partake of that of the cock, swine, and East-Indian dog."[16] But while (perhaps to smooth over these somewhat humbling affiliations) the article characteristically goes on to define the human's "intellectual and moral character" as the proper subject of the study of human nature in contrast to "the study of anatomy, physiology, phrenology,

13 Evans: *A Pedestrious Tour*, p. 182.

14 The period between 1825 and 1850 was already recognized by contemporaries as the (first) "golden age of periodicals." Frank Luther Mott: *A History of American Magazines, 1741–1850*, vol. 1. Cambridge: Belknap Press of Harvard UP 1970, p. 341.

15 "One of the People": Hints on Human Nature, Style, Etc. In: *The Knickerbocker* 26,6 (December 1845), pp. 536–543, here p. 536.

16 Ibid.

and gastrology,"[17] it remains unclear to what extent these capacities can in fact be assigned to the sphere of human life alone. This is because it is not only the "passions and affections" that humans share with other living creatures, but, if the human is indeed "an intellectual being," this as well is a characteristic shared with the rest of the animal world, as is evident in the fact that the human, "like the bee and beaver, builds, lays up stores of provisions for winter, or against time of need; and like these animals, forms communities and establishes governments."[18] This begs the obvious question: If humans have all of these characteristics at least to some extent in common with nonhuman beings, doesn't the study of human nature threaten to lose the specificity of its subject – or indeed its subject as such? Even though we learn that "in matters of conscience or moral sense, and religion, man is said to be *sui generis*,"[19] whether or not the study of human nature is not in fact always already the study of more-than-human nature is a question that remains unaddressed by the article's mostly anecdotal line of argument.

Related to arguments about the human as a being uniquely endowed with rational and/or moral capacities was another quality sometimes employed in definitions of human exceptionalism: the uniqueness of human sociality. As John Quincy Adams argues in the *American Whig Review*, while "[i]t is the property of all animated nature to be *gregarious*," humans alone may be considered truly social beings. "The beasts of the forest and the fields, are drawn by the laws of their nature together in *herds* – the birds of the air in *flocks* – the fishes of the ocean in *sculls*; reptiles *cluster* in the recesses of the earth, and the insect tribes no sooner quicken from their shells into life, than they people the sunbeam in swarms."[20] But, Adams argues, the *purpose* of this nonhuman propensity to congregate for the most part remains a mystery to us, because it doesn't seem to have one.

> It is neither conducive to the subsistence of the individual nor to the continuance of the species. It affords no means of intellectual communion, where there is no mind to cultivate; no accession of strength to resist the destructive power of the elements, or the ravin of superior animals. The pigeon, surrounded by myriads

17 "One of the People", p. 536.

18 Ibid.

19 Ibid, pp. 536–537.

20 John Quincy Adams: Society and Civilization. In: *American Whig Review* 2,1 (1845), pp. 80–89, here p. 80, original emphases.

> of others, is as defenceless as in solitude against the talons of the hawk. There are in natural history a few instances of animals, perhaps exaggerated by human wonder, who unite in common labor for a common benefit – like the beaver, the ant and the bee; they are rare examples of animals partaking of the social nature, but not of the principle of progressive improvement. They exercise no powers but such as have always been exercised by their species. Powers untaught and unteachable, and no more vivified with mind, than the tendril that seeks a hook for its support, or the ivy that creeps around the oak.[21]

As the *Knickerbocker* article discussed above indicates, however, Adams' rather Cartesian conception of the nonhuman animal world as governed by an unminded mechanicity or instinctuality, while still shared by many contemporaries, was increasingly being challenged by those who questioned the defining characteristics (though rarely the idea) of human exceptionalism. Even the previously neglected or abjected human animal body, perhaps necessitated by the wider post-Enlightenment acceptance of the human as, at least in his earthly, corporeal existence, part of the animal kingdom, could now be reconceptualized in the service of exceptionalist arguments. Indeed, while still insisting on the importance of an immaterial principle that raised humans above other animals, another article from the *American Whig Review*, published a few years after Adams' piece, explains that even in their *animality*, in their "organic and sensuous attributes," human beings are vastly superior to the rest of the animal world to such an extent that "[f]rom the ape to the man there is no transition, but an abyss of differences."

> In the man first appears the upright figure, beauty of outline, universal grace of motion, smoothness and purity of skin, a countenance equally beautiful in motion or repose; speech, distinct and varied; authority, and skill of hand. [...] His *senses* are infinitely appreciative and delicate; his *instincts* powerful and complete; his *intelligence*, *passion*, and *affection*, incomparably superior to those of any other organized being.[22]

21 Ibid. For Adams, the exceptional sociality of human beings is tied to another supposed aspect of human uniqueness: history, which "must necessarily have reference to the existence and condition of *Man*," and which is, in its nineteenth-century teleological conception, premised on a uniquely human form of sociality defined by the "principle of progressive improvement" (ibid., original emphasis). For the interconnection between humanity and historicity, also see the introduction to this volume.

22 Passions and Intelligence of Men. In: *American Whig Review* 16,95 (1852), pp. 541–551, here p. 541, original emphases.

As this brief selection of examples from antebellum magazines shows, contemporary zooanthropological imaginings were involved in reconfiguring conceptions of humanity and animality in an era of increasing ontological uncertainty, when traditional models of human identity and the metaphysical reassurances that had hitherto underpinned humanity's exalted status were gradually losing influence, and what it meant to be human was perhaps less certain than ever before. I would argue that, on the broader level of antebellum discourse, it was precisely the interplay between 'elevating' animal life (to some extent) and acknowledging human animality (with important reservations and qualifications) that cleared the epistemological and rhetorical grounds for a reaffirmation of human exceptionalism based on a different and more diverse set of parameters. On the other hand, however, this diversity of arguments employed to reconceive the "abyss of differences" between humans and animals in the pre-Darwinian decades, rather than bolstering exceptionalist dogma, also threatened to achieve the opposite: it produced an increasingly ambivalent and polymorphous discursive space in which the metaphysical self-certainty of the human being (or, rather, of Man as its white, 'civilized' incarnation) underwent a disconcerting transformation from a more or less confident claim into an open question.

The conceptual struggle with the human animal also involved otherwise unorthodox antebellum figures such as Henry David Thoreau. Well-known today for his attentive affection towards and interest in nonhuman beings, the variety of "brute neighbors"[23] he encounters during his time at Walden Pond, Thoreau exhibits a perhaps unexpected concern with, and even hostility towards, *human* animal life. In the chapter "Higher Laws" from his 1854 book *Walden*, he offers some remarkable ontological elaborations on the question of human animality. Emphasizing his trademark allegiance to wild(er)ness, he initially reflects in a rather positive tone on his awareness of "an instinct toward a higher, or, as it is named, spiritual life, [...] and another toward a primitive rank and savage one, and I reverence them both."[24] Thoreau acknowledges the way in which both 'instincts' co-animate human existence – they are distinct and perhaps contradictory, but they also complement each other, and it seems that both have their role to play in the development and vicissitudes of human life. It quickly becomes

23 Henry David Thoreau: *Walden*, ed. by J. Lyndon Shanley. Princeton: Princeton UP 1989, p. 223.

24 Ibid., p. 210.

clear, however, that, for Thoreau, it is the spiritual life which represents the true *telos* of both the individual becoming-human that characterizes each person's biographical development and the historical and cultural becoming of the human as a species. Thoreau establishes a hierarchy in which the value of the 'primitive' and the 'savage' is ultimately not determined on its own terms but with regard to its ancillary function for the worthier aspirations towards the 'higher' life. It doesn't take long, then, that Thoreau's conciliatory tone begins to change, perhaps because the vague romanticism of his initial gestures towards a primitive life and his feral fantasies of "ranging the woods, like a half-starved hound, with a strange abandonment"[25] are now confronted with the more tangible question of the animal corporeality of the human. "We are conscious of an animal in us," Thoreau writes, "which awakens in proportion as our higher nature slumbers. It is reptile and sensual, and perhaps cannot be wholly expelled; like the worms which, even in life and health, occupy our bodies."[26] Because the human is continuously threatened by the "inferior and brutish nature to which he [*sic*] is allied," the full realization of the *humanitas* of the human, the not-animal part of the human which supposedly constitutes the human being's true essence or destination, hinges on a practice of anxious spiritual regulation, or even violent exorcism, of the brute within – or, as Thoreau puts it: "He is blessed who is assured that the animal is dying out in him day by day, and the divine being established."[27] The antagonistic relation between the animal and the spiritual nature of the human thus manifests itself in the form of a developmental continuum from 'lower' to 'higher' modes of being, with the former characterized by the prevalence of animal physicality and the latter testimony to the fulfillment of human potentiality, which is attained precisely by emancipating oneself, as far and fully as possible, from all physical demands and necessities. As Simon Glendinning puts it, this "terminal achievement [...] in which man attains to what is most human, human in every part," is the embodiment of the fantasies of disembodiment characteristic of both humanist and Judeo-Christian anthropocentrisms, "the *termination* of

25 Ibid.

26 Ibid., pp. 219–220. For an insightful discussion of the "Higher Laws" chapter and Thoreau's conception of human animality, see Neill Matheson: Thoreau's Inner Animal. In: *Arizona Quarterly* 67,4 (2011), pp. 1–26.

27 Thoreau: *Walden*, p. 220.

man existing as a finite creature – the transcendence of, the freedom from all determination by, human animality."[28]

Echoing models of collective progression from savage to civilized states of social existence inherited from French and Scottish Enlightenment thinkers and their popularization of the 'four-stages theory,' Thoreau explains that "even in civilized communities, the embryo man passes through the hunter stage of development."[29] And, it seems, even in these communities not all humans are equally successful in fully transcending this primitive stage of human life. A case in point is the French-Canadian woodchopper, Alek Therien, who frequently visits Thoreau during his time at Walden Pond and in whom "the animal man chiefly was developed,"[30] while "the intellectual and what is called spiritual man [...] were slumbering as in an infant."[31] Therien's behavior is determined by an "exuberance of animal spirits,"[32] his thinking "primitive" and almost wholly "immersed in his animal life,"[33] and despite Thoreau's appreciation of the occasional glimmers of unrefined, 'natural' genius he recognizes in Therien, his portrayal of the woodchopper indicates the underlying predicament that troubles Thoreau's metaphysics of the human: that humanity is not simply a given but a potentiality that needs to be actualized through continuous individual spiritual and collective civilizational effort, and that any concept of the essence of the human being is unsettled by the disturbingly performative nature of being, or becoming, human. Anthropogenesis, it seems, is not a natural, linear unfolding of an innate capacity but realizes itself in the mode of ceaseless corrective attempts at keeping in check, and trying to emancipate oneself from, an animal nature from which escape ultimately remains impossible.

In his 1851 book *The Hunter-Naturalist*, Thoreau's less well-known contemporary, the journalist, naturalist and adventurer Charles Wilkins Webber, offers a similar distinction between the spiritual and

28 Simon Glendinning: From Animal Life to City Life. In: *Angelaki* 5,3 (2000), pp. 19–30, here p. 27.

29 Thoreau: *Walden*, p. 213.

30 Ibid., p. 146.

31 Ibid., p. 147.

32 Ibid., p. 146.

33 Ibid., p. 150. For a discussion of Thoreau's relationship with and attitudes towards Therien, see Robert W. Bradford: Thoreau and Therien. In: *American Literature* 34,4 (1963), pp. 499–506.

the animal aspects of the human by employing the broader difference between avian life and the earthy existence of quadrupeds to make sense of the dual character of the human being. Given the many traits that they, as living, breathing beings, share with humans, birds and beasts are expressive of "the most intimate relations to the life below us," but in their respective lifeways they also point beyond the fact of human-animal kinship in that they embody "separate and living types of our compounded selves."[34] Accordingly, Webber continues, while "we see in the bird the type of our intellect – of the soul," the beast represents "the type of our sensuous life – it appeals to our material and lower impulses. It prefigures and embodies individually those purely physical attributes which we find expressed in man the Microcosm."[35] In marked contrast to the lofty nobility of feathered beings, the wingless beast is forced to bear the ignominy of living "with its belly in the dust."[36] Mired in the struggle for survival and the vagaries of subsistence, it merely "lives to eat," while for birds, in their relative congeniality with the "higher intellection" of human life, "alimentation seems [...] rather a means than an end."[37] Unlike the truly 'animal animal' whose mode of being-in-the-world is limited to the sensuous and instinctual life of the body and its precarious environmental embeddedness, birds are reminiscent of the human capacity to transcend their own animality for the purpose of a higher life, guided by 'higher laws' (although it seems somewhat ironic that Webber's birds are able to raise themselves into the immaterial-incorporeal sphere of "pure ether"[38] by the very means of their specific *corporeal* endowments). However, if, for Webber, human existence is characterized by a precarious ontological intermediacy between divine transcendence and beastly immanence, he appears to be much less hostile towards and anxious about the human animal than Thoreau. In fact, while surely most "humiliating to a transcendental pride," he goes on to admit that "as yet the beast more closely approximates our sympathies, appeals to us through more numerous traits of consanguinity than the bird."[39] And while humans should continue to cultivate the

34 Charles W. Webber: *The Hunter-Naturalist. Romance of Sporting; Or, Wild Scenes and Wild Hunters*. Philadelphia: J. W. Bradley 1851, p. 18.

35 Ibid.

36 Ibid.

37 Ibid., p. 19.

38 Ibid., p. 18.

39 Ibid., p. 19.

spiritual aspect of their nature, Webber argues that it is equally important and necessary for them to be "true animals"[40] and to look back without shame to "that antediluvian era in which our giant progenitors wrestled hand to claw with their brute antagonists."[41]

The zooanthropological ruminations of Thoreau and Webber illustrate the second sense in which the term 'zooanthropological' can be understood in the antebellum context (and beyond): besides underlining the broader epistemological interdependence of conceptions of human and nonhuman animality, it also refers in a more specific sense to attempts at grappling with the realization that *anthropos* might indeed be fully immanent to the realm of animality – that (even civilized) humans were, in the words of Scottish Enlightenment philosopher Adam Ferguson, "animal[s] in the full extent of that designation."[42] As I will discuss in more detail in the next section, however, unlike Thoreau's, Webber's writing and the way it is shaped by his Western experiences also serves to illustrate how white antebellum Americans in their speculations about human-animal difference, human specificity and (the ethics of) human-animal relations frequently looked, or indeed took, to the West. Not all too surprisingly, a strong interest in the forms and modes of life – human, animal or liminally 'inbetween' – on and beyond Western frontiers is particularly evident in contemporary accounts of Western travel. But more than merely offering instructive or entertaining descriptions of 'foreign' regions or societies, generic narratives of exploration and adventure or utilitarian evaluations of Western nature and animals, antebellum zooanthropological curiosity about Western environments was a crucial aspect in philosophical debates about the differences between human and animal life – debates that were also of an inherently *political* nature. At the same time, travelers' implicit or explicitly articulated intentions of, to again quote Evans, finding "more correct views of human nature" in the West also served to legitimize their travels as an activity conducive to human knowledge production in contrast to the seemingly mindless or merely subsistence-oriented roaming of nonhuman animals and human savages, into whose 'haunts' their journey would lead them. Travelers, as an 1835 *Knickerbocker* article puts it, "trace human nature, by its action, and consequences, up to

40 Webber: *The Hunter-Naturalist*, p 19.

41 Ibid., p. 20.

42 Adam Ferguson: *An Essay on the History of Civil Society* [1776], ed. by Fania Oz-Salzberger. Cambridge: Cambridge UP 1995, p. 48.

its source," and if "they seek the home of the savage, [...] it is to developе his passions, his feelings, his wishes, the very powers of his intellect, when he is under no curb but that of nature and his own finite existence."[43] In its connection with the advancement of human knowledge, the very activity of travel was already indicative of the superiority of civilized humanity, with the curiosity of the traveler being an expression of their intellectual and imaginative faculties and thus of the 'spiritual' life idealized by Thoreau and others: "Divest human beings of curiosity, and we [...] linger on a mere animal existence,—capable only of mere animal pleasures,—unworthy of the high place in the scale of created beings, which it has been our favored lot to attain."[44]

The Animal Geographies of Westward Expansion

> There is something in the atmosphere of the broad prairie that gives to those who make it their home an air of boldness and independence. The wild mustang of the plain has a stride and a step which the farm-bred steed never acquires. So it is with the prairie man.[45]

> Again and again I looked toward the crowded hill-sides, and was sure I saw horsemen; and riding near, with a mixture of hope and dread, for Indians were abroad, I found them transformed into a group of buffalo. There was nothing in human shape amid all this vast congregation of brute forms.[46]

By the 1830s, "the great peculiarity of that newest of all possible worlds, called the Western Country,"[47] as James Kirke Paulding puts it in his 1832 novel *Westward Ho!*, was fast becoming a staple of Euro-American cultural identity as well as expansionist political ambition. While the Western environments of Paulding's novel are still chiefly those "eternal forests" of the myth-historical tradition associated with the late eighteenth-century hunter-explorer and frontier icon Daniel Boone, "roamed by herds of savage beasts and savage men"[48] and dotted by the

43 A Chapter on Travelers. In: *The Knickerbocker* 6,3 (September 1835), pp. 253–261, here p. 256.

44 Ibid., p. 254.

45 William G. Brent: Commerce of the Prairies. In: *The Knickerbocker* 41,1 (January 1853), pp. 41–44, here p. 42.

46 Francis Parkman: *The Oregon Trail* [1849], ed. by Bernard Rosenthal. Oxford: Oxford UP 1996, p. 77.

47 James Kirke Paulding: *Westward Ho! A Tale*. New York: J. & J. Harper 1832, p. 9.

48 Ibid., p. 74.

log cabins of fearless pioneers, others began to turn their gaze towards the farther and stranger domains beyond the Mississippi. Already in 1827, James Fenimore Cooper's *The Prairie*, the third installment of his Leatherstocking series, sees its protagonist, Natty Bumppo, relocate to the Great Plains, an environment that differed markedly from the familiar Eastern Woodlands and came with unique challenges, beginning with the very attempt at aesthetic description.[49] As Cooper explains in the revised 1849 introduction to his novel, in the face of ever-advancing American civilization and with the 'primevality' of his forests now increasingly disturbed by the settler's axe, the "philosopher of the wilderness" had emigrated beyond the Mississippi to spend the final years of his life as a trapper on the "denuded plains that stretch to the Rocky Mountains,"[50] a region Cooper himself never visited and 'knew' only through the few accounts that had been published by explorers and travelers. In the years that followed the publication of *The Prairie*, however, an increasing number of works based on actual personal experiences of travel into the trans-Mississippi West would be published, with Washington Irving's *Tour of the Prairies* (1832) and Francis Parkman's *The Oregon Trail* (first in serialized form in *The Knickerbocker* from 1847–49) ranking among the more prominent examples.

Wilderness was a well-established concept widely employed to characterize the bioregions of the antebellum far West, which, like much of the Great Plains, seemingly "resisted both agrarian settlement and white bodies."[51] The conceptual substance of wilderness, in the antebellum American case and elsewhere, has always been less about geo- or topographical specifics than about a contrasting juxtaposition of the geographies of civilized society – the rural and built environments east of the Mississippi and on the Atlantic seaboard – with those spaces imagined as yet beyond the transformative reach of white civilization. But as much as wilderness was and is a (European or Euro-American) human construct and an integral part of hegemonic discourses that

49 For early American encounters with and impressions of the Great Plains and the Rocky Mountains, see Anne Farrar Hyde: *An American Vision. Far Western Landscape and National Culture, 1820–1920*. New York: New York UP 1990.

50 James Fenimore Cooper: *The Prairie. A Tale* [1827], ed. by James P. Elliott. Albany: State University of New York Press 1985, p. 6.

51 Stephanie LeMenager: *Manifest and Other Destinies. Territorial Fictions of the Nineteenth-Century United States*. Lincoln: University of Nebraska Press 2004, p. 16.

underpinned racialized and gendered ontologies of the human, cultural discourses and imaginaries of wilderness should also be considered as references to forms of environmental and animal agency beyond those normally encountered or accepted in evidently anthropogenic and anthropocentric environments, where such forms of agency are usually strongly circumscribed. In turn, these forms of 'wild' environmental and animal agency also shaped the kinds of corporeal and intercorporeal experience of self-identified civilized Americans in environments in which they found themselves, in the words of Parkman, "suddenly brought back to the wants and resources of their original natures."[52]
Even a cursory look at some of the sources should be sufficient to demonstrate the omnipresence of animals and animality in antebellum writing about the trans-Mississippi regions. But it might be instructive to discuss in some more detail the specific ways in which, in the contemporary zooanthropoligical imaginary, Western environments figured as *animal geographies*, conceptualized here, in Harawayan parlance, as thoroughly 'naturalcultural'[53] spaces that interweaved cultural discourses and imaginings with forms of environmental materiality and (human-)animal (inter)corporeality. Strictly speaking, of course, almost all geographies – animated as they usually are by a multiplicity of living beings and forms of interspecies relations in varying degrees of intensity and visibility – would have to be characterized as 'animal' to some extent, which makes the term appear somewhat tautological. The reason I want to discuss the phenomenon of antebellum westward expansion under this heading has to do with the specifics of historical perception and experience. Contemporaries perceived and experienced life in Western bioregions as radically different from that in built or rural Eastern environments, and three interrelated aspects

52 Parkman: *The Oregon Trail*, p. 62. The reality of wilderness, its uncomplicated, straightforward material existence 'out there' or its social constructedness and problematic role as a constitutive element of settler colonialist discourse, has taken center stage in a debate that reverberates well beyond the field of American environmental history. For the standard work on the cultural significance of American wilderness, see Roderick Frazier Nash: *Wilderness and the American Mind*. New Haven: Yale UP 2014, first published in 1965 and now in its fifth edition. For an important problematization of the concept, see William Cronon: The Trouble with Wilderness; Or, Getting Back to the Wrong Nature. In: Id. (ed.): *Uncommon Ground: Toward Reinventing Nature*. New York: Norton 1995, pp. 69–90.

53 See Donna J. Haraway: *When Species Meet*. Minneapolis: University of Minnesota Press 2008.

should be particularly highlighted in this regard: the exceptional *presence* of animal life, the manifold expressions of animal *agency*, and the specific modes of *relations* between humans (both indigenous and Euro-American) and animals (both wild and domesticated) in Western environments. Given that in the East animal life was for the most part incorporated into human-shaped environments according to predominantly utilitarian aspects, with strongly regulated forms and spaces of human-animal encounter and interaction,[54] antebellum travelers who remarked on the wild liberty of the mustang, the thunderous pre-ecocidal immensity of bison herds – "a sea of life—of muscular power—of animal appetite—of bestial enjoyment!"[55] – or even the curious subterranean 'republics' of prairie dogs acknowledged the relative autonomy of animal bodies, movements and lifeways in expressly more-than-human environments that challenged Manifest Destiny's fantasies of (white) human supremacy, while, at the same time, providing the necessary stage for adventurous performances of Western 'conquest.' In antebellum accounts of Western travel, the often remarked upon presence of animal life in the trans-Mississippi West sometimes contrasted strongly with the supposed *absence* of human life in these environments. In the words of an 1845 *Knickerbocker* article which nicely captures this widespread perception, "[n]o human being may be the companion of the traveller in the immense solitude, yet will he feel that he is not alone; the wide expanse is populous with myriads of creatures; and, in the emphatic language of the red man, 'The Great Spirit is upon the Prairie!'"[56] And while Irving muses that "there is something

54 This is not to say, of course, that animals were somehow 'irrelevant' or absent in Eastern rural or urban environments. Pre-twentieth-century cities could be distinctly "anthrozootic" and characterized by a "near-constant contact" with animals "on streets and in homes, in slaughterhouses and rendering plants, stables and dairies, and at racetracks, dog-fighting pits and rat baits," as Scott Miltenberger points out in Viewing the Anthrozootic City. Humans, Domesticated Animals, and the Making of Early Nineteenth-Century New York. In: Susan Nance (ed.): *The Historical Animal*. Syracuse: Syracuse UP 2015, pp. 261–271, here p. 262. Rather, my point is that in the city (most) animals were quite rigorously incorporated into the routines of human life (as Miltenberger's list of spaces and practices of urban human-animal relations itself suggests), and the implications of this for expressions as well as human imaginings of animal agency should not be disregarded.

55 Thomas Jefferson Farnham: *Travels in the Great Western Prairies, the Anahuac and Rocky Mountains, and in the Oregon Territory*. New York: Greeley & McElrath 1843, p. 33.

56 Lewis F. Thomas: Sketches of the Great West. In: *The Knickerbocker* 25,3 (March 1845), pp. 189–196, here p. 196.

inexpressibly lonely in the solitude of a prairie" in comparison with the "loneliness of a forest," where "the view is shut in by trees, and the imagination is left free to picture some livelier scene beyond," he also notes that even this "desert world" supposedly devoid of humanity is nonetheless animated by manifold forms of animal life, its pervasive silence frequently being "broken by the cry of a distant flock of pelicans" or the howling and whining of a "scoundrel wolf."[57]

For Webber, Western environments, where "the civilized man, the savage and the brute have been brought into extraordinary relations,"[58] offered fertile grounds for pre- and proto-Darwinian delineations of human-animal difference and the ethics of interspecies relations, including and especially those between humans and other creatures. Appropriately enough, Webber's own biography in many ways epitomizes the recklessness of antebellum frontier adventure and Manifest Destiny. Moving from his home state of Kentucky to the conflict-ridden Texas frontier of the late 1830s to join a company of Texas Rangers, he later led an ill-fated expedition to Arizona Territory, attempted to improve transportation in the Southwest with a 'camel company,' and eventually died in Nicaragua while participating in William Walker's infamous mid-1850s filibustering exploits. In 1844, concluding his Texan adventures, Webber moved to New York to work as a journalist, serving for two years as editor for the *American Whig Review* and publishing several articles and stories about his Western experiences, the "erratic wanderings" which brought him into familiarity "with all wild, grotesque and lonely creatures that populate those infinite solitudes of nature."[59] In the introduction to his *Hunter-Naturalist*, a collection of accounts of wilderness and hunting adventure interspersed with natural historical and philosophical elaborations which was planned as merely the first book of a projected series, Webber explains how his books are supposed to bear testimony to the lived relationality of human and animal life and that this relationality must also be taken into account on the

57 Washington Irving: *A Tour on the Prairies*. London: J. Murray 1835, pp. 271–272. Of course, trans-Mississippi Western environments were never really devoid of human life, and the reasons for this Euro-American perception can be found less in the respective environments themselves than in the history of settler colonial racism and its physical as well as discursive erasures of indigenous societies and ecologies.

58 Webber: *The Hunter-Naturalist*, p. 30.

59 Ibid., p. 90. For biographical information about Webber, see Thomas W. Cutrer: Webber, Charles Wilkins. In: *Handbook of Texas Online*. https://tshaonline.org/handbook/online/articles/fwe08 (accessed September 5, 2016).

level of narrative presentation: "The wild creature and its Human peer must go together in our treatment—the one re-acts upon and modifies the other; let us exhibit the passions and the life of both."[60] The Western lives of "the Wild Indian and his Buffalo—the Trapper and his Beaver,"[61] Webber seems to suggest, are dynamic co-enactments in which the lifeways of animal species are interwoven with that of their respective human types. However, while the image of animals and their "Human peer[s]" (even if distinguished by capitalization) suggests that the "extraordinary relations" of Western life are characterized by a certain horizontality, the specific type of relationship that permeates Webber's wild Western scenes as well as his conception of interspecies life and ethics more broadly obviously contradicts this idea: Just like the book's eponymous figure of the 'hunter-naturalist' embodies two domains of practice and knowledge traditionally associated with forms of epistemic and physical violence expressive of a masculinist dominance over nonhuman beings, the relations Webber refers to throughout his book are neither harmonious nor symmetrical because they are those between hunter and hunted, predator and prey – and "man, in a world of pursuers and pursued, is chief hunter of them all!"[62] While for Thoreau hunting was a necessary developmental stage with some educational value that was (or should be) limited to "the thoughtless age of boyhood,"[63] neither the "sickly benevolence" of some of his contemporaries nor "baby ethics, *alias*, transcendentalism"[64] could distract Webber from the reality that Man was the apex predator in a universe defined by a relentless struggle for existence in which "the *strong*, of course, conquer."[65] But even if humans were taken out of the equation, Webber's conviction that violence was the defining principle of interspecies relations was apparently supported by the workings of the animal world itself – and for proof one needed only look at the "lustful battles of the animal tribes among themselves."[66] Unsurprisingly, after briefly mentioning the "savage contests of the canines, felines, &c,"[67]

60 Webber: *The Hunter-Naturalist*, p. 6.

61 Ibid.

62 Ibid., p. 17.

63 Thoreau: *Walden*, p. 212.

64 Webber: *The Hunter-Naturalist*, p. 21.

65 Ibid., p. 22, original emphasis.

66 Ibid.

67 Ibid.

Webber bolsters and further elaborates on his point by drawing on his own experiences with Western animal life:

> It is a fact, with regard to the habits of the Mustangs, or wild horses of our great prairies, which we have frequently observed personally, that the weaker stallions are invariably, after desperate contests, either killed or driven into solitary banishment, from which they never return to the herd, until their strength and prowess have been so far developed in the solitude, as to give them some hopes of being able to triumph in a renewed struggle with their conquerors. The mares, in the mean time, are passive observers, and surrender without hesitation, to whichever of the opponents may have demonstrated the right to approach them legitimately.[68]

In the 1850s, Webber's red-in-tooth-and-claw conception of animal life was, of course, not exactly a novelty, because it was both shared by an increasing number of contemporaries and had already been anticipated in earlier writings. Evans, for example, while traversing one of the Western hunting grounds, encounters a group of wild deer, who – as he surmises, because of his "garments of fur" – look at him "with rather an inquisitive than fearful aspect."[69] Evans is "only half disposed" to shoot the innocent looking creatures, but his canine companions are much less hesitant, pursuing and killing one of the group.[70] However, while, this scene of interspecies violence provides the context for Evans musings on "the lengthy, and complicated chain of destruction" and the "perpetual carnage" that suffuses the animal world, there is quite a different moral resonance to Evans observations.[71] In contrast to Webber's celebration of Man as the "chief hunter," for Evans, the role of Man is that of the "great devourer" – and although the "destruction of animal life" may be an unpleasant necessity for the support of human existence, "the life and comfort of animals should never be trifled with. It is the only life which they can live; their little light, once put out, is extinguished forever."[72]

While one might argue that the relations between Evans' Western travels and his reflections on animal life and humans' problematic role in the web of interspecies relations were of a coincidental rather than causal nature, throughout the antebellum decades the interconnection between far Western environments and ethico-ontologies of animal

68 Ibid.

69 Evans: *A Pedestrious Tour*, p. 93.

70 Ibid.

71 Ibid.

72 Ibid., pp. 93–94.

life and interspecies relations became increasingly visible. More widely read than Webber's writing, Parkman's account of his 1846 travels on the Oregon Trail underlines both this interconnection and the extent to which, in contemporary zooanthropological imaginings, the trans-Mississippi West epitomized the relentless struggle of animal life in a way that also naturalized, and offered a legitimizing framework for, the violence of Euro-American territorial expansion more broadly. A wealthy Bostonian plagued by an undiagnosed neurological disease which often left him nearly blind and weakened his body to the point of total immobility, Parkman attempted to overcome his condition by immersing himself into the invigorating harshness of Western wilderness environments. In Parkman's West, an environment that threatened to make "quick and sharp work"[73] of all those too weak to adapt to and cope with its unforgiving realities, "the human biped" was "reduced to his primitive condition."[74] In the unrelenting physicality of his journey, the privileged white Easterner Parkman imagined himself as both an animal body subject to the undifferentiating natural and animal processes that also affected all other organisms *and* as a specimen of civilized humanity who stood apart and above the worlds of nonhuman animals and savage indigenes, the boundaries of which remained consistently blurry and indeterminate. "No man is a philanthropist on the prairie,"[75] Parkman writes; and for him and likeminded contemporaries, the human and animal savagery that characterized Western life also exemplified the deeper truth of the animal nature of the human, a truth whose consequences could only be kept in check, but never entirely evaded, by the regulations and 'artifices' of civilized life. "Man is naturally an animal of prey," as Irving concludes from his own Western travels, "and, however changed by civilization, will readily relapse into his instinct for destruction," with his "ravenous and sanguinary propensities daily growing stronger upon the prairies."[76]

73 Parkman: *The Oregon Trail*, p. 183.

74 Ibid., p. 252.

75 Ibid., p. 128.

76 Irving: *A Tour on the Prairies*, p. 125. Charles Latrobe, who accompanied Irving on his tour on the prairies, found it "amusing to see the effect of the life we were leading [...] on the spirits of the most peaceable among us. There was the good, kind-hearted commissioner, whose career had never been stained [...] by [an] act of violence to beast or bird, girding himself in his own quiet way for the expected rencontre with biped or quadruped savages, and breathing destruction to the innocent skunks and

But while the realities of Western interspecies relations could be translated into an aggressive 'Darwinian' ethics à la Parkman, they were also suggestive of what might be described as a much less callous (and often neglected) ethics of creaturely commonality that was crucially based on, or at the very least strongly bolstered by, the corporeal experiences of and in Western animal geographies. Identifying this alternative strand of ethics is arguably complicated to some extent not only by the fact that both 'Darwinian' and 'creaturely' ethical perspectives frequently bleed into each other in the sources and are thus not always neatly separable, but also because – unlike the kind of social Darwinism *avant la lettre* espoused by the likes of Parkman and Webber, which was already approaching something like a semi-coherent ethical 'system' in antebellum discourse – the latter were of a much more situational and ephemeral, perhaps even epiphanic character. In the journal he kept during his overland trip to San Diego over the Santa Fé Trail and along the Gila River in 1849, John Robert Forsyth repeatedly comments, in a starkly and unsparingly corporeal language, on the violent fate of some of the domesticated animals accompanying the emigrant trains on their way to California. Among other incidents of animal death and suffering, Forsyth mentions how he encounters a mule and an ox, both abandoned by their respective trains, both about to meet their respective ends at the jaws of wolves, the ferocious embodiment of the Western struggle for existence. While the "poor mule," "a most miserable object skin & Bone & not even all his skin for if it had not been peeled from his lean sides for Whip Lashes it had certainly been lashed off," far from water and unable to walk, "would never again wet his burning throat,"[77] the ox is already being besieged by his predatory assailants. A "brave old fellow," the animal is fighting back valiantly, "but his hind legs were partly Knawed away," and with their growing numbers the wolves would soon "gorge their villaneous carcases with his quivering flesh."[78]

turkeys. There too was to be seen our friend Irving,—the kindly impulse of whose nature is to love every living thing,—ramming a couple of bullets home into a brace of old brass-barrelled pistols which had been furnished him from the armory at Fort Gibson." (Charles Joseph Latrobe: *The Rambler in North America, 1832–1833*. London: Seeley & Burnside 1835, pp. 205–206.)

77 John Robert Forsyth: Journal of a Trip from Peoria, Ill. to California on the Pacific in 1849, p. 64. The Bancroft Library, University of California, Berkeley, BANC MSS C-F 50 FILM, part 2, reel 1.

78 Ibid., p. 67.

A more extensive account of a similar scene, this time involving one of the train's own animals, the ox Tom, is perhaps worth quoting at some length for the way its language of violent (inter)corporeality resonates with both social Darwinist fatalism and an implicit recognition of the common threads of being that interweave creaturely lives across the supposed rigidity of species boundaries:

> When our Train amounted to 44 wagons Tom was considered the noblest Meekest & best trained animal in that vast cavalcade, but now alas to be entirely abandoned to the ravenous Wolves in a strange country to have his beautifully rounded loins, straight back, full & broad chest, delicate Head & full Black Eye torn & mangled by those ever rapacious monsters. the thought was too much & an irresistable tear trickled down my cheek. No Tom said I this shall not be your fate I will drive you on to where some more generous place will yield you a little grass & water & where your strength which you have expended in my service shall be renewed & you be enabled to fight for your life & I impulsively turned to where the feeble fellow stood trying to munch a mouthful of bitter dry weed. I believe In my soul the poor creature Knew me for he turned towards me & approached & as he had often done in the days of his Glory held forward his gentle head for me to pat & fondle I examined it carefully & then step'd round to drive him onward, but horrible! his thighs & legs were fearfully torn & lacerated [...] I turned & left him with a perfect sickness of heart I truly believe I Never had felt before. as long as the road gave me a view of him, I often turned round & still poor Tom was standing there gazing after my retreating figure.[79]

Not able to get Tom out of his head, for the remainder of the day Forsyth continues to be haunted by imaginary scenes of the beloved animal's violent death – of "poor Tom look[ing] round in Terror" while the hungry wolves "collect in hundreds" around him, as both the day and Tom's life are nearing their inevitable end.[80]

In *Corporal Compassion*, Ralph Acampora introduces the term "symphysis" in order to emphasize how interspecies encounters are mediated and shaped by affective-bodily experiences in contrast to the "more airy, psychic notion of sympathy" that moral theory and philosophy are usually preoccupied with.[81] For Acampora, symphysis is based on (but also meant to convey) the fact that humans share a "somaesthetic nexus" with other creatures, and the concept can be defined as a "proto-ethical feeling that assures us of another animal being's morally considerable

79 Forsyth: Journal of a Trip, pp. 90–91.

80 Ibid., p. 91.

81 Ralph R. Acampora: *Corporal Compassion. Animal Ethics and Philosophy of Body.* Pittsburgh: University of Pittsburgh Press 2006, p. 76.

capacity for conviviality."[82] Despite what Acampora describes as its essentially pre-reflexive character, he points out that symphysis "retains (at least residually) its affective aspects even upon reflection."[83] I want to argue that we can read Forsyth's account of the abandonment of Tom and his imaginings of the animal's lonely death as, at least in part, testimony to the symphysical experiences of interspecies-intercorporeal commonality the long journey on the overland trails inevitably entailed. The fact that Forsyth's writing takes the form of a journal of day-to-day experiences perhaps also allows us to credit it with a certain amount of experiential immediacy that doesn't characterize other forms of writing in the same way and to the same degree. This is not to say that we should naively interpret his account as somehow expressive of pure, unmediated experience: not only does it clearly involve a certain amount of self-stylization on the part of the author in terms of a civilized human's paternalistic care towards 'inferior' creatures, it arguably also reflects the ways in which racialized discourses of civilization sometimes functioned to conceptually unite civilized beings across species boundaries in opposition to the savagery of both wild predatory beasts and 'bestial' humans. Still, Forsyth's writing also serves as an example for the way in which Western animal geographies could be imagined and experienced in terms of a "creaturely 'carnosphere'" (to again borrow from Acampora) in a sense that emphasized the shared corporeal vulnerability of humans and animals beyond the violent ethics of (social) Darwinism.[84]

Somewhat in contradiction to Manifest Destiny's fantasies of a unidirectional imposition of civilized ways on savage environments and beings, already in the antebellum era Western environments were often regarded as spaces of inevitable corporeal transformation. As Stephen

82 Ibid.

83 Ibid., p. 77.

84 Ibid., p. 76. Acampora uses this term to refer to a broader transpersonal perception of creaturely commonality in the sense of a "quasi-mystical communion with the planet." I use it in a more limited sense here to refer to transspecific imaginings that are tied to the distinctly corporeal experience of (or vulnerable exposure to) a particular environment. For a discussion of the concept of vulnerability in the context of animal studies, see Dominik Ohrem: An Address from Elsewhere. Vulnerability, Wonderability and Creaturely Life. In: Id. / Roman Bartosch (ed.): *Beyond the Human-Animal Divide. Creaturely Lives in Literature and Culture*. Basingstoke: Palgrave Macmillan (forthcoming).

Tatum argues in an article on what he terms "topographies of transition," such topographies "depend upon, indeed are bound up with, the extra-linguistic realities of the 'country' and of laboring bodies. Though such topographies are always, on one level, images and representations, they are notable for their formal strategies in resisting allegory and symbol and returning us to the facts of place and the body."[85] I would suggest that we should be similarly attentive to the ways in which at least some historical sources (such as Forsyth's) are particularly expressive of "the facts of place and the body" and of the corporeal experience of Western environments as spaces in which bodies *as such* became highly visible in their capabilities and limitations, in their *presence*. Arguably, zooanthropological imaginings thus also reflect the fact that the material realities of Western life and travel were not only shaped by the presence and agency of nonhuman animals and environments but also by a heightened experientiality of *human* animality in the sense of a corporeal immersion in, and corporeal exposure to, forms of nonhuman materiality not subject to established Euro-American forms of environmental regulation. "The trials of a journey in the western wilderness can never be detailed in words," as Western explorer Thomas Jefferson Farnham emphasizes:

> To be understood, they must be endured. Their effects upon the physical and mental system are equally prostrating […]. Loneliness [is] coupled with a thousand natural causes of one's destruction; perpetual journeyings over endless declivities, among tempests, through freezing torrents; one half the time on foot, with nothing but moccasins to protect the feet from the flinty gravel and the thorns of the prickly pear along the unbeaten way; and the starvings and thirstings wilt the muscles, send preternatural activity into the nervous system, and through the whole animal and mental economy a feebleness, an irritability altogether indescribable.[86]

Seemingly not conveyable by means of linguistic description, the existential character of far Western travel could only be shared *experientially* – and this shared experientiality encompassed not only fellow human but also nonhuman creatures.

85 Stephen Tatum: Topographies of Transition in Western American Literature. In: *Western American Literature* 32,4 (1998), pp. 310–353, here p. 318.

86 Farnham: *Travels in the Great Western Prairies*, p. 113.

Western Humanimalities

Edwin James, who served as a botanist and geologist on Long's Rocky Mountain expedition, surely echoed the sentiments of many of his contemporaries with his belief that "[t]o travellers in such a country, any domesticated animal, however abject, becomes an acceptable companion."[87] But if Western travelers sometimes developed close and affectionate relationships with the animals that accompanied them in a way that, though usually remaining within the established framework of benevolent paternalism, potentially questioned the rigid ontological and ethical distinctions of the human-animal divide, such interspecies affinities among civilized beings stood in marked contrast to the ways in which whites regarded those members of their own species who happened to find themselves in the way of settler colonial expansion and at the bottom of their racialized hierarchizations of human life. For Parkman, whose narrative is replete with particularly abhorrent acts of epistemic and physical violence against both Western wild animals and indigenous humans,

> a civilized white man can discover but very few points of sympathy between his own nature and that of an Indian. [...] [A]n impassable gulf lies between him and his red brethren of the prairie. Nay, so alien to himself do they appear, that having breathed for a few months or a few weeks the air of this region, he begins to look upon them as a troublesome and dangerous species of wild beast.[88]

With an ambiguity in many ways characteristic of contemporary portrayals of Native American peoples, Parkman's 'Indians' are, on the one hand, "brethren" and thus seemingly located within the mythological bounds of the 'human family,'[89] while, on the other, the notion of an "impassable gulf" is strongly evocative of the 'abyssal' character of the divide that supposedly separates human life from that of all other living beings. Akin to the wild beasts that roamed Western landscapes, indigenous people's dubious humanity substantiated the precarity of their ethical considerability, pointing to the ways in which the recognition of creaturely commonality remained inseparable from, and was frequently broken through, the prism of race as well as other social categories

87 Edwin James: *Account of an Expedition from Pittsburgh to the Rocky Mountains, Performed in the Years 1819 and '20*, vol. 2. Philadelphia: Carey & Lea 1823, p. 213.

88 Parkman: *The Oregon Trail*, p. 237.

89 See Roland Barthes: *Mythologies*, trans. from the French by Annette Lavers. New York: Hill & Wang 1972, pp. 100–102.

constitutive of the relations of power and inequality among humans. In turn, contemporary distinctions between savage and civilized forms of life encompassed the lifeways of not only human but also of nonhuman beings: never simply congruent with the dichotomy of animality and humanity, savagery and civilization were notably transspecific concepts, with the "predatory expeditions"[90] of the human savages of the West not essentially different from the behaviors of their rapacious nonhuman counterparts, such as grizzly bears, cougars or wolves. But, as Parkman remarks, while there was not much to be feared from nonhuman wolves – "the greatest cowards on the prairie" –, "[i]n respect to the human wolves in our neighborhood, we felt much less at our ease."[91] Suggestive of how forms of human-animal relations could also function as indicators of civilizational status, the (to Euro-American eyes barely) domesticated animal companions of Western indigenes were living testimony to the latter's savage ways, with 'Indian' dogs in particular serving as a frequent object of critique and commentary by white travelers. In *Astoria*, Irving is repulsed by the appearance and character of the dogs who "swarm about an Indian village as they do about a Turkish town" and who retain the "savage but cowardly temper" of the wolf: "howling rather than barking; showing their teeth and snarling on the slightest provocation, but sneaking away on the least attack."[92] It is with similar sentiments that Ross Cox, after learning that one of his group's dogs has been killed for food, laments that

> there was no necessity to justify the murder of a civilized dog, while several of those which had been purchased [from the 'Indians'] at Oakinagan still remained untouched. [...] I would have preferred picking the bones of the most maigre of the Indian breed, to the plumpest of our own faithful companions. Their keen eye, sharp nose, and pointed upright ear, proclaim their wolfish origin, and fail to enlist our sympathies in their behalf; in consequence of which our repugnance to eat them in periods of necessity is considerably diminished.[93]

Especially in the American context, the concept of indigenous savagery had always been strongly associated with notions of unrestrained

90 Irving: *A Tour on the Prairies*, p. 75.

91 Parkman: *The Oregon Trail*, p. 287.

92 Washington Irving: *Astoria. Or, Enterprise Beyond the Rocky Mountains*. Philadelphia: Carey, Lea & Blanchard 1836, p. 223.

93 Ross Cox: *Adventures on the Columbia River. Including the Narrative of a Residence of Six Years on the Western Side of the Rocky Mountains, Among Various Tribes of Indians Hitherto Unknown*, vol. 2. London: Colburn & Bentley 1831, p. 33.

violence and cruelty – epitomized by the idea of a no-holds-barred 'savage warfare' that didn't shy away from shedding the blood of children, women and elderly people[94] –, and while such connotations remained influential in the nineteenth century, a more subtle underpinning of the 'savage ontology' of indigenous life came to the fore throughout the antebellum period. In this view, indigenous peoples' inability of transcending their 'external' natural environment by transforming it in a way that was in accordance with the requirements of civilization (especially with regard to patterns of habitation and land use) and with the claims of human dominion inherent to this concept was understood as causally related to their inability of transcending their 'internal' animal nature. 'Indians' were absorbed into and part of the very environments they, as members of the human species, were supposed to subdue, with the specifics of this causal relationship depending on whether savagery was conceptualized as primarily a result of environmental conditions or in biologistic terms as an innate inferiority. Accordingly, indigenous lifeways were frequently regarded as similar, if not identical, to the lifeways of nonhuman creatures, with the latter supposedly determined by an instinctual preoccupation with bodily subsistence that underscored not merely their being immanent to their environments but what might be described in Heideggerian terminology as their environmental "captivation."[95] In contrast to the self-governing subjectivity of civilized humans, the life of 'the Indian,' not unlike that of the 'poor-in-world' animal, was seemingly defined by a diminished form of relating to the world and themselves – their imagination "bounded by the lines of [...] sensible experience,"[96] their being wholly confined to the realm of material objects and relations: "abstract existence ['the Indian'] never conceived; the verb '*to be*' except as relating to time, place, and action, had no meaning in his [*sic*] language."[97]

While such dehumanizing representations often undifferentiatingly referred to the 'character' of 'the Indian' as such, emblematic of this

94 See, for example, John Grenier: *The First Way of War. American War Making on the Frontier, 1607–1814*. Cambridge: Cambridge UP 2005, p. 19.

95 The concept is developed in Martin Heidegger: *The Fundamental Concepts of Metaphysics: World, Finitude, Solitude*, trans. from the German by William McNeill / Nicholas Walker. Bloomington: Indiana UP 1995.

96 John Ludlum McConnel: *Western Characters: Or, Types of Border Life in the Western States*. New York: Redfield 1853, p. 34.

97 Ibid., p. 44, original emphasis.

discursive relegation of indigenous peoples to the realm of abject animal materiality are antebellum portrayals of the societies of the Great Basin region west of the Rocky Mountains, in particular the Paiute and Shoshone, often collectively referred to as 'Snake Indians' or 'Diggers' (the latter as a pejorative reference to the supplementation of their diet with edible roots). "Herding together among bushes, and [...] using their instinct only to procure food," as John C. Frémont describes them in the bestselling report of his 1840s expeditions, "these may be considered, among human beings, the nearest approach to the mere animal creation."[98] "In these Indians," he writes at another point in his account in reaction to a group of Paiute who didn't seem to welcome the presence of Frémont's expedition, "I was forcibly struck by an expression of countenance resembling that in a beast of prey; and all their actions are those of wild animals. Joined to the restless motion of the eye, here is a want of mind—an absence of thought—and an action wholly by impulse, strongly expressed, and which constantly recalls the similarity."[99] Echoing Frémont's sentiments, Farnham, in his *Travels in the Great Western Prairies*, describes the "Piutes" as "the most degraded and least intellectual Indians [...]. They provide nothing for future wants" and, frequently being reduced to starvation after harsh winters, "crawled upon their hands and feet, eating grass like cattle. These poor creatures are hunted in the spring of the year, when weak and helpless [...], and when taken, are fattened, carried to Santa Fe and sold as slaves during their minority."[100] In a follow-up volume focused on his Californian travels, Farnham includes the observations of a fellow Western traveler who, in a description that evokes the notion of an animal removed from its natural habitat and features a telling use of pronouns, recounts his experience with one of the kidnapped indigenes: "From the time it was brought into the settlements of California it was sad, moaned, and continually refused to eat till it died."[101]

And yet, while antebellum representations of trans-Mississippi indigenous societies exemplify the ways in which, at the intersections of

98 John Charles Frémont: *Report of the Exploring Expedition to the Rocky Mountains in the Year 1842, and to Oregon and North California in the Years 1843–44*. Washington, D.C.: Blair & Rives 1845, p. 212.

99 Ibid., p. 267.

100 Farnham: *Travels in the Great Western Prairies*, pp. 107–108.

101 Thomas Jefferson Farnham: *Travels in the Californias, and Scenes in the Pacific Ocean*. New York: Saxton & Miles 1844, p. 378.

zooanthropological and racial imaginings, human animality was displaced onto the bodies and lifeways of racialized others (thus allowing for the discursive emergence of white civilized Man as the pinnacle of humanity), I want to argue that Western environments tended to complicate this discursive strategy both in a general and in a more specific sense. First, the inevitable foregrounding of human corporeality in Western geographies confronted westering whites with the facticities of their own animal bodies, which, in their insistent, vulnerable materiality, frequently forced themselves into the travelers' writing. "But hunger!!," Farnham exclaims, "Every bud was fed; every bird had its nourishment; the lizards even were not starving. We were."[102] Ironically enough, antebellum travelers' accounts are not seldom characterized to a considerable extent by the same preoccupation with subsistence activities that supposedly relegated indigenous people to the uncultured domain of animal existence. If the civilized East was inhabited by the *human* animal (or, even, the human ~~animal~~), Western animal geographies tended to foreground the unwelcome presence of the human *animal*. This doesn't mean that an immersion into Western environments always resulted in *in extremis* situations of some sort, but rather that the exposure to and experience of these environments highlighted the animal vulnerability of human beings (particularly those unfamiliar with them) in the face of larger more-than-human forces not adapted to and, in fact, often counteractive to their needs and wants – an existential vulnerability shared by all living creatures, human and nonhuman, white and nonwhite. This primacy of human animality in Western environments is also evident in the forms of bodily practice expressive of the fundamental human dependence on nonhuman animal bodies in these environments (and indeed, though often beyond the thresholds of visibility and recognition, in all kinds of environments): in the way humans sustained their bodies by consuming the flesh of hunted animals or by otherwise making use of animal matter – for instance, by using the flammable excrement, usually referred to as 'buffalo chips,' left behind by herds of bison to warm their bodies and cook their food in woodless Plains environments; in the way they clothed themselves in the skins and furs of Western animals; and in the way they interpreted the diversity of behaviors, tracks and traces of animal bodies as environmental

102 Farnham: *Travels in the Great Western Prairies*, p. 131.

cues that were sometimes essential for survival. The heroization of Euro-American pioneers and frontiersmen in the mythology of westward expansion already emergent in the literature of the antebellum period is thus haunted by a certain tension between human agency and vulnerability, human activity and passivity, that is not often commented upon and perhaps drowned out to some extent by the boisterous chorus of Manifest Destiny and tales of frontier bravado. In fact, as already pointed out by botanist John Bradbury in his 1817 account of Western travels, the 'agency' of pioneers and frontiersmen in the 'conquest' of the West involved not only their clichéd "hardihood" but also a remarkably passive "capability of suffering."[103]

Second, this inevitable foregrounding of human animality was connected with a more specific type of concern already alluded to in the introductory section of this chapter: as much and as widely as the process and progress of westward expansion was understood as a reaffirmation of the dominion of white civilized humanity over savage forms of animal and animal-like human life, the transformative powers that Western environments undoubtedly wielded over civilized bodies evoked troubling questions about the fate of those individuals or families that lived or worked on or beyond the fringes of American society. What to make of those people who left behind – turned their back on? – American civilization in favor of the vagaries of the wilderness, where many of them, in the words of George Frederick Ruxton, "rival the beasts of prey" and "destroy human as well as animal life with as little scruple and as freely as they expose their own"?[104] Were these westerners really the vanguard of the march of American civilization, conquerors of a continental wilderness, or was it, in fact, the wilderness that did the conquering? More than merely about the habits of a geographically and socially marginal group of antebellum Americans, the lives of Western whites were of importance due to their seeming implications for the distinctions between humanity and animality, civilization and savagery. Writing about the "trappers of the Rocky Mountains," whom he refers to as a "'genus' more approximating to the primitive savage than perhaps any other class of civilized man,"[105] Ruxton illuminates the decivilizing

103 John Bradbury: *Travels in the Interior of America, in the Years 1809, 1810, 1811.* London: Sherwood, Neely & Jones 1817, p. 10.

104 George F. Ruxton: *Adventures in Mexico and the Rocky Mountains.* London: John Murray 1847, pp. 241–242.

105 Ibid., p. 241.

trajectory of civilized Man in Western environments in a language expressive of the interrelated twin specters of 'becoming animal' and 'becoming savage':

> Their lives being spent in the remote wilderness of the mountains [...], their habits and character assume a most singular cast of simplicity mingled with ferocity, appearing to take their colouring from the scenes and objects which surround them. Knowing no wants save those of nature, their sole care is to procure sufficient food to support life, and the necessary clothing to protect them from the rigorous climate. [...] When engaged in their avocation, the natural instinct of primitive man is ever alive, for the purpose of guarding against danger and the provision of necessary food.[106]

Reviled as "White Indians" by some, these men "may have good qualities, but they are those of the animal" and indeed "just what uncivilised white man might be supposed to be in a brute state, depending upon his instinct for the support of life."[107]

The ambiguous role assumed by the figure of the white westerner complicated discursive strategies through which human animality became almost exclusively associated with racialized otherness. Shy of a complete animalization, like 'Indians,' actual – that is, (semi-)permanent – westerners seemed to be suspended in, or veering towards, a state of liminal humanimality that was particularly associated with the concept and the spaces of the Western 'frontier' which, though notoriously vague in meaning, were often imagined as the "meeting point between savagery and civilization."[108] White frontiersmen not only inhabited the frontier in a geographical sense, they also *embodied* it in an ontological sense, pointing to the metamorphic agency that resulted from its dangerous intermixtures of civilized and savage, human and animal ways of being. What Derrida, in the epigram to this chapter, imagines as a process of ontological border-crossing that demands (or allows for?) a "surrender to the animal," for many antebellum Americans found its geographical expression in the spaces of, and beyond, the Western frontier. As sources and authorities of knowledge about the very environments which also reshaped their civilized humanity, white westerners

106 Ibid.

107 Ibid., p. 242.

108 This is, of course, the famous 1893 phrasing of Wisconsin historian Frederick Jackson Turner. See id.: The Significance of the Frontier in American History. In: *Frontier and Section. Selected Essays of Frederick Jackson Turner*, ed. by Ray Allen Billington. Englewood Cliffs: Prentice-Hall 1961, pp. 37–62, here p. 38.

were both subjects and objects of zooanthropological inquiry. To antebellum travelers like Bradbury, they provided first-hand information "concerning the nature and habits of animals, with which no men are so well acquainted," and who were even able to "imitate the cry or note of any animal found in the American Wilds, so exactly, as to deceive the animals themselves."[109] But in the eyes of others, these men's animal mimicry went well beyond the technique and tactics of the chase – at worst, it underscored the failure of their ontological acrobatics, that precarious act of walking the line between human and animal worlds of which supposedly only civilized whites were capable. What the antebellum fascination with Western life thus also highlights is that, only seemingly paradoxically, in its endeavors to pinpoint the differences between human and animal life, contemporary zooanthropological imaginings relied to a considerable extent on precisely those figures who were regarded as not neatly fitting into either category. As Erica Fudge, Ruth Gilbert and Susan Wiseman explain, it is precisely because the human being has "no sharp or evident frontier" that the shifting metaphysics of the human is crucially and self-constitutively dependent not only on the meta-figure of the animal but on an ensemble of "contrasting border-figures, partly human – or, rather, intermittently human and inhuman according to their context."[110] It is this epistemic situationality or even volatility of the human/animal that also evokes unsettling questions about the validity of both concepts.

Capturing the Derridean ambiguity of the term, for many antebellum Americans the "ends" of American Man lay westward in more than one sense: in the sense of 'his' continental *telos* as it was most visibly epitomized in the feverish expansionism of Manifest Destiny, but also in the spatial and ontological sense in which Western animal geographies both underwrote and challenged white American self-conceptions as the embodiment and actualization of human potentiality.

109 Bradbury: *Travels in the Interior of America*, pp. 106–107, footnote.

110 Erica Fudge / Ruth Gilbert / Susan Wiseman: Introduction: The Dislocation of the Human. In: Iid. (eds): *At the Borders of the Human. Beasts, Bodies and Natural Philosophy in the Early Modern Period*. Basingstoke: Palgrave Macmillan 1999, pp. 1–8, here pp. 2–3.

The Passenger Pigeon and Its Role in Perceptions of Manifest Destiny

Andrew Howe

The American bison was long foregrounded as the key biological casualty of nineteenth-century westward expansion on the North American continent. Embarrassingly, it wasn't until 1970 and with the publication of Dee Brown's *Bury My Heart at Wounded Knee* and the emergence of the New Western History that the widespread displacement and slaughter of indigenous groups during the process of continent-wide European settlement was contextualized in quite the same fashion.[1] A third casualty, however, exists at the roots of the re-examination of American Manifest Destiny and the numerous excesses associated with this expansionist ideology. The abrupt and surprising extinction of the passenger pigeon (*Ectopistes migratorius*) continues to trouble the American consciousness, standing as a symbol of permanent consequence resulting from a national agenda that privileged land and resource acquisition over ecological impact. In 2014, the pigeon attracted quite a bit of attention, mostly due to the 100th anniversary of the death of Martha – the last pigeon in captivity – in the Cincinnati Zoo. Despite a population numbering in the billions at the beginning

1 See Patricia Nelson Limerick's groundbreaking *The Legacy of Conquest. The Unbroken Past of the American West*. New York: Norton 1987, and ead. / Clyde A. Milner II / Charles E. Rankin (eds): *Trails. Toward a New Western History*. Lawrence: UP of Kansas 1991.

of the nineteenth century, the species was nearly extinct in the wild by 1900 due to habitat destruction, the fact that the pigeons were being used as a cheap food source, hunted for 'sport,' and due to other factors. The precipitous decline did not go unnoticed at the time, and along with the bison the pigeon became a symbol not only of ecological but also of national loss. In 1893, historian Frederick Jackson Turner famously declared the American frontier to be 'closed.' The end of the century ushered in an era of reflection, which included early anxieties regarding the impact of westward expansion and an increasing human population upon the environment.[2] Martha would become a celebrity and, upon her death, a symbol of human complicity in the extinction process.

This chapter explores the small but important role of the passenger pigeon in relation to changing perceptions of Manifest Destiny – a concept that was a nineteenth-century outgrowth of American exceptionalism linked to the process of territorial expansion and the (mythical) spaces of the western frontier. Following the Louisiana Purchase (1803) and later the Mexican Cession (1848), the size of the United States more than doubled. The sudden increase in cheap land came during a time when more and more immigrants were beginning to make their way to the United States. Fueled by the notion that the American destiny was one of continual westward expansion, and that widespread continental settlement would once and for all ensure that white, Euro-American interests would overwhelm indigenous resistance, settlers began to flood west. The frontier was a dangerous place, and a mythology of rugged individualism combining a strong work ethic with virile masculinity took center stage, with men like Kit Carson, James 'Grizzly' Adams, and Davy Crockett becoming household names. The desire for precious metals, resources, and – most importantly – land as well as the view that the indigenous groups already populating the continent were 'uncivilized' impediments to their procurement, resulted in the decimation or destruction of many Native American societies. In 1893, less than 100 years following the Louisiana Purchase, historian Frederick Jackson Turner noted that the frontier was officially closed, but that it lingered in the collective consciousness as a dominant force in the formation of the American 'character.' According to Turner: "Up

2 For a general discussion of American "postfrontier anxiety," see David Wrobel: *The End of American Exceptionalism. Frontier Anxiety from the Old West to the New Deal.* Lawrence: UP of Kansas 1993.

to our own day American history has been in a large degree the history of the colonization of the Great West. The existence of an area of free land, its continuous recession, and the advance of American settlement westward, explain American development."[3] Turner described a process whereby early trailblazers led to early settlers led to permanent settlements, the residents of which began clearing the forests in order to build the first towns, and so on, a rolling wave of smaller, and then larger, communities pushing ever westward.

This description of American expansion partially explains the ultimate demise of the passenger pigeon, with forests gradually sectionalized by logging in order to feed the increased need for lumber. It also resonates metaphorically with the pigeon, itself a species with a highly social structure, where scouts would locate likely areas of woodland for a nesting, with increasingly larger groups arriving until an area was overcrowded, with scouts then moving on to search for new possibilities. Of the more than 20 books and numerous articles written about the demise of the pigeon, Mark Avery's *A Message from Martha* perhaps best contextualizes the extinction within the greater context of American history. He is also the only author to link the pigeon's demise explicitly to Manifest Destiny: "the period when Progress marched across the continent and when the Wild West was tamed—when the West was won, the Wild was lost."[4] Avery goes on to note the toxic brew that resulted from dominant European notions of human-nature relations combined with American exceptionalism, explaining why the pigeons were hunted past the threshold of extinction, and the American bison to its very doorstep:

> The mind-set was that nature would provide, however much we asked of her, and this was established by the size of the country and its original richness in nature. Europeans coming to the New World were amazed by the abundance they found there. They had no reason to believe that passenger pigeons could ever be shot to extinction. Why should they? At the beginning of the century which saw the passenger pigeon's extinction Audubon and Wilson were reporting single flocks that numbered billions. The Bison were abundant in a way that no Europeans had seen grazing animals in their home continent. The European invaders took what they wanted and counted their blessings.[5]

3 Frederick Jackson Turner: The Significance of the Frontier in American History. In: Ray Allen Billington (ed.): *Frontier and Section: Selected Essays of Frederick Jackson Turner*. Englewood Cliffs: Prentice-Hall 1961, pp. 37–62, here p. 37.

4 Mark Avery: *A Message from Martha. The Extinction of the Passenger Pigeon and Its Relevance Today*. London: Bloomsbury 2014, p. 174.

5 Ibid., p. 214.

The nation's religious makeup did not help either, with continuing traces of the early colonial notion that the North American continent was a sort of New Jerusalem, a providential gift allowing colonial groups a refuge of plenty from the excesses of European nations fighting over resources.

The only thing more mind-boggling than the speed of continental westward expansion during the nineteenth century was the rapidity of the pigeon's decline. During the age of colonial exploration, the species was first described by Jacques Cartier on July 1, 1534 (Prince Edward Island, Canada).[6] Its range extended across the United States and Canada east of the Rocky Mountains. It was migratory but not with a predictable pattern, with flocks numbering in the millions (and occasionally, billions) moving with the seasons in search of food and setting up huge colonies once a good food source was located. At the time of European settlement, population estimates put the birds at 3–5 billion in number, perhaps a quarter of the continent's avifauna.[7] Certainly, this species was hunted by various indigenous groups, as pigeon bones have been discovered at numerous archaeological digs.[8] Margaret Mitchell, however, found only three stories involving the pigeon in indigenous lore, two involving the Feast for the Dead in Huron mythology and one involving a story of privation followed by plenty from the Attawandaron (Neutral Nation).[9] There is some indication that the birds were so plentiful, nestings resulted in inter-tribal cooperation, as there was no need to compete for resources.[10] The debate over the degree to which indigenous tribes hunted the pigeon continues today. Despite assertions that indigenous groups did not engage in wholesale destruction, reports exist of both Iroquois and Neutrals taking part in indiscriminate killing of adult birds, although anthropologists have wondered

6 Jacques Cartier: *Relation originale du voyage de Jacques Cartier au Canada en 1534*. Paris: Librairie Tross 1867, p. 41.

7 David E. Blockstein: Passenger Pigeon (*Ectopistes migratorius*). In: A. Poole / F. Gill (eds): *Birds of North America*, No. 611. Philadelphia: Birds of North America 2002, pp. 1–28, here p. 1; Arlie W. Schorger: *The Passenger Pigeon. Its Natural History and Extinction*. Caldwell: Blackburn 1955, p. 204.

8 Blockstein: Passenger Pigeon, p. 17; Joel Greenberg: *A Feathered River Across the Sky. The Passenger Pigeon's Flight to Extinction*. New York: Bloomsbury 2014, p. 32.

9 Margaret H. Mitchell: *The Passenger Pigeon in Ontario*. Toronto: University of Toronto Press 1935, p. 18.

10 Greenberg: *Feathered River*, p. 40.

Fig. 1
Passenger Pigeon.

From John James Audubon:
Ornithological Biography, or An Account of the Habits of the Birds of the United States of America: Accompanied by Descriptions of the Objects Represented in the Work Entitled The birds of America, and Interspersed with Delineations of American Scenery and Manners. Philadelphia: Dobson 1831–1849, vol. 1, pl. 62.

if this was a result of contact with Europeans and exposure to their hunting practices.[11] There is other evidence of surplus hunting, however, from before the colonial period, including stories of archery competitions and large-scale netting practices.[12] Regardless of the veracity of accounts of indigenous excess, clearly pre-colonial over-hunting was not substantial enough to impact overall population numbers. By the beginning of the nineteenth century, huge flocks sometimes numbering as many as a billion birds were being reported.

The two great ornithologists of the early American period – Alexander Wilson and John James Audubon – both marveled at the size of the flocks they witnessed. A mathematical computation of a super-flock Wilson reported would have the birds, if lined up from bill to tail, stretching around the equator more than 22 times.[13] And Arlie W. Schorger, using a conservative mathematical model, extrapolated from Audubon's notes regarding a single flock estimated to be over a billion birds, a fairly similar figure to the one provided by the famed naturalist.[14] The biggest nesting ever recorded, in Wisconsin during 1871, was 125 miles long and 6–10 miles wide.[15] Although the pigeon did have nonhuman and human predators prior to European settlement – hawks, falcons, crows, and certain indigenous tribes – the sheer size of the flocks made predation levels irrelevant.[16] Trouble was on the horizon for the pigeon, however, as by the early eighteenth century they were already being viewed as a public nuisance[17] and localized eradication efforts – although still in their infancy – were picking up steam. And during the nineteenth century, with a huge increase in population many began to see the pigeons as an easy and cheap food source.

European settlers turning to pigeons as a source of food was a practice that extended back into the early colonial period. By the time the first American cookbook – *American Cookery* – was published by

11 John Wilson Foster: *Pilgrims of the Air*. Widworthy: Notting Hill 2014, p. 141.

12 Greenberg: *Feathered River*, pp. 36–37, 44.

13 Errol Fuller: *The Passenger Pigeon*. Princeton: Princeton UP 2015, p. 56.

14 Schorger: *The Passenger Pigeon*, pp. 199–205.

15 Evidence that the 2014 flurry of interest involving the pigeon penetrated various forms of media is *One Came Home*, a young adult murder mystery set against the backdrop of this nesting. Amy Timberlake: *One Came Home*. New York: Yearling 2013.

16 Schorger: *The Passenger Pigeon*, pp. 208–211.

17 In 1703, the Bishop of Montreal went so far to symbolically excommunicate the pigeon due to the distress it was causing farmers. Avery: *Message from Martha*, p. 214.

Amelia Simmons in 1798, there were already multiple ways of preparing pigeons, including roasted, stewed, and potted.[18] It was not until the middle of the nineteenth century, however, with massive waves of largely European but also Asian immigrants flooding into the country, that the hunting of pigeons for food became widespread and commercialized. Writing about the local extinctions of the pigeon in Michigan and Pennsylvania, William W. Thompson notes that pigeon profiteering became common right before, but was disrupted by, the American Civil War (1861–1865). The practice continued immediately following the conflict and the 1870s ushered in widespread hunting to satiate the nation's increased need for a cheap source of food as well as for other uses (such as filling in city potholes and producing fertilizer for agriculture). Given its booming population and the prevalence of rail lines near areas frequented by the pigeons, Michigan became the leader in slaughter for food.[19] Following the war, there was a massive need to feed the increasing populations of large eastern cities, as well as Chicago, Detroit, Cleveland, and other cities in the upper Midwest and Great Lakes regions. In essence, the pigeons were the only supply that could readily meet the demand.

The technological might of a country rapidly industrializing was added to the clever inventiveness of the so-called 'pigeoners,' leading to numerous ways in which passenger pigeons were killed. Prices for dead birds ranged from $.75–1.25 per dozen,[20] so it was important to be able to kill in bulk in order to make a profit. Salt or lye traps were commonly employed to catch birds, smoke pots were set to disorient them, feed was placed under massive nets that were then dropped after enough birds took the bait, and tall poles were used to push squabs out of their nests.[21] Other pigeoners tried alternate methods: sulfur was burned under nests to release deadly fumes, pigeons were blinded with torches, vibrating poles were constructed along bluffs known to be popular flyways, and pigeons were shot at or hit out of the sky with paddles. Some

18 Foster: *Pilgrims*, p. 144. The heath hen, a gallinaceous bird of the Eastern United States and related to the Greater Prairie Chicken, was also hunted to extinction in the nineteenth century.

19 William W. Thompson: *The Passenger Pigeon*. Coudersport: Potter Enterprise 1922, p. 4.

20 Ibid., p. 6.

21 Captain Oran W. Rowland: *A History of Van Buren County, Michigan*. Chicago: Lewis 1912, p. 50.

people even flung potatoes at them.[22] Many of the deceased pigeons were drawn to their fate by 'stoolers,' pigeons trained to remain calm despite being attached to a pigeoner by a string, and to feed, fly, and generally act naturally in order to entice entire flocks to land.[23] Such pigeons were highly valued, as perhaps only one in fifty could be trained properly. Well-trained stoolers could sell for $5–10.[24] Any and all new technologies were immediately marshaled toward the industrialized slaughter, including dynamite, which after 1867 would occasionally be used to kill thousands of pigeons at a time, placed under huge sheets of tin with rocks, nails, and other projectiles that acted as shrapnel, flying up into the trees.

Other technological factors contributed to the pigeon's extinction. Much as the combination of transportation and communication technologies spelled doom for the indigenous peoples resisting the U.S. Army, so too did the twin developments in these areas impact the pigeon: "Railroads allowed access to nesting colonies and the telegraph provided a way for scouts who located colonies to inform the professional pigeon trappers, who numbered some 600–1,200 men."[25] Railroads also allowed pigeons to be shipped back east to feed the waves of immigrants disembarking in eastern port cities and looking for a cheap food source. The portable sawmill, which was introduced following the Civil War, allowed lumber interests to become more mobile, resulting in the depletion of previously untouched tracts of woodland. As Blockstein notes: "By 1880, about 80 % of the original forest of New England had been cleared."[26] And disturbingly, the large-scale killing of pigeons often took on a social dimension. Revelries were held at nest sites, where onlookers drank heavily and celebrated wildly as they watched the pigeon hunters net birds and bring down nest trees.[27] Shooting competitions were also commonplace; in some cases, the winner often shot

22 Greenberg: *Feathered River*, pp. 91–92.

23 Thompson: *The Passenger Pigeon*, pp. 13–14; Rowland: *History of Van Buren*, p. 50.

24 Greenberg: *Feathered River*, pp. 104–105.

25 Blockstein: Passenger Pigeon, p. 18. As Mark Avery points out, the Eskimo Curlew was also driven to extinction due to the combination of railroad and telegraph, with the American bison and Pronghorn antelope nearly suffering the same fate. Avery: *Message from Martha*, p. 215.

26 Blockstein: Passenger Pigeon, p. 18.

27 Foster: *Pilgrims*, p. 149.

over 20,000 birds.[28] One such shooting party is described in James Fenimore Cooper's 1823 frontier novel *The Pioneers*. After a huge flock arrives, the townspeople scramble to muster forth with every weapon they can find, including a horse-drawn cannon that they attempt to point up into the air. Cooper's message is of a proto-environmentalist nature, as after the slaughter a group of townspeople discuss the morality of killing so many pigeons for 'sport' and leaving essentially all of them where they lie. Cooper was ahead of his time writing about this issue in the 1820s. Cooper's daughter, Susan Fenimore Cooper, continued where he left off. Although lamenting the disappearance of the species from her area, she injected some humor into her study. After calculating speed and distance flown by a specific flock, she noted that a lost bird could easily make it across the Atlantic Ocean: "[W]hatever disputes may arise as to the rival merits of Columbus and the Northmen, it is very probably that American pigeons had discovered Europe long before the Europeans discovered them."[29] Although the Coopers were not alone in their concern over the mass killings,[30] there was very little traction when it came to local or state protection. An 1857 attempt to protect the pigeon from commercial hunting in Ohio was not too surprisingly rejected by the state senate, as at that point the bird was still prolific.[31] The pace of killing in the 1870s was frenetic, however, including the almost unbelievable estimate of a billion birds killed during 1878 at a single nesting near Petoskey, Michigan.[32] Given the huge pigeon population before the war, and the massive scale of killing after, it is no surprise that the anti-hunting laws that were passed came too late and were not very effective. For instance, Michigan did not fully clarify its ambiguous law until 1897, by which time the species was extirpated from the state and essentially extinct in the wild.[33]

28 Errol Fuller: *Lost Animals. Extinction and the Photographic Record*. Princeton: Princeton UP 2013, p. 64; Greenberg: *Feathered River*, p. 109.

29 Susan Fenimore Cooper ("A Lady"): *Rural Hours*. New York: Putnam 1850, p. 302.

30 Perhaps the strangest advocate of the pigeon was Junius Brutus Booth, the famed actor and father of John Wilkes Booth. Greenberg describes a strange and emotional communion undertaken by the actor with a basket full of dead passenger pigeons he had been given. Greenberg: *A Feathered River*, pp. 62–63.

31 Fuller: *The Passenger Pigeon*, p. 50.

32 Todd McGrain: *The Lost Bird Project*. Hanover: University of New England Press 2014, p. 55.

33 Fuller: *The Passenger Pigeon*, p. 64.

As the century drew to a close, a handful were reported in Pennsylvania in 1895 and a single pair in 1896,[34] no doubt a remnant that had failed to make the flight to Canada following the final nesting in that region a decade earlier. Reports of the last one seen in the wild come from Wisconsin, Connecticut, and Ohio. Most modern sources view the Ohio report to be the most believable, with a teenager shooting the last wild passenger pigeon in Pike County on March 24, 1900. However, at least one account recognizes a specimen claim from Indiana in 1902 (as it derives from 1912, a report of several birds seen by Theodore Roosevelt has generally been rejected).[35]

The fascination with the disappearance of the passenger pigeon was immediate, preceding the death of Martha in 1914. How could such a plentiful species completely disappear from the face of the earth? The acceptance of this extinction and a desire to understand it represented a major shift in thinking from just a century prior, when the prevailing attitude of the late Enlightenment period held that extinction was a local event and expeditions such as Lewis and Clark's Corps of Discovery expedition (1804–1806) were discovering new species and describing a landscape teeming with life. Thomas Jefferson, who in addition to serving as the primary author of the American Declaration of Independence and the fledgling nation's third president was also a naturalist of some note, was part of a scientific community that bought into a natural system predicated upon providential design. As Mark Barrow notes:

> To Jefferson and many of his contemporaries, the very idea of species extinction seemed anathema. Intellectuals of his day recognized that settlement often resulted in the local extermination of wildlife. But the complete disappearance of a species was another matter altogether. The loss of any organism across its entire range implied an unacceptable imperfection in God's creation, while violating deep-seated assumptions about the balance of nature and the great chain of being that proved central to Western understandings of how that creation was ordered.[36]

Even indigenous commentators had a hard time, initially, believing that the pigeon could go extinct. Simon Pokagon (1830–1899), the last chief

34 Thompson: *The Passenger Pigeon*, p. 7.

35 Fuller: *The Passenger Pigeon*, p. 68.

36 Mark Barrow: *Nature's Ghosts. Confronting Extinction from the Age of Jefferson to the Age of Ecology*. Chicago: University of Chicago Press 2009, p. 19.

of the Potawatomi of western Michigan, noted that at the beginning of his life the pigeons were "almost as inexhaustible as the ocean itself." He continues: "I had witnessed the passing away of the deer, buffalo, and elk, but I looked upon them as local in their habits, while these birds spanned the continent, frequently nesting beyond the reach of cruel man."[37] Despite the largely local focus when it came to beliefs about extinction, however, the nineteenth century saw a growing awareness about the potentially universal and permanent aspects of this phenomenon. During this time period, scientists, theologians, philosophers, and intellectuals in numerous other fields were already beginning to question the relationship between God, nature, and humanity. Particularly problematic in maintaining old views of the natural world were the presence of fossilized bones of animals for which there was no prior record, as well as geological observations that suggested an earth much, much older than had been previously entertained. Although the French naturalist Georges Cuvier had first proposed a theory of extinction in 1796 and by 1817 had revised the Linnaean classification of the animal kingdom to account for the ecological phenomenon, by and large extinction was still a controversial theory. Acceptance was grudging, initially amongst scientists and eventually the general population. By the mid-1860s, however, and the beginning of the widespread pigeon slaughter, that a species could disappear forever from all of its former habitats was both a familiar and accepted concept.

Hypotheses as to the reasons underlying the pigeon's extinction were numerous and varied, although one feature that most shared was a lack of awareness over the role that humans had played in the extinction process. Some blamed diseases such as canker, others a massive forest fire or a form of poison that had somehow tainted the pigeons' food supply.[38] Captain Oran W. Rowland, writing in 1912, points out that dead birds found floating in the Great Lakes and the Atlantic Ocean led some to suggest that various flocks had, over time, become disoriented and migrated accidentally over water, while still others cited a massive tornado in the Great Lakes region wiping out the entire population. Yet another creative theory of the time held that the pigeons had

37 Simon Pokagon: The Wild Pigeon of North America. In: William Butts Mershon (ed.): *The Passenger Pigeon*. New York: Outing 1907, pp. 48–59, here p. 53.

38 Thompson: *The Passenger Pigeon*, pp. 8–9; Schorger: *The Passenger Pigeon*, pp. 211–214.

relocated to South America or perished in the Gulf of Mexico attempting to make the journey.[39] The one factor often noted as a possible explanation that implicated 'man,' however, was the widespread cutting of woodland tracts.[40] Rowland came closer than most to approximating our contemporary understanding of the extinction:

> Their great wintering places in the south being broken up and the timber in the north that supplied them with such great quantities of mast, being cut down, so demoralized them that they could no longer exist in such vast bodies. Thus they scattered, and, like bees that abandon their hive, most of them could not survive an unsocial condition and finally died.[41]

Although he lacked the vocabularies and concepts of ecosystem biology, and was referencing the entire species rather than discrete flocks, Rowland is correct in asserting that the pigeons contracted below a critical mass of birds needed for survival. Today, there are two prevailing theories as to the reason such a threshold existed for each flock: one suggests a tipping point whereby predation began to outstrip breeding success, the other that the flocks were not large enough to send out enough scouts to find adequate feeding areas.[42] When all remaining flocks succumbed to one or both of these factors in the 1890s, the result was a tiny remnant living in zoos or private bird collections, eventually reduced to a solitary bird – Martha – in the Cincinnati Zoo.

Martha was a celebrity during her life and became an icon following her death on September 1, 1914. She dominated national news during a time of intense competition for newspaper headline space less than three weeks after the beginning of hostilities during World War I. The *Cincinnati Enquirer* broke out the purple prose upon her death: "Martha will be shown to posterity, not as an old bird with most of her plumage gone, as she is now, but as the queenly young passenger pigeon that delighted thousands of bird and nature lovers at the Zoo."[43] Her death as the final representative of a species that had gone from abundant to extinct in less than a century was significant for three reasons. First of all, record-keeping and public awareness had progressed to the point that, for the first time in history, humans were aware of the exact

39 Rowland: *History of Van Buren*, p. 46.

40 Schorger: *The Passenger Pigeon*, pp. 211–214.

41 Rowland: *History of Van Buren*, p. 46.

42 Blockstein: Passenger Pigeon, p. 19.

43 Fuller: *The Passenger Pigeon*, p. 118.

moment of a biological extinction. Secondly, Martha fit into a growing narrative during a decade of calamity that led many to question what had been viewed as the inevitability of progress (Meliorism). The extinction of the passenger pigeon was big news during a time of tragedy right after the outbreak of world war. Less than a week following her death, the Battle of the Marne began, signaling the beginning of trench warfare and a four year period during which as many as 25 million people died as a result of the war and 50 million from a virulent strain of influenza ("the Spanish Flu") shortly thereafter. The extinction of the passenger pigeon constituted a narrative that fit into this scary new world, where such institutions as science and technology no longer necessarily held all the answers and the frontiers of human progress resulted in mustard gas and species extinctions.

Thirdly, and most powerfully, Martha and the demise of the passenger pigeon provided ready-made symbols for a country in a state of transition. The frontier had 'closed,' and with that closure came a re-examination of frontier lives and myths that were cherished by the American populace. Successive waves of immigrants had remade the face of the North American continent, introducing new economic possibilities but also race and class-based anxieties into the American consciousness and cultural imaginary. Symbols can be powerful indeed, and the passenger pigeon and its plight proved to be one that could attach easily to growing concerns over the excesses of, and problems caused by, nineteenth-century American processes of nation building based on relentless territorial expansion. The pigeon has proven to be a very flexible symbol, representing immigrants, settlers, and indigenous groups, and even serving as a bit of a warped mirror for the American bison, the other well-known animal casualty of Manifest Destiny's 'conquest' of the West. An interesting relationship existed between the many immigrants arriving in the United States during the nineteenth century and the pigeon, itself a bit of an immigrant in search of food and land. Heeding New York newspaper editor Horace Greeley's famous call to "Go West, young man," and encouraged by the promise of cheap land and good job opportunities, many of these immigrants moved west, working in jobs that were either high risk or required no specialized experience. Many such immigrants helped to clear the forests as lumberjacks or loading cargo (including barrels filled with dead pigeons heading to market) onto trains heading east. They also turned to cheap food sources, including the pigeon.

Furthermore, as discussed earlier, the progressive rhythm of Frederick Jackson Turner's frontier settlement is reminiscent of a pigeon flock as it searches for a nesting site. In his famous essay on the pigeon, Audubon describes how a flock feeds in a linear fashion: "The rear ranks are continually rising, passing over the main body, and alighting in front, in such rapid succession, that the whole flock seems still on wing."[44] In the pigeon's continual movement in search of new resources, it shared a link with the westward expansion of a species that would eventually drive it to extinction. And much as with locust swarms, the passenger pigeon was reliant upon a boom/bust population cycle with a tenuous link to resources. Although it is a theory that is still being investigated, recent DNA work on the pigeon suggests that the European settlement of North America occurred during an extended peak in the boom/bust cycle, and that a population numbering in the billions was unusually high for the species and not at all sustainable. A DNA study conducted by Chih-Ming Hung at National Taiwan Normal University has suggested that during natural, pre-European crashes in the cycle, the population might have dipped as low as 50,000 birds. This finding is controversial, but an extended bust period in the cycle coming during the midst of massive habitat loss and new and unprecedented predation may help explain the rapidity of the extinction.[45] And finally, as the twentieth century progressed, and Americans began to better understand the complexity of holistic ecosystem dynamics, the pigeon was a ready-made metaphor for an American people beginning to ask more and more pointed questions about resource depletion, deforestation, and their own role in environmental catastrophe.

Writers of both European and indigenous background also noted similarities between indigenous groups and the passenger pigeon, not only in the correlation between extinction and what would later be termed genocide and the observation that many indigenous groups had (supposedly or factually) migratory cultural lifestyles, but also in some other areas.[46] Seventeenth century Jesuit missionary Paul Le Jeune noted the

44 John James Audubon: The Passenger Pigeon. In: Mershon (ed.): *The Passenger Pigeon*, pp. 25–40, here p. 31. This is a reprint of Audubon's chapter on the pigeon from his five-volume *Ornithological Biography* (1831–1839).

45 Susan Milius: Passenger Pigeon Had Ups, Downs. In: *Science News* 186,3 (August 9, 2014), p. 17.

46 In his discussion of what he terms "extinction discourse," Patrick Brantlinger notes how notions of the "vanishing savage" often served to rationalize or legitimize the

unpredictability of frequency in the appearance and numbers of both pigeons and indigenous groups: "In one season the turtle doves are sometimes found in such abundance that the end of their army cannot be seen when they are flying in a body; at other times in the same season they appear only in small flocks […] Our Savages are like them in this inconstancy."[47] To a European having spent the first 40 years of his life in France, and used to a relatively settled and sedentary lifestyle, the indigenous hunter-gatherer groups populating Quebec were more easily understood by Le Jeune when linked to another aspect of New World ecology. Not all such associations came from Europeans, however. Simon Pokagon was a widely published and well-known writer during the late nineteenth century. His work on the passenger pigeon, *How the Terrible Slaughter by White Men Caused Extermination of the 'Me-Me-Og,' or Wild Pigeon* was published posthumously the same year that Martha died in the Cincinnati Zoo. Pokagon identifies many connections between the pigeons and his people, including one deriving from an incident where he witnessed a man using grain soaked in alcohol to intoxicate and catch the pigeons despite being informed of the devastating effects of alcohol upon the Potawatomi:

> That wheat was soaked over night in whisky. His answer fell like lead upon my heart. We had talked temperance together the night before and the old man wept as I told him how my people had fallen by the intoxicating cup of the white man, like leaves before the blast of autumn. In silence I left the place, saying in my heart "Is it possible? Is there some of the white race in league with Maw-tehi-manito (the Devil) to deal out Ish-kot-i-wa-be (whiskey) to even the animal creation?"[48]

Known during his time as the "Redskin poet, bard, and Longfellow of his race,"[49] Pokagon was quite influential in the upper Midwest during a period where the 'Indian Wars,' although now taking place well to the west of his Michigan home, were still a subject of great concern. Pokagon communicated with and was considered an authority by William Butts Mershon, Rowland, and others writing about the decline of the pigeon, who could not ignore the powerful connections Pokagon drew between the treatment of the pigeons and indigenous groups. Mershon dedicates

genocidal aspects of settler colonial expansion. Patrick Brantlinger: *Dark Vanishings. Discourse on the Extinction of Primitive Races, 1800–1930*. Ithaca: Cornell UP 2003.

47 Quoted in Mitchell: *The Passenger Pigeon*, p. 16.

48 Rowland: *History of Van Buren*, p. 51.

49 This description is from a footnote introducing a reprinted article by Pokagon already cited above. Pokagon: Wild Pigeon, p. 48.

one of his volume's chapters to reprinting an 1895 article that Pokagon wrote for the monthly magazine *The Chautauquan*. Besides a general description of the pigeon, its social structure and the way it was hunted, the article not only conveys a critique of the pigeoners' hunting excesses but also subtly points to the (settler) colonial politics of naming: "The migratory or wild pigeon of North America was known by our race as *O-me-me-wog*. Why the European race did not accept that name was, no doubt, because the bird so much resembled the domesticated pigeon; they naturally called it a wild pigeon, as they called us wild men."[50] Following a discursive tradition already established in the antebellum era, some Euro-American commentators also linked the 'fate' of indigenous animal species with that of Native American societies. As Rowland notes: "The buffaloes have gone, the pigeons are extinct and other game, once so abundant, is rapidly disappearing and the Indians themselves are a disappearing race, rapidly journeying to their 'happy hunting ground.'"[51] In this regard, the prevailing attitude of the time still involved a justification or even celebration of Manifest Destiny, understood as a teleological process through which an expanding American civilization 'naturally' (if perhaps somewhat regrettably) displaced supposedly inferior indigenous societies and native animal species, human and nonhuman casualties of the transformative grasp of civilization. A minority view, however, one that began to gain some traction, involved a reassessment of the moral costs of Manifest Destiny and westward expansion, even though this reassessment was rarely separable from the more widespread nationalist nostalgia about a period of American history now finally fading into the past.

In the context of American perceptions of the nineteenth-century devastation of continental environments and animal populations, a word must be said about the American bison, as in essence the passenger pigeon's story is that of the bison's – except for the happy ending. Much like the pigeon, the bison were migratory animals hunted for their meat. They were also hunted for their hides, an alternative to more expensive clothing for a burgeoning middle class. By 1840, over 100,000 "buffalo robes" a year were being sold in eastern cities.[52] Steamships, and

50 Rowland: *History of Van Buren*, p. 48.

51 Ibid., p. 52.

52 Dale F. Lott: *American Bison. A Natural History*. Berkeley: University of California Press 2002, p. 173. For another seminal study see Andrew Isenberg: *The*

later railroads, allowed for easier access to herds, as well as the more rapid transportation of meat to eastern cities and their ever-increasing populations. In addition to symbolically devouring the bison, railroads quite literally did so, as leather straps cut from bison hides were used as fan belts in train engines. As Dale F. Lott succinctly states: "When the bison's hide could be tanned, their goose was cooked."[53] By 1870, the bison was all but extinct, down from a pre-colonial overall population estimate of 25–60 million animals. During the presidential administration of Ulysses S. Grant, concern over the future of the animal grew, and both professional and recreational bison hunters were excoriated.[54] An 1879 expedition to ascertain the population size of the "Southern Herd" indicates just how far environmentalism still had to come before the species was finally protected by President Theodore Roosevelt in 1905.[55] The 1879 expedition found that only 22 animals were left in this southernmost of the three historical North American herds. In order to pay back the debt incurred by this expedition, 12 of the 22 bison were shot, their carcasses laced with poison, with the hides from the 600 scavenging coyotes that subsequently perished sold to pay back the expedition creditors.[56] As Lott notes, the near extinction of the bison in the 1870s came at a time when, for a variety of reasons, Americans were beginning to question their complicity in its decline. The American Civil War had featured carnage unprecedented in the nation's history, and many Americans were beginning to feel a tension regarding what was happening to indigenous societies, even if support was high for military action against the Sioux and other groups that chose active violence over less visible forms of resistance or passive acquiescence. The Society for the Prevention of Cruelty to Animals (SPCA) had begun its work in 1866, and after a time also turned its focus to the diminishment of the bison. As Lott points out, the American bison became a powerful symbol whereas the beaver, hunted to near extinction only a few generations earlier, had never achieved a similar status. While the

Destruction of the Bison. An Environmental History, 1750–1920. Cambridge: Cambridge UP 2000.

53 Lott: *American Bison*, p. 176.

54 Ibid., pp. 178–179.

55 Larry Schweikart / Bradley J. Birzer. *The American West*. Hoboken: Wiley & Sons 2003, p. 262.

56 Lott: *American Bison*, pp. 175, 179.

beaver-killing 'mountain man' of the American imagination remained a trail-blazing hero, the bison hunter had come to be viewed as an agent of genocide, "quasi-criminals [...] greasy, dirty, conscienceless killers with the blood of millions of buffalo on their hands."[57]

Three aspects of the American bison's rise to symbolic status resonate with the passenger pigeon, which, although having a similar trajectory, found a very different end. First of all, it is obvious that a similar concern was not felt for the pigeon following the Civil War, a fact that can in part be explained by the general appeal of 'charismatic megafauna,' large animals and mammals that usually attract much more attention when it comes to human anthropomorphic concerns. Moreover, as Andrew Isenberg has shown, the bison figured as a powerful symbol of the American West and spoke to ideals of a rugged frontier life at a time when many feared a decline of national vigor and a 'degeneration' of (white) American masculinity.[58] Secondly, the scorn heaped upon buffalo hunters is interesting but not too surprising, as it is easier to single out a small, discrete group on the supply side for demonization than the millions of consumers whose demand constituted the engine driving this particular aspect of Manifest Destiny. Although looked upon as unsavory, the pigeoners were never held up to the same level of ridicule and outrage, at least not by those of European descent. In contrast, Pokagon referred to the pigeoners as "outlaws to all moral sense" and wondered about the providential "degree of punishment awaiting our white neighbors who have so wantonly butchered and driven from our forests these wild pigeons."[59] Still, Pokagon's criticism of the pigeoners' excesses seems to have been the exception. In large part, the lack of a more widespread condemnation of those plying this trade was because by the time the problem was fully realized, there were no more large nestings, and thus no more pigeoners. Those who had contributed to the extinction by engaging in that profession had already moved on to hunt or trap other species. And finally, there's the critical distinction that the American bison never went extinct. Indeed, the repopulation of the bison in various national parks, state parks, and on private lands and ranches has been one of the greatest success stories in the history of American conservation. Thus, the bison makes for a rather

57 Lott: *American Bison*, p. 180.

58 Isenberg: *Destruction of the Bison*, pp. 169–175.

59 Pokagon: Wild Pigeon, pp. 56, 58.

poor metaphor for the destructiveness of Manifest Destiny, as it comes with a built-in happy ending, one that does not resonate well with the nineteenth-century stories of destroyed or displaced indigenous societies, forgotten languages, destroyed cultures, and environmental degradation. The passenger pigeon, in contrast, with its permanence of consequence for the excesses of Manifest Destiny, makes for a much better prism through which to analyze this episode in American history. And finally, its extinction places it at the forefront of a conversation currently taking place about the ethics of cloning, or not cloning, extinct animals. Modern science has arrived at a place whereby genomic extraction and transfer to the embryos of cousin species is possible. The Long Now Foundation and other groups are advocating for this process to occur, and along with the wooly mammoth the pigeon is at the center of this discussion. The advantages of such a project are manifest. In addition to the greater scientific understanding that would attend the re-creation of such a species, Ben Minteer notes that "de-extinction is our opportunity to right past wrongs and to atone for our moral failings."[60] However, the issue is more complicated than that, and as Minteer also notes, the problems with such a venture outweigh the advantages. The placement of extinct species into ecological systems that have evolved without them could be disruptive, and the limited genetic diversity of such a population would make it vulnerable to diseases, which in turn could evolve to impact other species. And most problematically, Minteer notes that the Promethean spirit that attends this new science threatens to remove the permanence of outcome. Why invest resources in protecting a species when they can be recreated in a laboratory? As Minteer reminds us: "That is why there is great virtue in keeping extinct species extinct. Meditation on their loss reminds us of our fallibility and our finitude."[61]

The passenger pigeon is one of the world's most infamous biological extinctions, linked to the parallel downfall of Native American cultures and, in providing a cheap source of food for the huge numbers of Americans pushing westward during the nineteenth century, quite literally nourishing Manifest Destiny. It's extinction, it seems, has left an indelible mark upon the American psyche, if the numerous writings

60 Ben E. Minteer: When Extinction Is a Virtue. In: Id. / Stephen J. Pyne (eds): *After Preservation*. Chicago: University of Chicago Press 2015, pp. 96–104, here p. 101.
61 Ibid., pp. 103–104.

about this species extending from the time when it was the most plentiful bird on earth through the 100th anniversary of Martha's death in 2014 are any indication.[62] John Muir and Theodore Roosevelt, the Sierra Club and the Audubon Society, all came too late to help the pigeon, but may have in part been motivated by its demise. Different authors have focused upon different aspects of the extinction. Mark Avery notes that the bird was doomed from the start, perceiving the incompatibility of the mega-flocks and commercial aviation.[63] Others, such as Aldo Leopold, have focused upon the biological marvel of the species, denoting the flocks as "biological storms" and "feathered tempests."[64] Still others have linked the passenger pigeon to ecological crises of the day. An example of this phenomenon is *Once There Was a Passenger Pigeon*, written by Esther and Bernard Gordon.[65] Publishing their work in the mid-1970s, the Gordons were living in the shadow of DDT and other pesticides, explaining why they linked species such as the Osprey and the Bald Eagle to the pigeon. Although now plentiful, these two birds of prey experienced horrific population crashes in the 1950s and 1960s due to unwise uses of the chemical compound. And finally, the most common reflection involving the pigeon's extinction has involved the importance of memory. As Susan Morrison, author of a children's book on the pigeon reminds us: "It's a sad story. But it's a story we can learn from."[66] Frederick Jackson Turner notes that whereas the eastern seaboard was the frontier of the American colonies for the British and Spanish, the frontier as it moved westward became a uniquely American distinction.[67] It is a natural corollary, then, that any excesses committed during that period were uniquely American, including the destruction of the natural world in the name of 'progress.' The fact that thousands upon thousands of people made pilgrimages to the tiny aviary at the Cincinnati Zoo to see Martha indicates a shift in thinking, a curiosity about the past that is necessary before its

62 It is interesting to note that, whereas in 1914 Martha was commonly referred to by both the pronouns 'it' and 'she' (depending upon the author), today the latter pronoun is used almost exclusively.

63 Avery: *Message from Martha*, p. 225.

64 Blockstein: Passenger Pigeon, p. 1.

65 Esther S. Gordon / Bernard L. Gordon: *Once There was a Passenger Pigeon*. New York: Walck 1976.

66 Susan Dudley Morrison: *The Passenger Pigeon*. New York: Crestwood 1989, p. 7.

67 Turner: The Significance of the Frontier in American History, p. 39.

reevaluation. Martha may have been named after the first lady of the United States – Martha Washington – but she was the last of her kind, an inexorable marker of loss involving the excesses of the nineteenth century. Her kind had once darkened the skies over North America. Now, those thronging to catch a glimpse of Martha as the final representative of her species were the very species complicit in that event, swarming west across the continent in numbers that devastated the societies and ecologies they encountered.

Table of Figures

About the Contributors

Roman Bartosch is Senior Lecturer at the University of Cologne and has taught and published extensively on literary theory, ecocriticism and animal studies. He is the author of *EnvironMentality – Ecocriticism and the Event of Postcolonial Fiction* (Rodopi 2013) and *Teaching Environments* (Lang 2014, edited with Sieglinde Grimm) and presently works on a book on literary reception and affect.

Keridiana Chez is Assistant Professor of English at the Borough of Manhattan Community College, City University of New York. Her research is on nineteenth-century American and British representations of human-animal relationships, particularly as they intersect with cultural discourses of gender, race, ethnicity, and class. Her book, *Victorian Dogs, Victorian Men: Affect and Animals in the Nineteenth-Century British and American Novel*, is forthcoming in 2017 with Ohio State University Press.

Brigitte Fielder is Assistant Professor of Comparative Literature at the University of Wisconsin-Madison. She is currently working on two book projects, one on racial genealogies and interracial kinship in nineteenth-century American literatures, and one on overlapping discourses of race and species in the long nineteenth century. Her work has appeared in *American Quarterly*, *J19: The Journal of Nineteenth-Century Americanists*, *Studies in American Fiction*, *Early American Studies*, and *Women's Narratives of the Early Americas and the Formation of Empire* (Palgrave 2016).

Katherine C. (Kasey) Grier is Professor of History and Director of the Museum Studies Program at the University of Delaware. She is the author of *Pets in America. A History* (University of North Carolina Press 2006) and publishes the blog *The Pet Historian* (www.thepethistorian.com) about the material and visual culture associated with pet keeping in the United States.

Andrew Howe is Professor of History at La Sierra University in Riverside, California, where he teaches courses in film history, popular culture, and American history. Recent scholarship includes book chapters on fan-generated art involving HBO's *Game of Thrones*, the role of cemeteries and burial rites in the western genre, and the transformation of the Mohican myth in *Avatar*.

Michael Malay is a postdoctoral researcher at the University of Sheffield. He has published articles on Raymond Williams, Elizabeth Bishop and Ted Hughes. He is currently completing a monograph on representations of animals in modern and contemporary poetry.

Neill Matheson is Associate Professor of English at the University of Texas at Arlington, specializing in nineteenth-century American literature and culture. He has published essays on a wide range of topics and writers in the period. He has an ongoing interest in nineteenth-century literary and scientific writing about nonhuman animals and human-animal relations. Work on these issues includes two articles on Thoreau, focusing on animality in *Walden*, and animal figures and racial environmentalism in "Walking" and the *Journal*.

Dominik Ohrem is a doctoral candidate in the North American Department of the School of History at the University of Cologne. His research interests include American history, feminist philosophy and animal studies. He is currently working on his dissertation about animality and human-animal relations in the context of American westward expansion and co-editing the volumes *Beyond the Human-Animal Divide. Creaturely Lives in Literature and Culture* (Palgrave, with Roman Bartosch) and *Re-Encountering Animal Bodies* (Palgrave, with Matthew Calarco).

Olaf Stieglitz is Adjunct Professor in the North American Department of the School of History at the University of Cologne. His research interests include gender history, the history of the body, sport history as cultural history and the role of visual sources in historical writing. He is currently working on a research project titled "Modernity in Motion – Visualizing Athletic Bodies, 1890s–1930s."

Aimee Swenson is a doctoral candidate in the Department of Community Sustainability at Michigan State University. Her current research is situated at the intersections of human-animal relationships (specifically livestock), indigeneity, and land appropriation. Working broadly within traditional and contemporary shepherding populations, she is interested in the cultural importance of livestock in indigenous and isolated communities, and how that interfaces with governmental regulations and shifting demands in land use.